Painting of the River Thames at Kew by the botanical artist W.H. Fitch, who produced more than 10,000 drawings in his lifetime.

The Pagoda on a frosty day.

Ronald King

ROYAL KEW

Constable · London

First published in Great Britain 1985
by Constable and Company Limited
10 Orange Street London WC2H 7EG
Copyright © 1985 by Ronald King
Set in Monophoto Ehrhardt 11 on 13pt by
Servis Filmsetting Limited, Manchester
Printed in Great Britain by
BAS Printers Ltd, Over Wallop

British Library CIP data
King, Ronald
Royal Kew
1. Royal Botanic Gardens (Kew) – History
I. Title
580′.74′442195   QK73.G72K48

ISBN 0 09 466240 1

To
SIR GEORGE TAYLOR
WHO MADE SOME OF THE HISTORY
THAT THIS BOOK RECOUNTS
IN
MEMORY
OF
THE PLEASANT YEARS AT KEW

CONTENTS

ACKNOWLEDGEMENTS

The author and publishers are grateful to Professor E A Bell, Director of the Royal Botanic Gardens, Kew and Miss S M D Fitzgerald, Chief Librarian and Archivist of the Royal Botanic Gardens for permission to use the resources and facilities of the Library of the Gardens. They acknowledge with particular thanks permission to reproduce quotations from the manuscript works of John Smith and the plant collectors George Caley, James Bowie, George Barclay and William Purdie: from the 1773 Catalogue of Trees and Shrubs in the Gardens: the 1823 receipt for the sale of Hunter House: the Lindley note of February 11, 1840: certain volumes of the Kew Inwards, Outwards and Record Books: the 1873 letter of Sir Joseph Hooker about student-gardeners: and the manuscript work of William Dallimore.

The illustration on page 109 is reproduced by permission of the Keystone Press Agency Ltd. The remainder of the illustrations are reproduced by permission of the Controller, HMSO and the Director, Royal Botanic Gardens, Kew.

[6]

ILLUSTRATIONS

'Some of them will say, seynge that I graunte that I have gathered this booke of so many writers, that I offer unto you an heape of other mennis laboures and nothing of mine owne, and that I goo about to make me frendes with other mennis travayles. . . . To whom I answer, that if the honey that the bees gather out of so many floures of herbes, shrubs and trees that are growing in other mennis medowes, feldes and closes: may justelye be called the bees honeye . . . so may I call that I have learned and gathered of many good autores, not without great laboure and payne, my booke.'

From the *Herbal* of William Turner, Father of English Botany, who lived at Kew in the sixteeth century

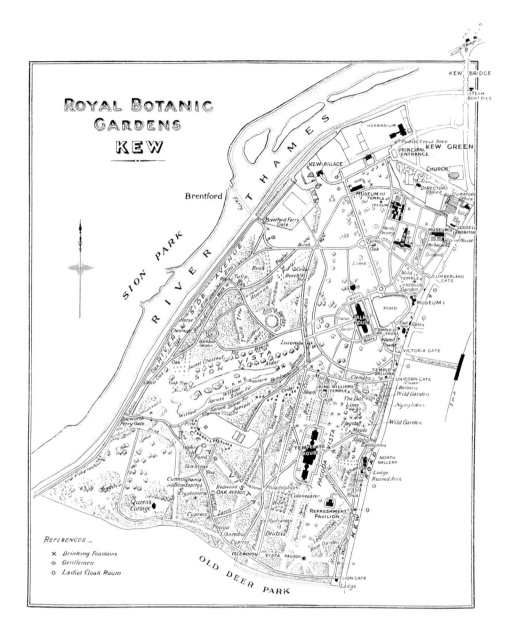

Gardens Map

[12]

I

PAGEANT

OF KINGS

'Through the wide wastes
Where the wildfowl called
The King came riding...'

The first question a gardener asks when moving to a new home is 'What is the soil like?' and this is perhaps the first question that ought to be asked about Kew. The answer will surprise most people. The natural soil of that beautiful garden is dry and hungry and water runs through it so fast that it is a common sight in the summer to see the sprinklers still at work when it is pouring with rain. The next question is, of course, 'How on earth did that garden, which contains specimens of more of the world's plants than any other, come to be founded on such an unsuitable site?' The answer to that question is part of the story that this book has to tell.

The Kew soil which drains away so quickly is underlain by gravel, deposited in past time by the Thames. Although Kew never felt the weight of glacial ice, the edge of the ice sheets that covered most of England from time to time up to 12,000 years ago came almost into the London basin where Kew is situated, and through the basin itself ran a Thames far mightier and more turbulent than the present modest stream. Rolled along by its current, greatly swelled by melting ice when the climate became warmer and the ice retreated, and broken and ground by constant knocking against one another, were innumerable small stones which accumulated in the bed and along the sides. Gradually the water ran away into the sea, and the Thames diminished year by year, leaving these stones as beds of gravel. The highest and earliest, deposited when the river was very wide, are now some way from the water. Kew Gardens, on the banks of the modern river, is situated on the newest and lowest of these deposits, called the Flood Plain Terrace. The top soil of the Gardens thus has, as sub-soil, the most perfect natural drainage that could be devised, since water runs very easily through the interstices between the stones.

The gravel did not remain in its pristine state on the surface. Carried down by the river, spread over the land by winter floods, and blown from elsewhere by the wind, came year by year leaves, twigs, branches, roots and even whole trees, and other detritus, to rot and spread into what, as time went on, became a scanty top soil, in which trees, shrubs and other plants could root and flourish. By the time Britain appears in history the land later to become Kew Gardens had developed into an area of scrubby woodland with here and there a marshy patch or shallow pool where the drainage had become impeded. At this juncture, the Romans turned their eyes on Britain and, by a twist of fate, one of the places that they passed through, and on which a mark of their passage was left, was, in all probability, Kew Gardens.

Julius Caesar, after a reconnaissance in 55 BC, decided to invade Britain and the next year 54 BC landed on the coast of Kent in force. Marching west he learned, he says in his *Gallic Wars*, that the Thames was fordable 'at one point only', but gives no indication of where the ford was other than that it was about 75 miles from the sea. A number of crossing places have been suggested, including one at Kew, a little up-river from the present Brentford Gate of the Gardens, where a ford is known to have existed from very early times. This ford has one piece of evidence in its favour that cannot be matched elsewhere.

Caesar says that when his troops reached the ford they found the bank of the river 'fenced by large stakes fixed along the edge and . . . similar ones . . . concealed in the river bed'. When the stretch of the Thames in which the ford was situated was deepened for navigational purposes in Victorian times the stumps of lines of stakes were found between Isleworth and Kew Bridge which seem to match up to Caesar's description. Brentford Urban District Council erected a memorial stone in 1909 on the north bank of the river to record this. The stone was inscribed on four sides; on that facing the river it bore the following:

54 BC At this ancient fortified town (Brentford) the British tribesmen, under Cassivellaunus, bravely opposed Julius Caesar on his march to Verulamium.

[14]

The identity of the place has recently been established by the discovery of the remains of oak palisades extending both along this bank and in the bed of the river ...

What happened when Caesar made his crossing? Let him speak for himself. When he reached the river 'he found large enemy forces drawn up on the opposite bank. . . . He sent the cavalry across first and then at once ordered the infantry to follow. But the infantry went with such speed and impetuosity, although they had only their heads above water, that they attacked at the same moment as the cavalry. The enemy was overpowered and fled from the river-bank.'

Walking amid the crowds admiring the trim and orderly Gardens of the present day it is difficult to envisage these happenings of the past: the jingling of harness and the stamp of feet as the Romans came up, the staccato orders of the centurions, and the shouts and splashings as they took to the water, the scuffling and blows as they hacked their way through and over the palisades to meet in the shallows of the other side the desperate but less well-armed and disciplined Britons. Outmatched, the latter soon gave way and fled, leaving, as silence fell once again, only the dead and dying among the useless stakes, their blood, mixed with the mud stirred up by the fight, floating away in reddish streaks on the sluggish Thames current.

Kew makes no further appearance in history until Anglo-Saxon times, when there seems good evidence in the *Anglo-Saxon Chronicle* that the ford at Brentford was used by both Saxons and Danes for the passage of armies that for long years fought for the domination of England. In the early years of the eleventh century King Edmund Ironside and King Canute crossed and recrossed the ford in the course of their battles several times, taking and retaking the settlement which had sprung up at Brentford and it seems likely that the saying 'there cannot be two Kings in Brentford' dates from this time.

Saxon and Dane divided England between them and in AD 1016 were united under Canute. Fifty years later they were conquered by the Normans. No trace of Kew, however, appears in the Domesday Book. It was still merely a featureless stretch of land within a loop of the Thames, occasionally hunted over, but otherwise unremarkable except for the river crossing. At the southern end of the territory, however, there was a place called Shene, a name which means 'beautiful', in the sense of shining. Here King Henry I, in 1125, had a substantial house, the land attached to which included Kew.

After Henry I the property at Shene, although apparently still a royal possession, was for two hundred years occupied by others. It was not until Edwards I's time that the king began to use it as a royal residence and it begins to be mentioned in historical documents, but from this period the royal association is probably continuous, most likely because access to it was easy by river both from London and Windsor and it was a comparatively safe retreat from the plague and other London inconveniences.

Kew had its part in this because, apart from the ford, it was used as a landing place by royalty and presumably others. An entry in Henry VIII's privy purse accounts for 1530 records that there was:

> Paid to the King's watermen, for their waiting from
> York Place to Keyho, with sixteen oars when the
> King's grace removed from York Place to Richmond   10s. 8d.

There is a long-standing tradition that the pond that still exists on Kew Green, though now confined by concrete into a quiet pool, is the remnant of what was formerly an inlet from the Thames, and that it was in this inlet that royal and other passenger barges could conveniently be moored.

The name 'Keyho' in the foregoing quotation is only one variation on 'Kew'. The name is probably of Middle English origin, a compound of *caye* or *keye*, meaning wharf or quay, and *ho*, derived from *hoh* meaning a spur of land, that is, the wharf or quay on the spur of land, the 'spur' being the land within the loop of the Thames. Many and remarkable are the changes that have been rung on it in various documents. It appears first in 1327 as 'Cayho'. In 1330 it is 'Kayho juxta Brayneforde'. In the year of the Black Death, 1348, it has become 'Kayhog', reverting in 1375 to 'Kayho'. In 1439 it appears as 'Keyhow', but in 1441 has become 'Kayowe'. Other later spellings are 'Kayo' (1483), 'Kayhough' (in the reign of Henry VII), 'Cayo' (1509), 'Keyowe' (1517), 'Kayhoo' (1522), 'Kyoe' and 'Kaiho' (1524), 'Cayhoo' (1530), 'Kaio' (1532), and 'Kewe' (1535). The last of these is the first appearance of what is virtually the modern name, but different spellings continue to appear long after this date, others being 'Cao' (1536), 'Keew' (1538), 'Keyomede' (in the reign of Henry VIII), 'Keyo' (1546), 'Kewe al Kyo' (1592), 'Ceu' (1607), 'Kewe-greene' (1609) and 'Kew al Kyo' (1648): a total in all of 24 different spellings.

One document has survived from the fifteenth century which throws a tiny beam of light on the standing of Kew at that time. A Patent Roll dated 28 September 1483 sets forth that a grant was made for life to:

> . . .the King's servant Henry Davy of the Office of Keeper of the King's Park called 'le Newpark' seven acres of meadow by the bridge of Chartesey, Co.

[16]

Kew Palace, built in 1631 for Samuel and Catherine Fortrey.

The Pagoda on a frosty day.

Old Richmond Palace as rebuilt by Henry VII in 1499. This Palace was much used by the Tudors and early Stuart monarchs but fell into disuse after Cromwell's time. The Palace demesne included the lands of Kew.

Middlesex, for the sustenance of the deer within the park in winter and the custody of the King's warren of the King's lordship of Shene, receiving 6d, 3d, 2d and 3d daily from the same from the issue of the King's manors or lordships of Shene, Petersham, Kayo, Hamme and the island of Crowet in the said counties with all other profits, and also 2d daily from the same issues for the repair of the paling and hedges of the same park.

From this involved sentence emerges the fact that Kew (Kayo) had achieved sufficient standing to be taxable, although at a lower rate than the neighbouring villages.

No record has survived of those who lived at Kew before the sixteenth century but a considerable amount is known about several of the people who had houses

[17]

there in Henry VIII's time, although we do not know precisely where they lived. None was more splendid than Charles Brandon, Duke of Suffolk, who married Henry's sister Mary. Charles' father had been standard-bearer to Henry VII, and was singled out for this reason at the Battle of Bosworth in 1485 and killed by Richard III. Charles, who was rather like his monarch, tall, sturdy and valiant, with a tendency to corpulence and a strong animal nature, seems to have been a favourite of Henry VIII from the first.

As part of the devious political dealings of the time Mary found herself betrothed to the King of France, Louis XII, and in August 1514 was married to him by proxy in London. She joined the King in October but he died two months later, on the last night of 1514. Charles, on whom Mary's mind had long been set, in spite of the fact that he had already at least one wife living, was already in Paris. Greatly to Henry VIII's annoyance, the couple married without waiting for his consent or that of the King's Council, many of whom wanted him put to death when they heard of it. The offence was eventually purged by the gift to the King of all Mary's plate and jewels and a bond of £24,000 to repay by yearly instalments Henry's expenses for the marriage with Louis. The couple had to live quietly for a time but by 1520 were back in favour and Charles accompanied Henry to the Field of the Cloth of Gold, which occurred in that year. From then on Charles took a prominent part in public affairs.

The residence of the Duke of Suffolk and Mary at Kew is mentioned in the Duke's will but the *Cygnea Cantio* of Leland, the traveller and antiquary, is the chief authority for it. He describes 'Chevo, vulgo Kew' as a 'villa elegans', distinguished by the hospitable residence of Mary, the French Queen, saying:

Ad Chevam hospitio Piae Mariae
Gallorum Dominae celebriorem

The house in which the couple lived was called Suffolk Place. Leland says that it was erected in the time of Henry VII and, according to report, was built by a steward of the royal household. Under the present Kew Palace, which was not built until the next century, is a fine vaulted stone crypt from an older building. Some have thought that this might be the foundation of Suffolk Place, but nothing definite is known to support this assertion, though it may well be true.

Another member of the royal circle who was resident at Kew was Charles Somerset, later Lord Herbert and Earl of Worcester. Born about 1460 he was an illegitimate son of Henry Beaufort, third Duke of Somerset. In his childhood he was probably an exile in Flanders, being knighted by the Archduke Philip before the battle of Bosworth. By his bearing in the battle he found favour with Henry VII, there being, among the accounts for Henry's coronation, an entry of 'three yards of cloth of gold' for the 'bastard Somerset'. He was appointed Chamberlain of Henry VII's household on 30 May 1508 and reappointed by Henry VIII the day after Henry VII's death, bearing as part of this office responsibility for the arrangements for the Field of the Cloth of Gold. He died in 1526, our knowledge of his residence at Kew being derived from his will which directed that, if he died at 'Kaiho' or anywhere near the Thames, his body should be carried by water to Windsor. The injunction was carrried out: he was buried in the Beaufort chapel at Windsor.

The ending of the Wars of the Roses and the more settled times that followed the advent of the Tudors afforded opportunity for continental influences to spread more freely in Britain, first the New Learning of the Renaissance and then the religious turmoil of the Reformation. By the end of Mary I's reign in 1558 many changes had, as a result, taken place in English society and much new effort had been stimulated. Some of the energy generated had begun to be turned towards finding out more about things that had long been taken for granted and had never been subjected to close scrutiny. The movement had its origin primarily in a desire to verify and establish correct texts for the authorities of the ancient world which had been rediscovered, but the work inevitably led on to further investigation which was eventually to evolve into modern scientific method.

Although it had not progressed very far by the 1550s, a start had been made in England in biology and in particular the study of plants, the science of botany. These events are not only related to the story of Kew in a general sense that modern Kew is concerned with botanical science, but in a more specific way because of a fortuitous but particular link with Kew which gave that place, for a short time at the beginning, a leading role.

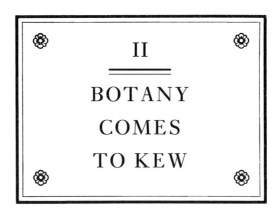

II

BOTANY

COMES

TO KEW

'For out of olde feldes, as men seith,
Cometh al this new corn fro yere to yere;
And out of old bokes, in good feith,
Cometh al this newe science that men lere.'

Chaucer: *The Parlement of Foules*

When the Roman Empire in the west went down before the barbarians, the botanical works of the great men of classical times, Theophrastus, Dioscorides and others, were preserved in the eastern Empire at Constantinople and much of the knowledge later passed into the Arab world. In the west, however, the study of plants virtually ceased for a thousand years. When it began again the first works were based on corrupt Latin texts illustrated by simplified and debased drawings which, as the originals from which they were copied were plants of southern Europe, were of limited use in northern European countries.

The invention of printing brought no improvement but in 1530 works began to be produced, at first in Germany, in which the illustrations of the plants had been drawn from the life and were clearly recognisable. Later works which followed in the course of the sixteenth century greatly improved the plant descriptions. A leading figure in England in this process was William Turner, who earned for himself the title of 'Father of English Botany'.

Turner was born at Morpeth, the son, perhaps, of a tanner. He gained the interest of Thomas, first Baron Wentworth of Nettlestead in Suffolk and in 1526 became a Fellow of Pembroke Hall in Cambridge. He was one of the group of young men who became the spearhead of the Reformation in England, being closely associated with two of the most famous, the martyrs Ridley and Latimer. Ridley taught him Greek.

The Protestant principles that Turner imbibed at Cambridge led him to become a preacher in the fiery demagogic mode of the time, and he also wrote polemical books supporting these principles. Fortunately for English botany, his second love, he managed, by absenting himself from England at the right time, to escape the violent end to which Ridley and Latimer came in Mary I's reign. They were burnt at the stake in Oxford in 1555. He did not, however, escape scot-free. His college work was ended in 1537 and Bishop Gardiner had him imprisoned, but he was able to go abroad at the end of June 1543.

Turner's attitude to botany at this time is set out in his preface to the 1568 edition of his *Herbal*. He says that:

> above thyrtye years ago ... beyng yet felow in Pembroke Hall in Cambridge where I could learne never one Greke, neither Latin, nor Englishe name, even among the Phisiciones of any herbe or tre, such was the ignorance in simples (medicinal herbs) at that time, and as yet there was no English herbal but one, all full of unlearned cacographees and falsely naming of herbes, and as then had neither Fuchsius, nether Matthiolus, nether Tragus written of herbes in Latin.

This is a fair summary of the situation in the 1520s. He set out to remedy the deficiency himself.

He first went to Italy, a visit which was of great importance to him as a botanist as it brought him in touch with the greatest minds of the time working in the plant world. Bologna university was ahead of all others at this time. He met and talked with the leading writers and workers and himself became an accepted figure in the learned world. From Italy he went to Germany, returning home on the accession of Edward VI in 1547. His career now took a new turn. He was appointed physician to Edward Seymour, Duke of Somerset, who was the greatest power in the land at this time, being Lord Protector, the King being a minor. Seymour had gained possession of Sion Abbey, on the other side of the Thames from Kew, the religious inhabitants of which had been dispossessed in the dissolution of the monasteries in the 1530s. As part of his job, Turner was given a house at Kew, to

[21]

Of cicerbita.

Cicerbita.

Cicerbita is named in greke sogchos: in Englische a sowthystel: in duche hasenkoel oz gense distel: in frenche lateron: it groweth common inough in all cuntries. There are twoo kyndes of sowthystel: There is one that is a wilde one, and hath moze pzyckes vpō it. and the other is but soft and tender, much desired to be eaten in meat: wyth a stalke full of cozners and hollow wythin: sumtyme red, with leues indented about the edges of thē. The other sowthostell is yet tenderer, after the maner of a tree: hauyng bzode leues, the leues departe the stalke whych groweth out in to bzaūches

The vertues

of Sowthystell.

The vertue of both is to coule and bynde, therfoze they are good foz the hoote stomake: and also foz inflāmatiōs, if they be layd vnto the place, the iuice of thē swageth the gnawing of the stomake, if it be dzonken It prouoketh also milke if it be layd to in woll. It helpeth the gatherynge together of mater, that is about the foundament, and the mother. Bohe the herbe & the roote is good foz them that are byten of a scozpion, yf it be layd to in the maner of an emplayster.

Of Cich oz ciche pease.

Cicer is called in greke erebinthos, in duch kicherns kicherbs: aud zisserne in frenche ciche ou pois ciches. Cicer is muche in Italy and in Germany I haue seen them in the gardine of the barbican in London and I haue it in my garden at kew. Cicer may be named in English ciche oz ciche pease, after the french tonge: cicer is described nother of dioscozides, nether of theophzastus, nether of plini sauing ÿ Plini sayeth, ciche hath a rounde cod, but other pulse haue longe and bzode after the figure of the seed, theophzastus saythe that ciche hath the longest roote of any pulse and that cicer differeth from other pulses by many pzoperties, first in that it is long in bzingynge furth the floure & doth hastely bzyngsozth the fruite, foz within. xl. dayes afterthat it is come vp it may be made persit, as some saye. It is also very fast & harde as wood, it is very ill foz new fallowid ground by the reasō that it wasteth it

R.ii.   vp

which he refers both in one of his letters and in one of the plant descriptions in the 1568 edition of his *Herbal*.

Living at Kew, Turner would have had to cross the Thames almost every day to Sion to attend his master. He complains bitterly about this in the Preface to his first *Herbal*, published in 1551, saying:

> I have more than three years bene a dayley wayter (i.e. in attendance, in the sense still preserved in Lady-in-Waiting) and wanted the chefe part of the day most apte to study, the mornynge, and have bene long and sore vexed with sycknes ... For these thre yeares and an halfe I have had no more lyberty but bare three weekes to bestow upon ye sekyng of herbes, and markyng in what places they do grow.

References in his books indicate that Turner grew exotic plants in his garden. It is an extraordinary and apt coincidence that the 'Father of English Botany' should have had such a garden at the precise spot where, two hundred years later, the national botanic garden was to arise. His garden had, of course, no direct connection at all with the later garden, although at least one important Victorian reference work was sufficiently misled by the coincidence to say, quite incorrectly, that 'the foundation of Kew Gardens is attributed to William Turner'.

In 1550 Turner obtained preferment as Dean of Wells and left his residence at Kew. He did not enjoy his situation very long, however, before Mary I came to the throne and he had to flee abroad again for the duration of her reign. While he was at Kew Turner must have been a familiar and well-loved figure to the local people as he wandered through the lanes and the surrounding villages on his botanical excursions, although they may have thought that he was not quite right in the head as he went about 'sekyng of herbes'. He was not a scientist in the modern sense, his primary intention being to interpret the true meaning of the past rather than to break new ground, but he went about his work in a methodical and painstaking manner which approximated to scientific method. He examined and checked all the authorities he could find and looked at his plants with the painstaking eye of the specialist in the light of what they said, and he tried to establish their true names.

Opposite: The page of the *Herbal* of William Turner, 'Father of English Botany', in which he says of the chick pea that 'I have it in my garden at Kew.'

He made no attempt to classify plants, his *Herbal* being arranged in alphabetical order, but with his efforts the methodical study of plants began in Britain.

As he wrote in English Turner's usefulness was limited on the Continent and his influence thereby that much less, but he was the first in Britain to show an interest in the study of plants that was to occupy the time and energy of many able and eminent men of his own nation in the years to come, and which was eventually to create the climate of opinion in which the foundation and maintenance of a national botanic garden at Kew could be accepted as a legitimate and worthwhile charge on national resources.

III

CHOICEST

FRUIT

'A heav'nly paradise is that place
Wherein all pleasant fruits do flow ...'

Thomas Campion (d.1620)

One of those who lived at Kew in Queen Elizabeth I's reign was her favourite Lord Robert Dudley, whom she made Earl of Leicester in 1564. He lived in a house called the 'Deyrie House', the site of which is not known. It seems likely, however, that it was not far from the present Kew Palace, although that had not yet been built. This notion receives some support from the long-used name of the area adjacent to it on the riverside, now used as a car park. This piece of ground by the Brentford Gate of the Royal Botanic Gardens has long been known as 'Queen Elizabeth's Lawn'. On this lawn there formerly stood a great elm, supposed to have been planted by Mary I, but called 'Queen Elizabeth's Elm' because she is said to have sat under it, perhaps in the company of Leicester. It was described in early Victorian times as 'a most beautiful specimen of luxurious vegetation'. It was blown down in 1844 and the top made into a kitchen table for Osborne House, Queen Victoria's retreat in the Isle of Wight.

The account given of Queen Elizabeth's favourite magician, John Dee, in John Aubrey's *Brief Lives*, reveals another resident of Kew in Elizabeth I's time, his own great grandfather, Dr William Aubrey, who was a cousin of John Dee and his intimate friend. 'Dr Aubrey's country house was at Kew and John Dee lived at Mortlake, not a mile distant', says John Aubrey. 'I have heard my grandfather say they were often together.' Some of their correspondence has survived. Dr Aubrey, a 'Doctor of Lawes', was a man of some importance at the court of Queen Elizabeth, who had an affection for him and called him her 'little doctor'. He was one of the delegates for the trial of Mary, Queen of Scots and was 'a great stickler for the saving of her life, which kindeness was remembered by King James atte his coming-in to England, who asked after him, and would probably have made him his Lord Keeper, but he died a little before that good opportunity happened. His Majestie sent for his sons, and knighted the two eldest, and invited them to court, which they modestly and perhaps prudently declined.'

Another resident of Kew in Elizabeth I's time was Sir John Puckering, a distinguished lawyer who was Speaker of the House of Commons in the sessions of 1584–5 and 1586–7 and Lord Keeper of the Great Seal from 1591 to 1596. Sir John left behind him the character of being a pliant person who made himself useful in scenting out conspiracies, and was none too nice in the disposal of ecclesiastical patronage. J E Neale, in *The Elizabethan House of Commons*, is much harder on him. He says Puckering was a man whom Elizabeth might have described as a 'greedy grasper', a notoriously corrupt person for whose death little grief was shown. Neale's condemnation of the 'mercenary Serjeant Puckering' springs primarily from consideration of the 'catalogue of lamentations' he put up in 1595, when he was 'successfully begging one hundred pounds land in fee farm from the Queen, and with naive and typical effrontery, while about to entertain her with prodigal magnificence at his Kew home, claimed that he had served her as Lord Keeper at a net loss of £1,000 a year'. He claimed also that the loss of legal fees and expenses of office as Speaker in 1584–5 and 1586–7 amounted to £2,000 and that he never received £400 fee for those four sessions as Speaker, which was 'recompense meant me by Her Majesty'. Neale comments, in reference to this last statement, that 'lest another notch be cut in the mythical tally of Queen Elizabeth's meanness, let us add what he conveniently forgot to say, that he had asked for his fee as Speaker to be set against a debt which he owed the Queen'.

Sir John Puckering seems to have entertained Queen Elizabeth at his house at Kew on more than one occasion. In the Harleian collection of manuscripts in the British Museum is one entitled 'Remembrances for Furnyture at Kew, and for her Majestie's entertainment, 14 August 1594', which would appear to have been drawn up by Sir John Puckering's steward. The writer calls it a 'Memorial of things to be considered if her Majestie should come to my Lord's House':

[26]

1st. The manner of receivynge, both without the house and within, as well by my lorde as my ladye.

2nd. What present shall be given by my lorde, when and by whome it shall be presented, and whether any more than one.

3rd. The like for my ladye.

4th. What presents my lorde shall bestowe on the ladies of the privye chamber, and gentlemen ushers and other officers, clerks of the kitchen, or otherwise.

5th. What rewards shall be given to the footemen, gardes and other officers.

6th. The purveyed diet for the Queen, wherein are to be used her own cooks, and other officers for that purpose.

7th. The diet for the lordes and ladies, and some fit place for that purpose specially appointed.

8th. The allowance for the diet of the footemen and gardes.

9th. The appointment of my lorde's officers to attend on their several offices, with sufficient assistants unto them for that time.

10th. The orderynge of all my lorde's servants for their waiting, both gentlemen and yeomen, and how they shall be sated to their several offices and places.

11th. The proporcyon of the diett fitted to each place of service; plate, linen and silver vessels.

12th. To furnishe how there will be uppon a suddeyne, provision of all things for that diett made, and of the best kinds, and what several persons shall undertake it.

13th. As it must be for metes, so in like sort for bredd, ale, and wynes of all sorts.

14th. The like for bankettynge stuff.

15th. The sweetenynge of the house in all places, by any means.

16th. Grete care to be had, and conference to be had with the gentlemen ushers how her Majestie would be lodged for her best ease and likinge; far from heate, or noyse of any office near her lodgynge; and how her bedchamber may be kept free from any noyse near it.

17th. My lorde's attendance at her departure from his house and his companye.

[27]

Ladies diett for bedchamber; ladies, some lodges beside ordinarie. Lord Chamberlayne in the house. Lord of Essex nere, and all his plate from me, and diett for his servants at his lodgings.

We do not know whether a visit followed this memorandum but an account has survived of a visit of the Queen in the following year to Sir John's house at Kew, when she was entertained on 11 December 1595, with 'prodigal magnificence'. A contemporary letter reported that 'Her majesty is in good health; on Thursday she dined at Kew, my Lord-Keeper's house, who lately obtained of her Majesty his suit for £100 a year, land in fee farm. Her entertainment for that meal was exceedingly costly. At her first lighting she had a fine fan, with a handle garnished with diamonds. When she was in the middle way, between the garden gate and the house, there came running towards her one with a nosegay in his hand and delivered it to her with a very well-penned speech. It had in it a very rich jewel with many pendants of unfirld diamonds, valued at £400 at least. After dinner, in her privy chamber he presented her with a fine gown and juppin (petticoat), which things were pleasing to Her Highness, and to grace his lordship the more she, of herself, took from him a salt, a spoon and a fork of fair agate.'

A fourth owner of property at Kew in Queen Elizabeth I's time was Sir Hugh Portman, descendant of a Somerset family of lawyers closely associated with royalty, owners also of the Marylebone property, Portman Square, which still preserves their name. Precisely what property Sir Hugh owned at Kew is not known with certainty but the researches of W L Rutton seem to have cleared up the matter so far as it is capable of being elucidated. Sir Hugh died in 1604; although his will gives no information about his property, inquisitions post-mortem into his estates mention two houses that he owned at Kew. The first of these is described as a 'capital messuage in Kewe' and the second as 'one other messuage called 'le Deyrie House', with all its appurtenances, two gardens or orchards, a pigeon house, and a rood of pasture.'

The Deyrie House was Leicester's house, which the Portmans doubtless acquired after his death in 1588. The 'capital messuage' may have been Sir John Puckering's house. The Portmans and Puckerings were related, Sir Hugh's brother, Sir John Portman, having married Sir John Puckering's daughter. No evidence exists, however, to identify the sites of either of these houses.

If Sir Hugh Portman possessed the house which preceded the present Kew Palace his heirs had sold it by 1630 to Samuel Fortrey, who pulled the old house down to its foundations and rebuilt it, incorporating beneath the western two-thirds of the house the existing vaulted cellar or crypt with a brick-lined well. He

[28]

commemorated the work by building the initials of himself and his wife and the date 16$_{SC}$31 (the letters stand for Samuel and Catherine Fortrey) above the entrance, where they may still be seen, almost as fresh as the day they were placed there. Samuel Fortrey was of Flemish parentage, being born on ship when crossing the Channel from Dieppe to England, where his parents took asylum from the persecution of the Spanish in the reign of Elizabeth. His father or grandfather was John or Nicholas de la Forterie of Lisle in Flanders, and his wife was Catherine, daugher of James La Fleur of Hainault.

Kew Palace is an attractive red-brick building seventy feet long and fifty feet in depth. It formerly had a wing on the south side which has been pulled down. The style of the house seems to have catered for a limited clientele. Traditional timber-framed houses of the Tudor type were still being built in the provinces and the wealthy were employing Inigo Jones to make buildings in the Palladian style. Rich merchants around London wanted something different from either of these. They did not wish to appear old-fashioned nor, on the other hand, to follow the new classical fad. The gabled brick house was devised to meet their requirements.

The designer seems to have enjoyed his commission and took full advantage of his opportunities to use brickwork in an ornamental way. This is laid in Flemish bond, that is, with the sides and the ends of the bricks alternating, which at that time had not been used in England. The building is of three storeys, the main fronts consisting of three gables with double-curved sides crowned with pediments which are alternately triangular and segmental, again at the time a new design feature, as were the brick crosses of a mullion and a transom incorporated in the windows. There is rustication around all the windows and the centre bay is ornamented by superimposed pilasters except on the top floor where columns have been used. The windows are also pleasantly arched.

The interior of the Palace is very simply arranged, with a cross passage through from the present main doorway to the river doorway: there are two main rooms to the left and two to the right of the passage. A certain amount is left of the original decoration. The ceiling of the Queen's Boudoir is quite possibly Jacobean, but, if not, is probably eighteenth century work designed by William Kent. The room on the ground floor called the King's Dining Room contains some traces of seventeenth century work: the overmantel, to which an oblong panel was added in the eighteenth century; the strapwork plaster decoration, with grotesque masks, over the inner doorway; and possibly the Tudor rose in the ceiling.

The panelling in the King's Breakfast Room is of early seventeenth century work and is divided into bays by fluted pilasters with carved composite capitals and strapwork bases. There is also seventeenth century panelling and strapwork in

[29]

the Library. The Queen's Drawing Room on the first floor retains its early seventeenth century frieze and fireplace and there is reset seventeenth century panelling in a small connecting-room leading to the Queen's Bedchamber. Samuel and Catherine Fortrey would therefore recognise a few familiar things if they returned now to their old home. One or two items seem to have come from the house they pulled down, notably some restored and reset linen-fold panelling in the Library Ante-Room and a Tudor fireplace in one of the rooms on the second floor. No doubt when the house was newly-built they were proud of their new home, which symbolised their prosperity and was a mark of their rising status.

There was formerly a small colonnade at the back of the house, under the balcony which is still present, from which a flight of steps led down to ground level. Eighteenth century maps, the earliest which show the Palace, do not indicate any garden on this side of the house. The land between the Palace and the river was a tree-fringed grazing paddock, with paths or roads. In latter years trees and shrubs were scattered over almost the whole area. No formal garden had certainly existed there since the early part of the eighteenth century. Before the embankment of the Thames was raised the area was probably partially flooded at the highest tides and it seems probable that it was never at any time developed as a garden for this reason, although the Deyrie House which may have preceded the present Kew Palace building is referred to in the inquisitions into the Portman estate as having two gardens and a rood of pasture. This could, however, have been at the side of the house.

There is an interesting entry in the Court Roll for Richmond for 1647. Samuel Fortrey:

> . . . surrendered in Court all that his Capital Messe and Customary Tenement with the appurts scituate in Kijo als Kew within the manor of Richmond and all and singular the Barns Stables Edifices Orchards Gardens Plots Court Yards Proffitts and Easments Whatsoever belonging to the said Messe and Tenement and one Close of Land containing by Est Seven Acres of Land more or less adjoining to said Messe or Tenement with all and singular Woods Underwoods Ways Waters and Fisheries adjoining to the said Close of Land belonging to or appertaining to the Use of himself and Theodora his wife and his heairs forever who were admitted accordingly Rent 7s.10d. and other services. Fine 20s.0d. Theodora being no tenant before.

This entry also brings out that there were gardens attached to the house at that time. The seven acre close of land 'more or less adjoining' the house may be the area between the Palace and the present day Herbarium block.

Two years after this, on 26 March 1649, Kew Palace was leased to Edmond Prideaux for three years. There is no direct evidence to support the notion, but it seems very possible that the Edmond Prideaux who took the house was the eminent lawyer and politician on the Parliament side who bore that name. He was a member of the Long Parliament and Solicitor-General in the 1640s but apparently had conscientious scruples about the line followed by the regicides as he resigned when the King's trial became imminent. From 6 April 1649, a few days after he took the house, he became Attorney-General, retaining this office until his death in 1659. For many years he managed the postal services and by 1649 had established a regular weekly service about the kingdom. He made a great fortune from the posts and his legal practice and appears to have been a sound Chancery lawyer, highly esteemed by his party as a man of religion. On 31 May 1658 he was made a baronet for his 'voluntary offer for the mainteyning of thirty foot-souldiers in his highnes army in Ireland'. Whether he held Kew Palace for three years only or for longer is not known, but he may well have continued there until his death in 1659 as he was still in office and no doubt required to be within easy reach of London.

The diarist John Evelyn introduces another resident of Kew. Returning on 27 August 1678 from a visit to Windsor he:

> ... went to my worthy friends Sir Hen:Capels (bro:to the Earle of Essex) it is an old timber house, but his garden has certainely the choicest fruits of any plantation in England, as he is the most industrious, and understanding in it. ...

This 'old timber house' was at Kew: it stood on the site marked by a sundial to the right of the Orangery some seventy or eighty yards in front of Kew Palace. When the house was later bought by Prince Frederick of Wales it contained a collection of portraits. These had been the property of the wife of Sir Henry Capel: she was Dorothy Bennet, daughter of Sir Richard Bennet, who was the son of Thomas Bennet, citizen and mercer, Sheriff of London and Middlesex in 1613–14.

The description of the house suggests that it was in the Tudor timbered style and built before Kew Palace, probably in the sixteeenth century. It may, indeed, be one of the two houses owned by Sir Hugh Portman. On the other hand, it is possible that Thomas Bennet built it because a number of the portraits, which probably formed the original nucleus of the collection, are inscribed in a uniform way and seem from their date to have been brought together early in the seventeenth century, a reasonable inference being that they were bought to furnish the walls and gallery of the newly-built house. The view has, however, also been advanced that they were collected by Sir John Leman, Dorothy Bennet's ancestor on her mother's side whose portrait, now at Hampton Court, was in the collection.

Lady Capel was very highly connected, her father Richard Bennet being first cousin to Henry Bennet, Earl of Arlington, Secretary of State to Charles II and member of the famous 'Cabal' which governed Britain in his reign. Henry Capel was himself of high birth, being the second son of Arthur, Lord Capel of Hadham, by Elizabeth, daughter and heiress of Sir Charles Morrison of Cassiobury. He was created KB at the coronation of Charles II. Both Sir Henry and his brother were noted gardeners, Arthur at Cassiobury and Sir Henry at Kew. The garden which Evelyn saw was on the south side of the house in the area which is now the broad sweep of lawn, the largest open area in the Royal Botanic Gardens, to the south-west of the Orangery.

On 30 October 1683 Evelyn visited Sir Henry at Kew but found that he was away and therefore returned home. Not, however, gardener that he was, before looking over his friend's house and appraising the alterations. He notes that Sir Henry had repaired 'the old timber house' and 'roofed his hall with a kind of cupola, and in a niche installed an artificial fountain', but the room seemed to Evelyn to be 'over-melancholy' and capable of much improvement by 'having the walls well painted a *fresca*, etc'. He admired 'the two greene-houses for oranges and myrtils communicating with the roomes below', which he thought 'very well contriv'd' and considered 'a cupola made with pole work between two elmes at the end of a walk, which being covered by plashing the trees to them ... very pretty'. He deplored, however, 'too many fir-trees in the garden'.

Five years later, on 28 March 1688 Evelyn visited Sir Henry again, commenting that his 'orangerie and myrtetum are most beautiful, and perfectly well kept'. Sir Henry was 'contriving very high palisadoes of reedes, to shade his oranges in during the summer, and painting those reedes in oil'.

Sir Henry's garden was by now very well known and an account of it by J Gibson, who had visited it in 1691, was included in a paper read to the Society of Antiquaries on 3 July 1694, which contained descriptions of a number of gardens and nurseries he had visited:

Sir Henry Capell's garden at Kew has as curious greens (evergreens), and is as well kept as any about London. His two lentiscus trees, for which he paid forty pounds to Vesprit (a nurseryman), are said to be the best in England, not only of their kind, but of greens. He has four white striped hollies, about four feet,

The original specimen of *Rosa hugonis* growing at Kew from which the species was described and named.

above their cases, kept round and regular, which cost him five pounds a tree this last year, and six laurustinus he has, with large round equal heads, which are very flowery and make a fine show. His orange trees and other coarser greens stand out in summer in two walks about fourteen feet wide, enclosed with a timber frame about seven feet high, and set with silver firs hedgewise, which are as high as the frame, and thus to secure them from wind and tempest, and sometimes from the scorching sun. His terrace walk, bare in the middle, and grass on either side, with a hedge of rue on one side next a low wall, and a row of dwarf trees on the other, shews very fine, and so do from thence his yew hedges with trees of the same at equal distance, kept in pretty shape with tonsure. His flowers and fruit are of the best, for the advantage of which two parallel walls, about fourteen feet high, were now raised and almost finished. If the ground were not a little irregular, it would excel in other points, as well as in furniture.

The 'lentiscus trees' (*Pistacia lentiscus*) were recent introductions into Britain from the Mediterranean. Sir Henry's interest in such novelties prefigured the Kew interest of later years in exotic plants. His garden was a worthy forerunner of the botanic garden to be established in after years on the same site.

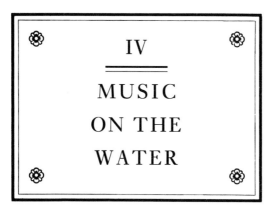

IV

MUSIC
ON THE
WATER

'They all stayed, until it was
late, upon the water to hear the
Prince's music, which sounded
much sweeter than from the
shore.'

Lady Bristol

The Capel estate included only that part of present-day Kew which lies between the modern Holly Walk (formerly Love Lane) and the Kew Road. The remainder, between Love Lane and the Thames, was part of the grounds of Richmond Lodge, a house, long since demolished, which stood in what is now the Old Deer Park. This had been part of the demesne of old Richmond Palace but in 1707 Queen Anne gave a lease of it for three lives to James Butler, Duke of Ormonde. He was, however, attainted as a Jacobite on 20 August 1715 and forfeited the property leaving it, however, in very good condition. A report by John Macky, who saw it in 1714, commented that 'above all, the woods cut out into walks, with plenty of birds singing in it, makes it a most delicious habitation'. Kew, to which this partly refers, is still a sanctuary and refuge for wild birds which may, as in Macky's day, be heard singing there.

When George II and his wife Caroline were Prince and Princess of Wales they quarrelled with George I and were expelled from his court. In 1721 they bought the Richmond Lodge estate, and thus part of the old royal manor of Richmond came back into possession of the reigning family. George I died in 1727 and Caroline was given possession of the Richmond Lodge estate, including the portion that later became part of Kew Gardens. At the same time, however, developments were taking place on the Capel estate and the village of Kew which adjoined it to the north.

There were by 1710 some eighty houses in the Kew area, mainly in the vicinity of the Green, and in 1712 the inhabitants applied to Queen Anne for leave to build a chapel for their convenience and accommodation, on the site of an 'ancient gravel pit upon Kew Green'. Permission was given for enclosing so much as would amount to 100 feet square and the Queen gave £100 towards the cost of the building, which amounted to £600, the remainder being found by subscription.

It was also necessary to find money for an endowment before the church could be consecrated. A sum of £80 was raised with which land was bought in Essex. One of the trustees for the purchase was Sir Charles Eyre, who lived in what was afterwards known as 'the Queen's house' on the site of the present Lower Nursery. Another trustee was Christopher Appleby, whose family possessed land incorporated into the north-eastern end of Kew Gardens. The third trustee was John Lely, son of the famous court painter, Sir Peter Lely. Sir Peter had spent part of the considerable fortune he had made from painting on acquiring a country house and small estate at Kew which his son had inherited. This house and land was on or slightly to the west of the present Herbarium building. Sir Peter Lely was the first of several painters of renown who found the Kew environment congenial to them, and who have some part in the Kew story.

Various bequests were made to the new church in the succeeding years, including one by Lady Capel, who survived her husband and lived in the 'old timber house' until 1721. She left £10 per annum to the church and also founded a trust to benefit a dozen schools in various parts of the country, including one at Kew, which still exists. John Lely was one of the Trustees for the school at Kew. There was doubtless a good deal of mutual respect and trust between the Capel and Lely families, who had been neighbours for so long.

Lady Capel was buried in Kew church, which had been dedicated to St Anne, and which at that time was very small, consisting of little more than a nave and a north aisle. Her monument is composed of different marbles, and shows a flaming urn under a tented canopy, with a pediment above, supported by Corinthian pilasters, fluted, and surmounted with the family arms; at the sides are weeping boys, and at the bottom, cherubs. An inscription describes her as having:

... dy'd retyr'd in this place, on 6 June 1721, without issue, aged 79, having always supported, during the course of many years, the character of piety, vertue, charity and goodness, in every station and circumstance of publick and private life. She was, in her life time, an eminent benefactress to this place, and at her death, extended her charitable care to every part of the kingdom, to which she had any relation or tye.

When Lady Capel died, her house, as she had no children, passed to her grandniece, Lady Elizabeth Capel, granddaughter of the first Earl of Essex. Lady Elizabeth had married Samuel Molyneux in 1717, when he was 28, and in 1721 the couple came to live in the Kew house, the 'old timber house' that Evelyn saw, so that both Richmond Lodge and the Kew House had new occupants in that year.

As a principal residence of the Prince and Princess of Wales Richmond Lodge soon became a centre of gaiety. A great number of the nobility drove down by road in their coaches, or came by water in their barges, during the summer months. Lady Bristol, Lord Hervey's mother, who was one of the Princess's ladies, wrote that:

> Yesterday there was a horse race for a saddle the Prince gave; 'Twas run under the terrace wall for their Royal Highnesses to see it. There was an infinite number of people to see them all along the banks; and the river full of boats with people of fashion, and that do not come to court. . . . They all stayed, until it was late, upon the water to hear the Prince's music, which sounded much sweeter than from the shore. Everyone took part in the Prince and Princess's pleasure in having this place secured to them when they almost despaired of it, and though such a trifle, no small pains were taken to disappoint them.

The last sentence of this refers to the efforts made by George I, pursuing his malice against his son, to block the purchase of Richmond Lodge.

The Prince and Princess hunted several days a week from Richmond, going out early in the morning and coming back late in the afternoon, riding hard all day over rough country. Anything that the Prince enjoyed he rather tended to overdo, irrespective of whether others in his entourage were enjoying themselves as much. The hunt was well-attended, but many of the Maids of Honour would have shirked the violent exercise if the Prince would have let them off. Alexander Pope the poet, who lived at Twickenham and was frequently at court, wrote of one encounter:

[37]

I met the Prince, with all his ladies on horseback, coming from hunting. Mrs Bellenden and Mrs Lepel took me under their protection (contrary to the laws against harbouring Papists) and gave me dinner, with something I liked better, an opportunity for conversation with Mrs Howard. We all agreed that the life of a Maid of Honour was of all things the most miserable, and wished that every woman who envied it had a specimen of it. To eat Westphalia ham in a morning, ride over hedges and ditches on borrowed hacks, come home in the heat of the day with a fever, and (what is worse a hundred times) with a red mark on the forehead from an uneasy hat; all this may qualify them to make excellent wives for foxhunters, and bear abundance of ruddy-complexioned children. As soon as they can wipe off the sweat of the day, they must simper an hour and catch cold in the Princess's apartment; from thence (as Shakespeare has it) to dinner with what appetite they may, and after that, till midnight, walk, work or think, which they please.

In her early years in England, Caroline was anxious that her elder son Prince Frederick should be brought over from Hanover. He was growing up a stranger to her, and the accounts of him which were reaching her were far from reassuring. The failure to bring him to England meant that he was brought up as a German with German interests and tastes and in consequence regarded his future position as Electoral Prince as of no less importance than any he could occupy in England. His mother, whom he did not see for fourteen years, and who never set foot in the Electorate again, came to hold the view, after the birth of her second son William, that Frederick should stay in Germany.

With the death of George I in the autumn of 1727, which occurred while the Prince and Princess were at Richmond Lodge, Caroline's opportunities, now she was Queen, to make changes on the estate, which now became her property, were greatly increased. Her lands, however, included only about half of modern Kew. Developments had also been taking place which concerned the other half, that to the east of Love Lane, now the residence of Samuel Molyneux.

Samuel Molyneux was an intelligent and cultivated man. In his early twenties he had attracted the attention of the Duke and Duchess of Marlborough, being with them at Antwerp during the winter of 1712–13. He was sent by the Duke on a delicate political mission to the Court of Hanover in 1714, when the Duke had to establish his position with the man soon to be his King. He came back to England with the Royal family and when George I became King had ingratiated himself so much that he became secretary to George Augustus, the Prince of Wales, a post he retained until the Prince succeeded to the throne in 1727.

Molyneux was greatly interested in astronomy and optics. He made the acquaintance of James Bradley, who was some years younger than himself but who had, under the influence of an uncle, early developed a genius for astronomy, and had been elected a Fellow of the Royal Society on 6 November 1718, when he was still only in his middle-twenties. In 1720 Molyneux obtained a living for Bradley, who was not in affluent circumstances, and he was elected to the Savilian Chair of Astronomy at Oxford in 1721. He carried out a good deal of his work at Wanstead, where his uncle lived, and continued there after his uncle's death in 1724, but the basic work for two of his most important discoveries was carried out with Samuel Molyneux in the Capel house at Kew.

Robert Hooke, remembered most as a brilliant microscopist but also eminent in other fields, had supposedly detected a large parallax for the star λ Draconis. This so puzzled and intrigued Bradley and Molyneux that it was decided to investigate the matter further. For this purpose, on 26 November 1725 Molyneux had a $24\frac{1}{2}$ foot telescope fixed in the direction of the zenith in 'the old timber house'. The telescope moved on an axis at the top. It was supported by some ironwork, which was fixed very strongly to a 'large stack of brick chimneys which were quite within the house and scarce at all exposed to the weather, and were very strong old built chimneys, some part of the house being near three hundred years old'.

On the north side was fixed a small brass screw which touched the lower end of the tube with its point, being directed southward. The telescope was gently pressed against the point of this screw by a string passing over a pulley, with a small weight on the end, which pulled it northward. The telescope could therefore be moved with the greatest nicety by rotating the screw. For reasons which need not be set out, the telescope must have been located on the south side of the house. From later plans it seems likely that the only chimney which faced the south was in the eastern of the two compartments which flanked the centre of the garden front. This is where it was probably located, passing through the floors of the house with its top immediately under the roof of the building.

The first observation was made by Molyneux on 3 December 1725. It was repeated by Bradley 'chiefly through curiosity' on 17 December when, to his surprise, he found the star pass a little more to the southward. This unexpected change, which was in the opposite direction to that which could have been produced by parallax, continued, in spite of every precaution against error, at about the rate of one second of arc every three days; and at the end of a year's observations the star had completed an oscillation 39 seconds in extent.

The source of this inexplicable movement could not at first be surmised. It was

[39]

found also in other stars, varying in degree with their latitude. A movement of the earth's axis was at first postulated and a check made on a star on the opposite side of the pole. The drift of this star was, however, insufficient to support this explanation as accounting for the whole of the change. The possibility of refraction as a cause was also discussed and rejected. Bradley now transferred his activities to Wanstead and accumulated a further year's observations, but was still unable to explain them until he accompanied a pleasure party on a sail on the Thames in September 1728. He noticed that the wind seemed to shift each time the boat was put about and a question put to the boatman elicited the reply that the changes in the direction of the vane at the top of the mast were merely due to changes in the boat's course, the wind remaining steady throughout. This was the clue he needed. The explanation of part of the apparent change lay in the movement of the earth itself in its orbit, which must cause an annual shift in the direction in which heavenly bodies are seen.

Bradley announced this memorable discovery of the 'aberration of light' in a letter to Sir Edmund Halley, the Astronomer-Royal, which was read before the Royal Society on 9 and 16 Jan 1729. When, however, this had been fully accounted for the observations had shown from the beginning a further slight progressive inequality. Bradley watched this carefully for twenty years before he committed himself to publishing another discovery. He was able to announce in 1748 that his first idea that a movement of the earth's axis had caused the apparent change in the direction of the star was, in fact correct: although not the whole cause, it was a contributory factor. The earth nodded slightly on its axis as it rotated, due to the pull of the moon: he had discovered what is known as the 'nutation of the earth's axis'.

Samuel Molyneux would undoubtedly have continued to co-operate with Bradley. He did assist in setting him up with his telescope at Wanstead but he unfortunately inherited a brain disease from his mother and had a seizure in the House of Commons which eventually resulted in his death on 13 April 1728. He was no sleeping partner in Bradley's investigations: his description of the instrument used at Kew and his observations are an integral part of the early investigations. There are also papers by him on the grinding and polishing of optical glass. He might well have made some mark in the scientific world had he lived longer. As it was, his death put the 'old timber house' and the estate at Kew on the market. Destiny dictated that it should fall vacant at a time when George I's grandson Frederick, whom we left as a boy in Hanover, should, as Prince of Wales and heir to George Augustus, now George II, be looking for a country house. He was successful in acquiring it and thus another piece of the royal manor of Richmond followed Richmond Lodge and its lands back into royal possession.

[40]

V

QUEEN
CAROLINE'S
KEW

'You may strut, dapper George
But 'twill all be in vain;
We know 'tis Queen Caroline,
Not you, that reign.'

From the time that Caroline became Queen in 1727 until her death she virtually governed England with Robert Walpole. She did not merely reign, but ruled. They first discussed matters together, decided on a course of action, and she then brought the King round to her way of thinking. The onlookers were not fooled: it was perfectly clear to them what was happening as the rhyme quoted above, which was current during this period, illustrates.

Walpole obtained £100,000 a year for her from Parliament, plus Somerset House and Richmond Lodge. Caroline continued to use Richmond a great deal and spent large sums on developing the gardens, for which she employed Charles Bridgman, who was one of the first to make a move away from the formal garden then in fashion. Horace Walpole wrote of Bridgman's work in 1785 that though he:

> still adhered much to strait walks with high clipt hedges, they were his only great lines; the rest he diversified by wilderness, and with loose groves of oak, though still within surrounding hedges. ... As his reformation gained footing, he ventured farther, and in the Royal Garden at Richmond dared to introduce cultivated fields, and even morsels of forest appearance. But this was not till

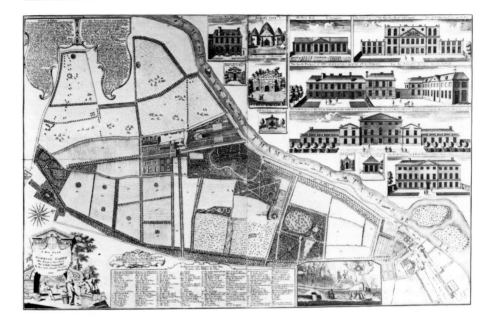

Plan made in 1748 by Robert Greening showing both Queen Caroline's Richmond Lodge estate and Prince Frederick's White House at Kew, together with elevations of the Palaces and other buildings, including Merlin's cave and the Hermitage, on these estates.

other innovators had broke loose, too, from rigid symmetry.

Caroline's interest in great men and their works was reflected in the embellishments with which she adorned her garden. Two of these were unlike anything seen in England before and were considered very peculiar indeed, although they would not have occasioned surprise in anyone familiar with Continental gardens. Both were designed by William Kent, who began working for Caroline soon after 1730: one of the buildings was called the 'Grotto' or 'Hermitage' and the other 'Merlin's Cave'. Grottos had been a feature of European gardens since Renaissance times and date, indeed, to the classical era. Hermitages, complete with resident anchorites, had also been a common feature of large gardens in Continental countries. The name 'Grotto' seems somewhat displaced for Queen Caroline's building, which was Gothic in style and contained busts of famous men. 'Merlin's Cave' was not a cave at all but a thatched building that looked rather like a collecion of beehives. It had a set of life-size wax figures round a table, one of whom was the wizard Merlin. Who the others were, and whether one represented Queen Elizabeth I or not, and what was the purpose and meaning of the scene, gave rise to much discussion.

A work by Edmund Curll, an unscrupulous publisher of very doubtful reputation, published in 1736 and entitled *The Rarities of Richmond* purports to identify all the figures, but it is doubtful, from the satirical tone of the work, how much value can be placed on the supposed identifications. One of Caroline's protégés was a poet named Stephen Duck, who had been employed as a thresher before he was brought to notice for his literary work; his wife showed visitors around Merlin's Cave. Curll's account is as follows:

> Since the legendary Story of Merlin, our British Wizard, hath been thought worthy of Royal Regard; inasmuch that an Edifice is now erected to his memory, for the benefit of honest Stephen Duck and his wife: in order, therefore, the better to suit her place, I shall *thresh* out, from the Monkish Historians, the entire feats both of him and his namesake which, as a Necessary Woman, she may recite to the numerous Visitors to the Cave, more especially the Ladies.

Curll continues:

> In the Royal Gardens of Richmond, about a mile distant from the Palace, through several fine walks and agreeable labyrinths (the ground being most beautifully laid out) you arrive at Merlin's Cave. The Denomination of this Place is ... an impropriety; because it is a building above Ground. It is a thatched Edifice, and very Gothique. The Room is circular, supported by four wooden pillars, and the walls, at present bare. At each end of the Room are a few Books in three small Niches (though it is not doubted but that Mr Duck's stock will daily increase). The Library appears in the neat Plainness of Quakerism, all the Books being covered with White-Vellum, and their Names written, in an indifferent Hand, upon their Backs. In the middle of this Room Mrs Duck conducts you to six waxen Images, the handy work of Mrs Salmon, all taken from the Life, and said to represent the following Persons, viz.
>
> I.   Merlin from Mr Ernest, Page of the Back-stairs to the Prince of Wales.
> II. Queen Elizabeth, from Miss Paget.
> III. Her Nurse (By some called a Witch) from a Tradesman's Wife in Richmond.

[43]

To Her most Excellent Majesty
QUEEN CAROLINE
This View of the HERMITAGE,
in the Royal Garden at Richmond.
And of the Heads of Hon.ble Rob.t Boyle Esq.r Jn.o Locke Esq.r
S.r Isaac Newton Will.m Wollaston Esq.r & of y.e Rev.d D.r Sam.l Clarke
Done after the Marble Bustos placed therein,
is most Humbly
Dedicated.

IV. Henry the Seventh's queen from Mrs Margaret Purcell, Dresser to her Majesty (By some said to be the Countess of Suffolk).

V. Minerva from the Honourable Mrs Poyntz.

VI. Merlin's Secretary, from a Youth named Kemp, one of the Duke of Cumberland's Grenadiers.

Curll next describes the postures and positions of the waxen figures:

I.   Merlin sits at a Table, in a musing Posture, with his Conjuring-Wand in his Hand, Books and Mathematical Instruments before him, his Eye cast towards that shelf (in the Nich next him) whereon stands the Life and Predictions of the late celebrated Duncan Campbell the North British Conjuror.

II.   On the other side of the Table stands his Secretary.

III and IV.   On the Right Hand of Merlin, are Queen Elizabeth, and the old Beldam, before-mentioned.

V and VI.   On the Left Hand of the Secretary are Minerva and King Henry VII's Queen.

The Hermitage or Grotto was easier to understand and during the years 1732 and 1733 there was much praise in the *Gentleman's Magazine* for the Queen, Michael Rysbrack, the sculptor who made the busts with which it was ornamented, and the personages portrayed. Curll's account of the Hermitage is as follows:

Having paid our Devoirs not to old, but to young Merlin (who, bye the bye, as here represented in his Molten Image of Wax, does not show a Person above Thirty Years of Age) and had some chit-chat with Mr Duck who informed us that (in Imitation of Mr Pope) he was printing his Barnean Hymns, and other Rustique Rhythms by subscription, we took leave; and by our Guide, was conducted to Mr Bridgman's Ground; in whose Territories, as a Gardener,

Opposite: The Hermitage, one of the curious buildings with which Queen Caroline furnished the gardens of the Richmond Lodge estate.

stands the Hermitage. In our way we could not help admiring the beautiful and most delightful Terras next the River Thames; after which we pursued our journey, and were (through a great Number of close Hedge-Alleys, neatly clipt) led up to this Building. The Architecture of which is very Grotesque, being a Heap of Stones thrown into a very Artful Disorder, and curiously embellished with Moss and Shrubs, to represent rude Nature. The entrance of this Pile is adorned with a Range of Iron Palisades finely gilt. A Person attends to open the Gates to all Comers. Upon entering you behold, elevated on high, a very curious Busto of the Honourable and justly celebrated Robert Boyle Esq., incompassed with Rays of Gold. And on each side of him below, are placed Sir Isaac Newton; Mr Locke; Dr Clarke and Mr Wollaston, author of the Religion of Nature delineated.

In 1732 the *Gentleman's Magazine* printed the following verse:

> With Honour, thus by Caroline placed
> How are these venerable Bustos graced!
> O Queen! With more than regal title crown'd
> For Love of Arts and Piety renown'd!
> How do the Friends of Virtue joy to see
> Her Darling Sons exalted thus by thee?
> Nought to their fame can now be added more
> Rever'd by Her whom all Mankind adore.

Other verses in Latin and English followed month by month. When she was Princess of Wales Caroline had welcomed any literary man of eminence to her court at Leicester House. The King and Walpole, however, despised literature and she could not, against this combination, fulfil promises made in her earlier days. Her inability to help drove Swift, Gay and Pope into enmity towards her. She must have been very hurt by Swift's verses in the *Gentleman's Magazine* of April 1733:

On the Grotto:

> Lewis the living genius fed,
> And raised the Scientific Head;
> Our Q—, more frugal of her Meat
> Raises those heads which cannot eat.

[46]

Answer'd

> Our Queen, more anxious to be just
> Than flattered, rears the living Bust
> To chosen Spirits, learned Tribe!
> Whom, Lewis like, she cannot bribe.

There was a more effective reply:

> Since Anna, whom bounty thy merits had fed,
> Ere her own was laid low, had exalted your head
> And since the good Queen to the wise is so just,
> To raise heads from such as are humbled in dust,
> I wonder, good man, that you are not envaulted.
> Pr'y thee, go and be dead, and be doubly exalted.

Which Swift characteristically capped with:

> Her majesty never shall be my exalter;
> And yet she would raise me I know, by – a halter.

Four of the subjects of the busts, Newton, Locke, Boyle and Bacon are historical figures, but Clarke and Wollaston have been forgotten. Samuel Clarke died in 1729, renowned as a philosopher and theologian and vigorous opponent of the Deists: his friend and contemporary, William Wollaston, followed a similar line. Five of the busts (Bacon is the absent one) are at Kensington Palace.

It was not only the general public who were puzzled by Merlin's Cave. The King also regarded it as proof of the Queen's folly rather than her wisdom. When the Queen told him that she had heard that the *Craftsman*, the Opposition paper run by Bolingbroke, had attacked her hobby, Merlin's Cave having been described by that journal as 'an old haystack thatched over' she got no sympathy. 'I am very glad of it,' he said, 'you deserve to be abused for such childish silly stuff, and it is the first time I ever knew the scoundrel (Bolingbroke) in the right.'

The Keeper of Merlin's Cave, Stephen Duck, also came in for a good deal of satire. He was, according to Joseph Spence, 'for many years a poor Thresher in a Barn, at Charleton in the County of Wilts., at the wages of four shillings and sixpence per week till taken notice of by ... Queen Caroline'. 'Considering the

[47]

difficulties the poor Fellow lay under,' says Spence, 'the inclination for knowledge must have been very strong in him.' He must have had some ability and a good deal of application, for when his day's work was done, he taught himself the rudiments of grammar and a smattering of history and science. These labours bore fruit in poetry. 'The Spectators improved his Understanding, he said, more than any other thing. The copies of verses scattered in those pieces, helped on his natural Bent that way, and made him willing to try, whether he could not do something like them. . . . What first gave him a higher Taste of Poetry than he had been us'd to, was Milton's *Paradise Lost*. . . . Stephen read it over twice or thrice with a Dictionary, before he could understand the language of it thoroughly. This, and a sort of English grammar . . . have been the greatest use to him in anything.'

Duck seems to have been a likeable and modest fellow for he said himself that 'he could not think highly of' his own poems. 'Gentlemen, indeed', he said, 'might like 'em, because they were made by a poor Fellow in a barn; but . . . he knew as well as anybody, that they were not really good in themselves.' Spence lent him books and found the means to print some of his poems in pamphlet form, including *The Thresher's Labour*, a poem descriptive of his own life. These poems were shown to Lord Tankerville and Dr Alured Clarke, Prebendary of Winchester, who arranged for them to be brought to the notice of the Queen.

Caroline was greatly interested in the fact that these poems were written by a poor thresher and had Duck brought to her. She was so pleased with his manner and address that she settled a small pension on him, and in 1733 made him one of the Yeomen of the Guard. His poems were widely praised and, thus encouraged, he wrote more, the Queen's patronage ensuring a large sale. Duck in due time took holy orders, to which he always had a leaning, being ordained by the Bishop of Salisbury. Shortly after his ordination, the Queen appointed him Keeper of Merlin's Cave where, as we have already seen, Edmund Curll met him.

Curll makes no secret of his view of Duck. A note in the *Rarities of Richmond* makes one of his party, described as an 'Arch-Wag', say impromptu:

> What! Merlin's Cave! Exposed to sun and air,
> Z. . .ds, 'tis a Barn, and Duck's the Thresher there.

Another note in the same work, referring to Duck's intention to print his poems, says 'His works, at present, sell but for sixpence; which is a groat (fourpence) more than they are worth' and finishes with the couplet:

But Stephen thinks his reputation safe
While Fops subscribe, and Fools are pleased to laugh.

Greater men than Curll exercised their wit on poor Stephen: Swift wrote:

The thresher Duck could o'er the Queen prevail;
The proverb says, 'No fence against a flail',
From *threshing* corn he turns to *thresh* his brains
For which Her Majesty allows him *grains*,
Though 'tis confest that those who ever saw
His poems, think them all not worth a *straw*.
Thrice happy Duck! Employed in threshing *stubble*
Thy toil is lessened and thy profits double.

Duck was sensitive to these attacks and they may well have had something to do
with his later troubles. They were not entirely warranted, at least in the case of his
poem *The Thresher's Labour*. Robert Southey said in 1831 that 'the picture of rural
occupations' in this poem, 'here drawn from the life, is very different from what we
find in pastorals; but the truth of the description is not its only merit, for there are
passages in it which would have done no discredit to more celebrated names.'

Caroline remained Duck's constant friend, and preferred him successively to a
chaplaincy at Kew and the cure of souls at Byfleet in Surrey. His end, however,
was an unhappy one. He became deranged and threw himself into the water near
Reading in 1756 and was drowned. The kindness of his friends at court did not
cease on his decease and his family were allowed to retain his apartments at
Richmond. His son was buried at Kew in 1801, at the age of 73, and one of his
daughters, aged 79, in 1804. Sir Richard Phillips, in his *Walk to Kew* (1816)
mentions two more as still alive at that time and calls them 'relics of a former age'.
They were buried at Kew in 1816 and 1818, both 80 years old.

It is not now possible to determine precisely where Merlin's Cave and the
Hermitage were situated but from a comparison of old maps there seems little
doubt that both were in the area occupied by the modern botanic gardens. The
former was probably at the south-eastern corner of the lake in the southern part of
the Gardens, although that was not in existence at that time, being made in the
nineteenth century, and the latter at the north-western tip of this lake. A pile of
stones, remains probably of these buildings, remained for many years in the
Gardens, some being used for the rock garden made in 1882, but dispersed again in

[49]

One of the first five *Sophora japonica* trees introduced into Britain, planted in Kew around 1750 and still surviving there, though showing considerable signs of age.

the 1960s when the limestone in the rock garden was replaced by sandstone.

The King believed that the money expended by Caroline on Richmond Gardens came from her own resources and would not look at her plans, saying that he 'did not care how she flung away her own money'. Walpole, however, helped her from the Treasury without the King's knowledge and when she died she was in debt to the amount of £20,000. Caroline allowed the Richmond Lodge gardens to be opened to the public when the royal family was not there and a contemporary report says that 'the walks are full of company every evening to the great advantage of the town and the neighbourhood'. For the first time, some of the lands of the Royal Botanic Gardens were opened to visitors, the beginning of its long tradition as a place of public resort.

Some reflection of Caroline's daily life at this time may be gained from the letters of Peter Wentworth. On one occasion he recalls that on a Sunday, in the evening:

> . . . the Queen commanded me to order her a chaise and one horse, and a coach and six to follow, for Monday, at six o'clock in the morn, and six Life Guards and two Grenadiers, and your humble servant on horseback, which was to be kept a great secret. When I had put Her Majesty into her chaise with Princess Mary, she bid me ride and tell the Colonel of the Guard not to beat the drum as she passed out of St James's. We drove to the foot ferry at Kew, where there was a barge of four oars which carried Her Majesty, Princess Mary, Mrs Purcell and I to the Queen's house at Kew. We had a fine breakfast, with the addition of cherries and strawberries we plucked from the garden.

'The Queen's house at Kew' was not Richmond Lodge, but another house which stood at the northern extremity of the Richmond Lodge gardens to the west of the present Kew Palace in the modern Lower Nursery area.

The Queen had purchased this house from Lady Eyre, whose husband, Sir Charles Eyre, died in 1729: his tomb is in Kew churchyard. Lady Eyre had acquired it in 1722 from Sir Richard Levett, a Lord Mayor of London, whose wife died in that year. Sir Richard's will shows that he possessed two houses at Kew, one a copyhold messuage held of the manor of Richmond, which is probably this one and the other 'a capital messuage called Kew' which is the present Kew Palace. He had acquired the latter in 1697 from the last descendant of the builder to own it, William Fortrey. Caroline also leased Kew Palace, there being a record in 1728 of her daughters, the princesses, living in a house at Kew 'over against where Mr Molyneux lives'. Not yet regarded as a Palace, it became known as 'the Princess Royal's house'. Unfortunately, Caroline did not live to enjoy these possessions for long. She was taken ill on 9 November 1737 and died from an internal rupture, which she had concealed for a number of years, on 20 November 1737.

VI

PRINCE FREDERICK'S KEW

'... A handsome house to lodge a friend,
A river at my garden's end,
A terrace walk, and half a rood
Of land, set out to plant a wood.'

Jonathan Swift

Frederick, still in Hanover, was impatient with procrastination over his possible marriage to Wilhelmina, Princess Royal of Prussia, and started to take action on his own account. This annoyed his father, George II, so much that he gave orders that the Prince should be brought over to England. He landed on 7 December 1728, his arrival being deliberately played down by his royal parents.

The cause of George and Caroline's dislike of their son is not known. He had a childish streak but this seems to have been no more than pleasure in foolish pranks such as a schoolboy might enjoy, smashing windows and joining, incognito, some of the wild young bloods who paraded the streets at night. Even those who disliked him, however, had to concede that, for the first few years after his arrival in England, he behaved with considerable patience in the face of great provocation. Several surviving letters testify to the very favourable impression he made on his first arrival.

Prince Frederick of Wales, who grew exotic plants in the garden of the White House before the botanic garden was formally established, and thus began the collection on which the Royal Botanic Gardens, Kew was founded.

[53]

When Samuel Molyneux died on 13 April 1728 his wife, Lady Elizabeth Capel, left the 'old timber house' precipitately with Nathaniel St André, a court anatomist, and married him on 17 May 1730, incurring the Queen's displeasure. Dismissed from the court, Elizabeth and her husband had to retire to the country and put the house at Kew on the market just at the moment that Frederick was looking for a country establishment. He decided to take the lease and on 26 March 1731 bought the furniture and goods of this house and another, possibly two others, the doubt arising because a 1734 map shows the Prince as possessing two auxiliary houses at Kew, one of which is probably the house adjacent to the Main Gate of modern Kew and the other on the site of the present Herbarium.

The goods acquired with the 'old timber house' included the series of historical portraits mentioned earlier which had come to Lady Capel from her ancestors. The collection had probably been augmented by Lord Capel who, according to Vertue, 'collected many portraits of Eminent men as well of this Nation as of other parts of Europe'. Horace Walpole thought little of them when he saw them in September 1761, merely recording them as 'a room full of old heads in pannels, which have long been in the house; many are imaginary, all very bad, two very curious, Mary of Burgundy, wife of Maximilian, and the Duke of Norfolk, who was killed at Bosworth, probably an original picture, undoubtedly of the time'. The latter picture is now at Windsor Castle. Twenty other portraits seem to be identifiable at the present day as having come from Lady Capel's collection. With one or two exceptions, which are at Holyroodhouse, these are all now at Hampton Court.

The Prince was greatly interested in pictures, and is reckoned to be the most enthusiastic royal collector between Charles I and George IV. His first care, however, when he acquired his new residence, was the virtual reconstruction of this ancient building, both inside and out. For this purpose he turned to William Kent. Plans and elevations of the house as it was left by Kent are shown in Sir William Chambers' book on the gardens and buildings at Kew published in 1763. The third plate in the book shows a five-bay three-storey middle block with a big pediment, lower two-bay pavilions with smaller pediments, and long single-storey wings. Although it was called a palace, it was hardly palatial in appearance or size.

Queen Caroline had had some interest in science: she gave, for example, great support to Lady Mary Wortley Montague in her efforts on her return from the East to introduce inoculation as a means of combating smallpox. This interest passed on to her son, the scientific antecedents of the house created by the work in it of Samuel Molyneux and James Bradley being carried on to some extent by Frederick, as Lady Anne Irwin, Lady-in-Waiting to the Princess of Wales, explained in a letter she wrote from the White House in 1737:

> The Prince lives retired, seeing no company. We have a new amusement here which is both very entertaining and instructive. Dr Desaguliers has a large room fitted up at the top of the house, where he has all his mathematical and mechanical instruments at one end and a Planetarium at the other; which is an instrument he has invented which is much superior to the Orrery, and shows the motions of the heavenly bodies in a plainer and better manner. The Doctor reads lectures every day which the Prince attends diligently. I have gained some credit by the little knowledge I have in astronomy ...

In addition to his efforts in connection with the White House William Kent carried out another notable work for Frederick. The Thames was still a much-used highway and Kent designed for his use a magnificent Royal Barge. This splendid vessel which brought the Prince upriver on the many occasions he came to his country home, was profusely decorated with carved and gilded ornament and provided with seats for his favourite French horns. Kent's commission extended even as far as designing uniforms for the watermen who manned it. The barge, which was twelve-oared, was built in the yard of John Hall, which was on the south side of the Thames opposite Whitehall, in 1732. Kent brought together, as he did for the White House, a talented team of craftsmen. Their work may still be seen today, in all its original splendour, as the barge has survived and is on display in the National Maritime Museum at Greenwich.

Although Parliament granted the King £100,000 per annum for Frederick, he disgorged only a small part of this to the Prince until in 1735 a threat to appeal to Parliament caused him to carry out his obligation. He then not only granted the full £100,000 per annum but agreed to a separate establishment and to the Prince getting married. The King suggested Princess Augusta of Saxe-Gotha, whom he had seen on his visit to Hanover in 1735. Negotiations were successful and the Princess landed at Greenwich on Sunday, 25 April 1735.

The Prince was pleased with his bride, who had a pleasant expression and engaging manner which soon won her popularity. Lord Hervey described her as:

> ...rather tall and had health and youth enough in her face joined to a very modest and good-natured look to make her countenance not disagreeable, but her person, from being ill-made, a good deal awry, her arms long and her motions awkward had, in spite of all the finery of jewels and brocade, an ordinary air which no trappings could cover or exalt.

[55]

A contemporary print of the White House drawn in the eighteenth century by Joshua Kirby, the King's Drawing Master, who lived in a house, long since demolished, near the Brentford Gate.

To this Lord Egmont added that she was 'much pitted with the smallpox'. Comments from others were more generous and, in truth, there was nothing more wrong with her than the gawkiness of a seventeen year old.

The wedding on 27 April 1735 was noteworthy for the splendour and richness of the costumes, which were said to excel anything seen before in England on such an occasion. Augusta's behaviour after her marriage was exemplary. She refused to get involved in the bad feeling between Frederick and his parents, showing a foretaste of the judgement and force of character she exhibited as a mature woman. She could not, however, prevent an explosion between her husband and the King over the birth of her first baby which led to history repeating itself. Just as his own father, George I, had expelled George II when Prince of Wales from St James', so now George II expelled Prince Frederick and Princess Augusta. They settled first at Norfolk House and then, exactly as George Augustus and Caroline had done, took up residence at Leicester House and, exactly also as they had used Richmond Lodge, began to spend much time at the White House.

There they lived a simple outdoor life. Frederick was keen on cricket and not only arranged matches but took part in them; he also played at tennis and baseball. He walked very often in the meadows and lanes around Kew, including among his companions a dog which the poet Alexander Pope had given him with the following couplet engraved on its collar:

> I am His Highness's dog at Kew
> Pray tell me, sir, whose dog are you?

Another of his companions was the poet James Thomson, who had lived in Kew Foot Lane since May 1736. His famous poem *The Seasons* which pre-figured the Romantic movement by depicting Nature in a truthful and unaffected manner, as distinct from the artificial classicism of Pope, had been published in the 1720s. During the years at Richmond he revised it and added new material, some of the inspiration for which came from the royal gardens so near his home and the fields and lanes surrounding Kew, which he must have grown to know well, as he was a great walker.

At Kew Frederick was interested not only in Kent's work on his house but in the reputation he had also made as a landscape gardener, and employed him to lay out the garden there, himself working away enthusiastically in the gardens. Horace Walpole implies that the changes that were being made were substantial, saying that Frederick 'began great works in the garden' at Kew, but does not specify the works in detail. This interest in gardening was not a personal foible. It reflected a national interest among landowners in landscape gardening which was growing year by year and led to the formation of a number of famous gardens in the period 1730–1750. The idea of gardening had extended to comprehend the whole estate, not in the formal manner practised by Le Nôtre in France in the seventeenth century, but in a way which took account of and enhanced the innate virtues of the terrain. All the fashionable world now gardened in this way and royalty, in its greatness, must emulate and surpass its subjects. And so the stage was set, on the ornamental side, for the great developments soon to take place at Kew.

Frederick was in the van of change. In his few acres attached to the White House he had not much scope for landscaping, but he had adequate room to indulge a taste for exotic building. Vertue visited Kew in 1750 and saw 'a new Chinesia summer hous' which became known as the House of Confucius. This had been designed about 1747 by Joseph Goupy, the Prince's Cabinet Painter, and was decorated as the name suggests with subjects relating to Confucius, the furnishings being designed by Kent. There was also an 'India House' on which work was being done in 1750. A preliminary study was made for a Moorish

'Alhambra' in that year also, but this was not built at that time. Frederick had plans for a construction which was to represent Mount Parnassus but this also came to nothing. Thirteen Renaissance statues by Pietro Francavilla were bought for him in Italy but he died before these arrived in England. All these taken together represent a considerable effort on Frederick's part to create a memorable garden at Kew.

Side by side with the interest in landscaping had grown an interest in plants from other countries, which had begun to come in considerable numbers, particularly from America. There was also great interest in plant science, stimulated by Stephen Hales' book published in 1727 which, under the name *Vegetable Staticks*, demonstrated experimentally the basic processes of plant physiology. In the 1740s and 50s also Georg Dionysus Ehret, probably the greatest botanical illustrator who has ever practised that art, was working in London and lionised by the nobility.

Frederick was well aware of the influx of new plants and interested himself in the circles where such plants were discussed and grown. He was also well aware of what was being done in plant science, since he was in the habit of riding over from Kew to Teddington, where Stephen Hales held the living, to see the experiments in which he was almost constantly engaged, Hales being interested in many things apart from physiology. After his marriage, Princess Augusta frequently accompanied him on his visits to Teddington and came to have a high regard for Dr Hales.

Frederick's interest in botanical science was further stimulated by an acquaintanceship he formed in 1747. John Stuart, third Earl of Bute, was said to have come into the Prince's circle accidentally when asked to join in a game of cards in the Prince's tent to while away the time while the weather cleared after a shower at Egham races. They soon became friends, enjoying one another's company because of a mutual interest in plants.

Bute seems to have been making efforts to obtain exotics before this meeting, but it may be that Frederick's enthusiasm encouraged him to start. Writing to John Bartram, the American plant collector, on 2 June 1747 Dr John Mitchell asked him to get a parcel of seeds for the Duke of Argyll and requests him to send as many as he can afford for five pounds, saying: 'If they please, I doubt not he will desire more – as well as my Lord Bute, who gave me this commission. They desire chiefly flowering trees and shrubs.' G S Boulger writes:

He (Bute) seems ... to have planned the collection of plants from all quarters of the globe; for as early as 1750 a letter states that 'the Prince of Wales is now about preparation for building a stove (hothouse) three hundred feet in length; and my Lord Bute has already settled a correspondence in Asia, Africa, America, Europe and everywhere he can.'

Unfortunately, this project was never brought to fruition. In March 1751 Frederick caught cold and died. According to Horace Walpole the Prince, who already had chest trouble:

Last Tuesday was se'nnight . . . went to attend the King's passing some bills in the House of Lords; from thence to Carlton House, very hot, where he unrobed, put on a light unaired frock and waistcoat, went to Kew, walked in a bitter day, came home tired, and lay down for three hours, upon a couch in a very cold room at Carlton House, that opens into the garden. Lord Egmont told him how dangerous it was, but the Prince did not mind him . . .the Prince relapsed that night. . . .

In a letter of 1 April 1751 Walpole adds that 'the imposthumation is supposed to have proceeded, not from his fall last year, but from a blow with a tennis ball some years ago'.

The funeral provided for Frederick was of the poorest and quite unbefitting the heir to the throne. He was the subject of what may well be the cruellest epitaph ever compiled. The first two lines and the last line of this epitaph are almost the only thing that many people know about him:

> Here lies poor Fred
> Who was alive and is dead:
> Had it been his father,
> I had much rather;
> Had it been his brother,
> Still better than another;
> Had it been his sister,
> No one would have missed her;
> Had it been the whole generation,
> Still better for the nation;
> But since 'tis only Fred
> Who was alive and is dead
> There's no more to be said.

The King himself said, 'This has been a fatal year for my family. I have lost my eldest son but was glad of it.' Modern criticism has taken the line that the malice directed towards him both in his lifetime and afterwards had very little foundation. Much of the behaviour which seems objectionable and misguided was the only answer he could conceive to action taken against him. The considered verdict of a modern historian, Averyl Edwards, in *Frederick Louis, Prince of Wales*, is that:

> ... the impression left by a careful examination of unbiased contemporary references, and the surviving fragments of his own letters and writings, is of a man called to fill a position of extreme difficulty and outstanding importance, without any education or preparation. Inconstant, wayward and late to develop, the Prince, though dangerously responsive to kindness and flattery, yet possessed latent capacities which, had he come to the throne, would in all probability have made his accession less disastrous than has been generally supposed.

Those active in the plant world had a truer view of the Prince than his enemies. In his *Life of Peter Collinson* Brett James says, referring to the 1740s, 'Kew Gardens ... were even then beginning to be the Mecca of botanists, and Collinson and his friends thought highly of the Prince for his love of plants'. Such was the Prince's interest in them that Dr John Mitchell, writing to John Bartram on 30 March 1751, ascribed his death to his devotion to them, it having resulted from his 'contracting a cold by standing in the wet to see some trees planted, which brought on a pleurisy'. Peter Collinson himself wrote to John Bartram on 24 April 1751, saying:

> The death of our late excellent Prince of Wales has cast a great damp over all the nation. Gardening and planting have lost their best friend and encourager; for the Prince had delighted in that rational amusement, a long while: but lately he had a laudable and princely ambition to excel all others. But the good thing will not die with him; for there is such a spirit and love of it, amongst the nobility and gentry, and the pleasure and profit that attends it, will render it a lasting delight.

This is undeniable evidence that, in the last few years of his life, Frederick had begun to form a collection of exotic plants in his garden at Kew. It has been customary to claim that his wife Princess Augusta was the foundress of the Royal Botanic Gardens, and to date the formal foundation of the Gardens to 1759, when

William Aiton was put in charge. Sir William Chambers, working at Kew at that time, says that 'the Physic or Exotic Garden was not begun before the year 1760'. This seems less than just to Frederick. Perhaps the truth is that Frederick, whose character had been so sedulously blackened, was rather too dubious a personage to be acceptable as the founder of the august Royal Botanic Gardens and it was deemed preferable to accord the honour of foundress to his respectable wife. Nevertheless, Frederick began the planting of exotic plants at Kew and the history of the collection is continuous from that beginning. The title of founder of these Gardens more properly, therefore, belongs to him rather than his wife.

VII

PRINCESS AUGUSTA'S GARDEN

'It is well done, and fitting for a princess'

Shakespeare: *Anthony and Cleopatra*

Life in the Princess's family gradually returned to normality as the death of Prince Frederick receded into the past, and the round of duties and pleasures customary in the lives of those of royal blood was resumed. Some idea of the way the family entertained themselves may be obtained from a note which appeared in the *Gentleman's Magazine* in the summer of 1755, which related to Prince George's seventeenth birthday. In celebration of this:

> A pleasure barge, built by John Rich Esq, was launched in the gardens of Kew, and named the Augusta. It was formed in a taste entirely new, and made to imitate a swan swimming; the imitation is so natural as hardly to be distinguished from a real bird except by the size of it. The neck and head rise to a height of eighteen feet; the body forms a commodious cabin, neatly decorated and large enough to contain ten persons; and the feet so artfully contrived as to supply the place of oars, which move it with any degree of velocity. The novelty of the design, and the elegance of the execution, afforded a particular pleasure to the royal family who were present.

This fanciful vessel, floating on the lake at Kew, may be seen in a contemporary print.

George was beginning to grow up and a map of 1754 shows that he had already been allocated the present Kew Palace, sometimes called 'The Dutch House', as a residence. Augusta had retained the friendship of the Earl of Bute after her husband's death and George himself had great respect and affection for him, to whom he took the place of a father, so far as anyone was able to do so. As soon as he reached the age of 18 his grandfather, George II, made an attempt to break the bond and to induce him to make a separate establishment either at St James's or Kensington, but George would not move and, moreover, insisted that Bute should be appointed Groom of the Stole. Other appointments were made to afford the Prince a properly constituted household, but none of those introduced into the circle obtained any position of influence with him and he turned more and more to Bute for guidance and friendship.

As soon as the Prince's household was formed Princess Augusta, on the advice of Bute, appointed Sir William Chambers as her architectural advisor and tutor in architecture to the Prince of Wales. The results of this appointment very soon began to show themselves and a transformation was effected in the grounds of the White House that obliterated most of the work done in Frederick's time.

The new design for the garden divided the grounds of the White House into three parts with a peripheral belt, a feature first used by Philip Southcote in his popular *ferme ornée*, from which the idea may have been derived. The first area to the north of the lake, a stretch of water larger than the present Palm House lake but including that lake, contained the White House. South of the lake were two irregular meadows each surrounded by a ha-ha. Sheep and cattle grazed in these meadows, as in a *ferme ornée*, and among the trees and in various parts of the garden Chambers scattered a variety of buildings in different architectural styles.

Chambers retained in his scheme a certain amount of the work already in existence but the House of Confucius was moved in 1758 to a site 'at the head of the lake'. A Gothic cathedral designed by Muntz, which stood on the western periphery in the southern half of the estate was preserved, as were garden seats designed by William Kent. The first of the new buildings designed and erected by Chambers himself was a Gallery of Antiques, which was built in 1757. Although this is known to have been of classical design, its overall appearance is a matter of guesswork as it has long since disappeared. It seems to have stood in the southern part of the estate not far south of the lake. Several other buildings were being planned in 1757 as an Alhambra and Temples of Pan and Arethusa are stated to have been completed during 1758. Of these only the Temple of Arethusa, a small

[63]

Ionic style building of four columns now situated just south of the Palm House lake, has survived. Commemorative plaques recording the Kew dead in the two World Wars have been affixed to the wall of this Temple, which is now used as a garden arbour.

The Alhambra is the Moorish building for which a preliminary study had been made in 1750. Walpole had a poor opinion of it, saying that it was 'ill-imagined, and ... like the buildings of no country'. The Doric Temple of Pan was in the northern part of the Gardens 'in a retired solitary walk' to the east of the lake. Chambers also built some covered seats in 1758.

A start was made in 1758 on a new bridge across the Thames at Kew. The *London Gazette* of May 1759 reported that 'the workmen employed in the new bridge at Kew work double tides, in order, if possible, to finish the bridge against the fourth of June, for the convenience of the Quality, who shall that day (George III's birthday) pay their compliments to His Royal Highness.' It was finished in time and formally opened on that day but royalty had a special advance privilege:

> On Friday last (1 June) Their Royal Highnesses the Prince and Princess Dowager of Wales, with the Royal family, passed over the new bridge at Kew. His Royal Highness the Prince was pleased to make a present to the proprietor of £200, and ordered 40 guineas to be given to the workmen.

On the opening day 3,000 went across the bridge and there was 'a large meeting of Gentlemen in the neighbourhood who dined together upon the occasion, and in the evening there was a bonfire and illuminations at Kew Green'. The lower orders were not forgotten, as one hundred workmen were entertained at dinner and 'the healths of the King and the Heir Apparent were publicly and uproariously drunk!'

At this time the Seven Years War, which had begun in 1756, was well under way. To commemorate the victory at Minden on 1 August 1759 Chambers was asked to build a Temple of Victory. This Ionic style building stood on the mound now occupied by the flagstaff. During 1759 Chambers also built what remains one of the sights of the modern Gardens, the Ruined Arch. This is beautifully illustrated in his book in plates showing it from the north and south sides

Opposite: The Maidenhair Tree (*Ginkgo biloba*) which was planted c.1750. This tree, a native of the Far East, is a 'living fossil', remains of such trees being found in ancient geological strata. It is no longer known in the wild, having survived in temple courtyards.

[64]

[65]

respectively, the latter giving a glimpse of the Temple of Victory on its mound in the distance through the Arch. Chambers built it to provide a passage for carriages and cattle over one of the principal walks of the Gardens. His intention was 'to imitate a Roman Antiquity, built of brick, with incrustations of stone'. The Arch may still be seen today very much as Chambers built it, but the Temple of Victory has disappeared.

It seems probable that the large glasshouse, the building of which had been projected by Frederick in 1750, was built in 1759. It was 144 feet long. It lay east and west, the centre being occupied by a 'bark stove', formed of tan bark in pits in which pots could be plunged to benefit their occupants by the gentle and constant warmth generated by the fermentation of the bark. The two ends of the glasshouse formed two 'dry stoves'. As this was the first great glasshouse built in Kew for the cultivation of exotic plants, the event was something of a landmark. It stood on a site a few yards to the south-west of the present Ferneries and remained in being for a hundred years, not being pulled down until 1861. A wisteria which grew over it for many years was preserved on an iron framework and, one hundred and twenty-three years later at the time of writing, may still be seen growing over that framework, though much less vigorous than it was, in the shade of the large Maidenhair Tree, which itself had been planted in the 1750s.

The victories of 1759 established the English-speaking nations as the economic masters of the world, although the Seven Years War still had several years to run. In that same year, apt to the time, the first step was taken to put the exotic plants at Kew on a formal scientific basis and thus begin the fashioning of the instrument which was to prove so useful in the investigation and exploitation of the plant resources of the British Empire which now came into being. A young Scots gardener, William Aiton, who had been working for five years under Philip Miller at the Chelsea Physic Garden and thus had experience of the cultivation of a wide range of plants, was put in charge of the collection and ran it under the direction of Bute acting for the Princess.

The new garden occupied between nine and eleven acres immediately to the east of the White House and was divided into two nearly equal parts. The southern part was called the 'Physic Garden' because it contained the collection of herbaceous plants including those thought to be useful in medicine. This part also contained a collection of grasses and a special collection of British and alpine plants. The northern part, called the 'Arboretum', was devoted to trees and shrubs. The herbaceous plants in the Physic Garden occupied an area of about one acre. The plants were set out in long single rows with an alley between each row. The beginning of each genus was marked by a cast-iron label with the name of the

SIR JOHN HILL, M.D.
KNIGHT OF THE POLAR STAR.
First Superintendant of the Royal Gardens at Kew.

Sir John Hill, described as the 'First Superintendent of the Royal Gardens at Kew', a post about which nothing is known but who published an early list of plants cultivated at Kew. The print, which is taken from Thornton's *Temple of Flora*, shows also the White House.

[67]

genus painted on it and each individual species was marked by a smaller iron label bearing a number which referred to a list in a book called the *Herbaceous Book*. The collection of grasses was arranged in concentric circular beds in a piece of ground one hundred feet in diameter adjacent to the icehouse, which may still be seen. It was surrounded by a lilac hedge. The soil was very poor, the upper layers having been scooped out in earlier times to make the hillock of the ice house. The other collections were enclosed by clipped hedges of lilac and hornbeam.

Early records of the plants in the Garden have not been preserved but the lists published by William Aiton in his *Hortus Kewensis* of 1789 give the dates of introduction of the plants into England and are thus some guide as to when they may have arrived in the Garden. The Arboretum received a notable augmentation of its collection in the spring of 1762. The Duke of Argyll possessed an estate at Whitton in Middlesex in which, from 1720 onwards, he planted all the rare trees and shrubs he could obtain. When he died in 1761 all the trees that were young enough to be moveable were offered to Princess Augusta for her botanic garden at Kew. Some of the old trees which still remain in the gardens near the Orangery, the Maidenhair Tree (*Ginkgo biloba*), the False Acacia or Locust Tree (*Robinia pseudacacia*) and perhaps also the Eastern Plane Tree (*Platanus orientalis*) may be from this collection.

John Smith I, the great Curator of early Victorian times, who came to work at Kew when many of the trees planted in the early days had reached a substantial size, recorded that the western side of the botanic garden was occupied by species of oak (*Quercus*), plane (*Platanus*), poplar (*Populus*), ash (*Fraxinus*), walnut (*Juglans*), and elm (*Ulmus*), the north and part of the east by pines (*Pinus*), birches (*Betula*), maples (*Acer*) and others, while lime (*Tilia*), crab-apple (*Pyrus*), hawthorn (*Crataegus*) and species of small shrubs occupied the centre. What were considered rare and special trees were planted round the Temple of the Sun, a small circular classical building erected by Sir William Chambers in 1761, which survived until 1916 when it was smashed by a falling Cedar of Lebanon. Among these grew the first introduced plant of the well-known berried shrub *Aucuba japonica*. A tea plant (*Camellia sinensis*) also grew under the protection of rhododendrons for many years, but was killed by the severe cold of January 1838.

Next to the botanic garden was a Flower Garden and Menagerie, both of which were probably in existence before 1760, but have long since disappeared, as has the Theatre of Augusta which Chambers built in that year. A second building built in 1760, the Temple of Bellona, still, however, survives. This was built originally in the northern part of the Gardens, not far from where the T-range of glasshouses now stands. It has an attractive elliptical dome, painted blue on the interior.

[68]

A View of Lord Bute's Erections at Kew, with some Part of Kew Green, and Gardens

Engraved for the Political Register

A view of the houses on the south side of Kew Green with the White House in the background engraved in the early 1760s for a political pamphlet directed against Lord Bute and Princess Augusta. The letter 'L' shows the gate from Lord Bute's house giving access to 'B', the grounds of the White House 'A', Princess Augusta's residence, facilitating the alleged immoral relationship between them. Most of the houses on Kew Green may be seen today very much as they are shown in the picture, but the White House was pulled down by George III.

When George II died suddenly in 1760, the messenger sent to tell the new George III the news found him out riding. He returned at once to Kew Palace and waited for the official call. Later in the day the carriage of the great William Pitt came clattering over the new Kew Bridge and across Kew Green, with his servants in their smart blue and silver livery, to greet the new King and learn his wishes, and the new reign began. George III created a very favourable impression at the beginning of his reign but it soon became clear that the long domination of the Whigs had ended. In a reshuffle of offices in March 1761 Bute was brought into the Cabinet and at the same time a house was provided for him at Kew. He took up residence in a dwelling which Queen Caroline had owned which comprises the oldest part of Cambridge Cottage. Chambers undertook the design and arrangements for necessary alterations. The King wanted peace and the Tories constituted themselves a peace party but the general public was still war-minded. When Pitt resigned office early in October 1761 the country was flabbergasted and George's popularity fell with a thump.

Responsibility for the fall of their idol was attributed by the people to the influence of Bute and Augusta, now no longer the widow of a powerless and unpopular Prince but the powerful mother of a King. On all sides blame was laid on the King for dispensing with the services of the man who had led them on to great victories. Insults and filthy insinuations about his mother and Bute were hurled at him wherever he went. The London mob, ever ready to enjoy itself, seized every opportunity to rush about the city, carrying with them as symbols a jackboot (a play on Bute's name) and a petticoat, which they ceremoniously burnt to express their hatred. Bute had to have a bodyguard and even with this had some dangerous experiences at the hands of the rabble.

The King was married on 17 September 1761 to the German princess, Charlotte Sophia of Mecklenburg-Strelitz, who received Richmond Lodge and its gardens as part of her marriage settlement. Horace Walpole, who visited the adjacent gardens of her mother-in-law Augusta at the White House in 1761, thought little of the buildings so far erected. The Princess, he says, had 'laid out great sums ... it is said, £30,000', but 'there is little invention or taste shown. Being on a flat Lord Bute raised hillocks to diversify the ground and carried Chambers...thither, who built some temples, but they are all of wood and are very small.'

Augusta felt free, as mother of the reigning King, to embark on something more elaborate than had hitherto been erected on the estate. Walpole dates the commencement: 'In 1761 the Princess began a very high tower in the garden built after the model of the towers of Pekin, Nankin, etc. It was to cost £12,000.' The 'high tower' was the Pagoda, which disputes with the Palm House the title of the best-known building in the Royal Botanic Gardens. The building is octagonal in shape and of ten storeys. The first storey is 26 feet in diameter and 18 feet high, the diameter and height of successive storeys diminishing by one foot each, the total height being 163 feet. Each storey was finished with a projecting roof, covered with plates of varnished iron of different colours, and round each of them was a gallery enclosed by a rail. All the angles of the roof were adorned with large dragons, eighty in number, covered with glass of various colours. The ornament at the top

An eighteenth century print showing the Pagoda as it was when first built, with the ornamental dragons on the corners of the roofs, and the nearby Alhambra and Mosque, the latter standing on the hillock which in modern times has been occupied by the Japanese Gateway.

was gilt. The external ornaments have long since disappeared, but the building must have been a brilliant sight when it was new. Although gaily painted, its appearance today must be very drab compared with what it was like when newly built. Very soundly constructed of grey stock bricks it is as sound today as when first erected.

The completion of the new building caused a considerable sensation. The *London Gazette* for 20 July 1761 reported that, '... On Saturday a great number of

[71]

Chambers' Orangery as it is in modern times.

persons of distinction were at Kew Gardens to view a curious Chinese summerhouse, twelve stories high.' The artist Richard Wilson painted a picture of it as seen from across the lake. The *Universal Museum* carried a picture of it in 1764, but was unimpressed by its size. 'In comparison', it said, 'with the stupendous originals' which existed in the East, which it had previously described, 'we must look upon that at Kew almost in the same light as the little models of the latter which we see in the toyshop.'

Although there seems no contemporary reference to it, another noble building must have been recently completed or in course of erection at this time. The elegant Orangery which still stands at the northern end of the modern Gardens is the finest architectural work possessed by Kew. It is regarded as a fine example of the eighteenth century classical revival, designed and executed by Sir William Chambers with considerable taste and skill. It is not a large building, comprising

[72]

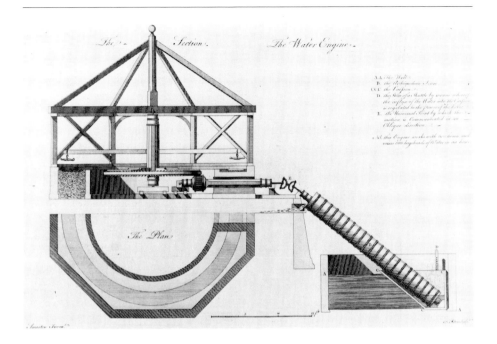

A section through Smeaton's pumping engine which for many years provided the Gardens' water supply.

one large room only 145 feet long, 30 feet wide and 25 feet high, but all the components of the design are balanced one with the other and combine to form a harmonious and pleasing whole.

Near the Pagoda on the western side is one of the small hillocks raised by Chambers. This is now occupied by a slightly reduced replica of a Japanese gateway but in 1761 Chambers built on it a mosque which had three doors, over each of which there was an Arabic inscription in golden characters. These inscriptions, which are quotations from the Koran, may be translated as follows:

> Let there be no coercion in religion
> There is no other God but God
> Make not any likeness unto God

[73]

Two small temples are mentioned by Chambers without giving the date of the building, but it seems likely that they had been built by 1762. The Temple of Aeolus is of interest because of its design. It was circular in shape with eight pillars but within the pillars was a seat which revolved on a pivot, so that it could be turned to provide the most advantageous position relative to the wind. The present-day Temple of Aeolus, which stands on the Mound on the north side of the Palm House Lake, is a rebuilding of the original without the revolving seat. The second building was a Temple of Solitude, which has not survived.

The improvements in the gardens of the White House meant that an improved water supply had to be provided. The famous engineer John Smeaton was given the task of satisfying this need. He built a pumping engine over an existing well. His specification required 'the engine to work with an Archimedes screw, 2 feet 8 inches in diameter and 24 feet long'. The screw was turned by a horse moving round a circular track 24 feet in diameter. The engine was designed 'to raise 1,200 hogsheads in four hours', a hogshead being about 50 gallons and the water being raised about eleven feet. There was also 'a small pump, to be worked occasionally by the engine, for raising water ... to the cistern in the kitchen garden.'

Although the King and Bute pushed the Peace of Paris through Parliament towards the end of 1762 it was against popular will and Bute was forced out of office in April 1763. Not before, however, Chambers had been commissioned to design and build a temple in the Gardens to commemorate it. It seems likely that this temple was not far from the Orangery. It has long since gone.

The departure of Bute from the political scene and the completion of Chambers' last ornamental work in the gardens of the White House mark the end of the period which may be regarded as dominated by the notions of Frederick, Bute and Princess Augusta. Ideas for further development along different lines were already in George III's mind, and he now began to take steps to turn them into reality.

VIII
═══
THE KING'S
PLANS

'What new creation rises to my view?'

Henry Jones 1767

The gardens of Richmond Lodge must have passed into the hands of George III little altered from the state in which Queen Caroline had left them and had, perhaps, begun to look a little old-fashioned. In the 1750s Lancelot ('Capability') Brown had come to the fore as the fashionable garden designer and had developed the ideas of Bridgman, Kent and Southcote into a style of his own, which had become very popular. In July 1764 George appointed him Royal Gardener, and moved his residence to Hampton Court. The King seems to have set him to work immediately on a plan for Richmond Lodge grounds and there is in the archives of the Royal Botanic Gardens a plan entitled 'Richmond Gardens with the proposed alterations, 10 December 1764' which is doubtless his work.

George III must have found the period after Bute's resignation a very tiring time politically because of the Wilkes affair and the continuing animosity against Bute which at one stage compelled the King to ask him to retreat to his wife's estate at Luton. These worries may have been a contributory cause to a serious illness which he suffered in the early months of 1765. He fell sick on 12 January, the cause of his illness being given out as a 'violent cold'. There was no doubt, however, that it was something much more serious than a cold since it kept him away from public business for the best part of three months. Rumour leaked out that his mind was affected and that at times he had to be put under restraint. It seems very likely that this illness was the first attack resulting from the disease porphyria which, following the work of Dr Ida McAlpine, her son Dr Richard Hunter and Professor C Rimington, was the most probable cause of the breakdowns which he suffered in later life.

The caricatures and satires on Bute and Princess Augusta continued unabated. They were libellous in the highest degree and not infrequently obscene. Once such piece of political invective appeared in March 1765, just as the King was recovering from his illness. It is of interest because it has attached to it what was called 'A true and accurate Plan of some part of KEW GREEN'. This purported to show that Bute had a house on the Green, which appears to be part of the modern Cambridge Cottage, in which his family resided, but had also built for himself another house on the Green, now called 'King's Cottage' 'to study in' and '*where none of his family resides*' (the italics are in the original), which was 'kept for him by one C. . ., a German, who is brother to the Ps of Ws WOMAN; and was formerly a menial servant to the Duke of St Albans; but now HOUSEKEEPER to LORD BUTE. By means of which LUCRATIVE post he is at present become a Man of considerable Property and Fortune.' This house is shown as having a walk leading down the garden to a door 'in the P D of Ws Garden Wall', there being no similar door in the Princess's garden from the house in which his family lived, the implication being that the house in which he was supposed to study was merely a blind for secret assignations with Princess Augusta. The houses shown in the picture are still standing, very little changed, on the south side of Kew Green adjacent to the Main Gate.

The Rev William Gilpin, the writer on forest scenery and picturesque beauty, visited Kew on 22 May 1765. As might be expected, he preferred nature unadorned to nature improved by the art of Chambers' buildings. He began his walk from the house and went down the east side of the garden first:

> The first view, upon the entrance, is that of the lawn before the house, which is very noble. The clumps are beautiful and very well disposed; and the buildings have a good aspect. The serpentine walk, into which you are next carried, has no fault but the want of variety. It might have admitted, here and there, a view of the lawn. The first opening is very fine.

He was so impressed with the view that he appended a drawing of it. Approving of

[76]

the Temple of Victory and the Theatre of Augusta, he found fault with a small Palladian bridge, which he thought a 'disagreeable object'. He continues:

> As you advance further, the Pagoda terminates the view. It is a whimsical object, but has a very good effect. As you approach it, the Moorish temple on one side and the mosque on the other make a disagreeable irregularity.

He found fault with 'little and unmeaning' patches of trees and, from the Pagoda, turned back on his tracks, still on the east side:

> The ruin (the Ruined Arch) is a very good one, and has a good effect but the view of the Temple of Victory as you walk along through the Arch is affected and disagreeable.

He found that the hillocks gave an unpleasant irregularity to the ground to the left of the Temple and at this point began to bear away towards the west:

> From the Temple of Victory you have a beautiful view of the house, over the lawn; only the Temple of Bellona is affectedly seen through the trees. From the colonnade the same view improves upon you. Towards the Gothic Temple the ground is finely laid out; only the trees still offend. The view is still beautifully varied as you walk along the side of the water.

Continuing round the head of the lake:

> As you pass the Chinese temple (the House of Confucius) the view opens on you still more nobly. The objects are all great, the water, the lawn and the thick wood beyond it. As you pass on (and look back) you have a view from the Seat to the Pagoda; which is one of those views in which the art of the introduction plainly appears and gives it an affectation. The Temple of the Sun appears to be introduced for no kind of purpose. The Greenhouse is very noble and the aviary very trifling; as it is not improvement of nature, but rather the reverse.

He concedes, however, that there were difficulties in constructing the garden arising from the terrain because it was dead flat and variety thus difficult to obtain. On the whole, despite his criticisms, he was favourably impressed.

At the same time as George III conceived the notion of getting Brown to modernise the grounds of Richmond Lodge, and put the work in train, another

The Queen's Cottage, built in 1772 as a summerhouse for Queen Charlotte and her family at the southern end of Kew Gardens.

idea occurred to him or was suggested to him. This was the possibility, eventually, of amalgamating Richmond Lodge gardens and the gardens of the White House. He took the first step towards this in 1765, obtaining an Act of Parliament in that year which gave him power to close the ancient road by the river between West Sheen Lane and the Horse Ferry at Kew, along which, in his day, William Turner had probably botanised, but which had fallen into disuse since Kew Bridge had been opened in 1759. In return for the power to close the riverside road, the Act required the King to convert the lane from Richmond to the new Kew Bridge into a properly metalled highway able to take vehicular traffic. The *London Chronicle* of 28 February 1767 duly informed its readers that, 'His Majesty is making an elegant road, 40 feet wide, from Kew Green to Richmond, on which he has employed 200 poor men during the hard season of the year.'

The year 1767 saw the publication of a poem on Kew by Henry Jones, an Irish playwright who was a protégé of Lord Chesterfield. The poem, in two cantos, is

[78]

pedestrian and uninspired, but contains one fact not noticed elsewhere. The interior of the Temple of the Sun was coloured red:

> Thy gilded gates unfold! Thy crimson cell
> And burnished cover, now blaze upon the sight
> With dazzling radiance, and delight the scene.

This must have been one of the most resplendent interiors of Chambers' small temples.

The first work which listed the plants in the botanic garden was published in 1768. This, the *Hortus Kewensis* of John Hill, must not be confused with the later *Hortus Kewensis* of William Aiton, published in 1789. In 1760 Hill, a protégé of Bute, had been appointed to the post of gardener at Kensington Palace, a sinecure worth £2,000 a year, but his connection with the botanic garden at Kew is not clear. In some works he is referred to as the Superintendent of the Botanic Garden and may have briefly held or been promised this post before William Aiton was appointed. After his death his widow claimed that he had been badly treated by Bute:

> The first employment that Lord Bute proposed ... was the disposing and superintending a part of the Princess of Wales' Garden at Kew, destined for botany, which was to contain all the plants known upon earth. In order to do this he formed a correspondence with men of distinguished learning everywhere: receiving and giving seeds. Even myself, after the fatal event of his decease ... expended many pounds upon the occasion for which, like him, I was never repaid.

It seems likely from this that Hill never held any official position at Kew and never enjoyed anything more formal than Bute's patronage there. Nevertheless, to compile his *Hortus Kewensis* he must have been a frequent and accepted visitor to the garden in the first few years of its existence and must have been allowed access to its records. His wife continues: 'His attendance was ... at least once a week required at Kew.' He may have given more assistance or had more influence on the garden than is usually supposed. Other circumstances reveal him as a somewhat bizarre and eccentric character and, like Prince Frederick, his dubious reputation may have discounted any good that he did. That said, his *Hortus Kewensis* is of limited use only, since it comprises a list of plants without date of introduction or reference to origin.

There now enters this story the first of the great names associated with the Royal Botanic Gardens as a scientific institution. Son of William Banks of Revesby Abbey in Lincolnshire, Sir Joseph Banks attended first Harrow and then Eton and at the age of 14 developed an interest in plants. In 1760 he went to Oxford and, finding no botany lectures there, induced Israel Lyons to come from Cambridge. Banks' father died in 1761 leaving him an ample fortune of which he obtained control on coming of age in 1764. In this year he made the acquaintance of William Aiton. He had left Oxford in 1763 but his attainments in natural history had been recognised and he had no difficulty in obtaining admission as a Fellow of the Royal Society in 1766. During that summer he went to Newfoundland to collect plants, coming back via Lisbon. He is credited in the *Hortus Kewensis* of William Aiton with the introduction of two new species from this voyage: these were his first recorded contributions to the Kew collections.

After his return he got to know the Swedish botanist, Dr Daniel Solander, and formed a friendship with him that was to last as long as Dr Solander lived. Solander had been a favourite pupil of the great botanist Linnaeus and when Banks came to know him was assistant librarian at the British Museum. Following the discovery of Tahiti and other hitherto unknown Pacific islands by Wallis and Carteret a project was formed ostensibly for observing the transit of Venus, due on 3 June 1769, from Tahiti, but in reality for further exploration, particularly to locate the supposed southern continent. Captain James Cook was put in charge of the *Endeavour* with instructions to proceed to Tahiti for the observations and then to make exploration southward. Sir Joseph Banks' interest in exotic plants induced him to obtain permission from Lord Sandwich, First Lord of the Admiralty at the time, to accompany the expedition at his own expense. He took with him Dr Solander, two artists and two attendants.

The famous voyage of the *Endeavour*, with its discovery of Australia and the naming of Botany Bay near where the city of Sydney now stands, is too well-known to be repeated here. Even at this early stage, Banks set to work to try out plants native to one place in another. He planted seeds of water melons, oranges, limes and other fruits and vegetables obtained in Rio de Janeiro, achieving some success in germination. By this voyage his interest in plants, and the wealth of plant products of the world, was so stimulated that he spent the rest of his long life in encouraging the collection of plants and the exploitation of the plant kingdom. When he returned to England, the King's collection of exotic plants at Kew was ready to his hand, and around the Kew collection his efforts centred.

The voyage of the *Endeavour*, which began on 25 August 1768 was not, however, completed until 12 June 1771 and in the intervening years George III

The Orangery with summer bedding and orange trees in tubs standing outside.

The Palm House with spring bedding in the foreground.

Sir Joseph Banks, who was *de facto* Director of the Gardens from 1772 to 1820

had come to an important decision with regard to Richmond Lodge. His rapidly increasing family, six of his fifteen children having already been born, was causing such pressure on space by 1769 that something had to be done. He had considered replacing Richmond Lodge with a new palace almost as soon as he had come to the throne and the project had been in his mind ever since. According to the journal of Mrs Papendiek, one of Queen Charlotte's German ladies:

In ... 1769 ... the ...court ... remained late in the season at Richmond, as His Majesty was greatly occupied in digesting plans with Sir William Chambers for a new palace at Richmond, the lodge now occupied being too small for the increasing family.

[81]

The design which the King was considering was the third in point of time that Sir William Chambers prepared for him and the only one that got further than the drawing board. Mrs Papendiek records that, when she wrote, many years after the event, 'the model of the excellent design fixed upon' could 'be seen by the public in the apartments at Hampton Court.' Two models of palaces designed by Chambers were, in fact, preserved at Hampton Court until 1922, when they were destroyed, but not before photographs of them had been taken by the Royal Institute of British Architects. Mrs Papendiek continues:

> A part of the Richmond Gardens already formed was marked out as a private garden round the palace; the site of which was to be near the Richmond end, opposite to Sion House, with an uninterrupted view of the river up and down, of the hill, the Cholmondeley walk and part of the green.

Lady Mary Coke dates for us the start of the work. She wrote in August 1770 that the King had:

> ... laid the foundations of a lodge (alas not a palace) in Richmond Gardens, very near where the old one now stands. It is to be 140 feet and to be built on arches as I suppose to command a greater prospect.

The population of Kew had continued to increase and by 1769 the congregation had assumed sufficient importance for Kew to be erected into a separate parish. The boundary of the new parish ran roughly east and west across the modern Royal Botanic Gardens through the northern part of the area where the Temperate House now stands. It was no doubt drawn, at the time it was fixed, in relation to clearly marked existing boundaries or objects but these are not now identifiable. The next year saw the church on Kew Green enlarged at the King's expense, the design being provided by J J Kirby, the King's Drawing-Master, who lived in a house next to the Brentford Ferry which has long since been pulled down. The nave was lengthened and the north and south aisles added to provide a building of the size and dignity consonant with its new role as a parish church. Economy still prevailed to some extent, the south aisle being separated from the rest and used as a charity school-house, with lodging for the beadle. The parishioners were not over-keen on the extension of their church as it meant they would have to find more money for its upkeep.

George III was particularly interested in astronomy. So much so that, when the impending transit of Venus approached he decided that he must have an observatory of his own from which to study it. Sir William Chambers was commissioned to design and erect the building known as the Kew Observatory which still stands in the Old Deer Park upon a low artificial mound. When the transit occurred on 3 June 1769 the King made the critical observation of the first contact between the discs, Dr Stephen Demainbray being put in charge of the Observatory as the first 'King's Observer'. The building has long since ceased to be used as an astronomical observatory but the instruments that were formerly housed in it may be seen in the Science Museum at South Kensington. The interior of the building has been altered since George III's time but its pleasing external appearance is almost unchanged. Nestling among the trees, of which an ancient Cedar of Lebanon may be a survivor from the days of Queen Caroline, it provides a fine focal point to the view seen from the south.

It seems probable that in 1770 the garden at Kew was visited by that remarkable youth, Thomas Chatterton. He was in London in that year and composed a poem of 3,000 lines entitled *Kew Gardens* which has nothing about the Gardens themselves but comprises a farrago of abuse of many people from Princess Augusta and Bute downwards, most of whom are unidentifiable. The poem has little merit, being merely a vehicle for rancour and envy. Shortly after it was written, on 25 August 1770, three months before his eighteenth birthday, he committed suicide in his lodging at Brook Street, Holborn.

By 1770 Brown had probably swept away the whole of the works of Bridgman and Kent in the gardens of Richmond Lodge, including 'Merlin's Cave' and the 'Hermitage'. At this time, too, he probably completed the destruction of the village of West Sheen which stood in the Old Deer Park and thus, to satisfy George III's desire to be a farmer, converted the whole of this area, once so populous and associated with so many famous names, into the parkland it has ever since remained. In 1767 it had been necessary to construct a ha-ha, which still exists, alongside the towpath between Kew and Richmond to prevent the royal cattle from straying. Although all the buildings other than the Lodge itself and the new Observatory had been removed, the Richmond Lodge estate was not entirely denuded of ornamental buildings: one other building was erected, a two-storeyed cottage of brick with timber framing and a thatched roof, which still stands in a quiet part of the grounds of modern Kew. Built in 1772, it is known as the Queen's Cottage, being designed as a summerhouse for Queen Charlotte and used for many years by the royal family for this purpose.

The modern Rhododendron Dell is probably a creation of Brown as it appears on a map of 1771. Tradition says that the work of excavation was carried out by soldiers of the Staffordshire militia under Brown's direction: there were, of course, always soldiers quartered at Kew when it was a royal residence. First known as the Laurel Vale, it did not acquire its association with rhododendrons until the introduction of the Asiatic rhododendrons in the mid-nineteenth century, when it was replanted. The walk through the Dell, known as Hollow Walk, another walk to the Dell across the Palace lawn, which was known as the Princess's Walk, and a third from the Dell past the Azalea Garden known as Stafford Walk, all of which still exist, were also laid out by Brown.

On 12 June 1771 the *Endeavour* came to anchor in the Downs and Captain Cook's first great voyage was over. Banks and Solander came ashore with their plants and specimens and it was soon seen that in quantity and quality the biological material collected on the voyage of the *Endeavour* was better by far than anything previously brought to Europe. The results so far as live plants were concerned, however, were meagre, the problems of transporting them over such great distances through all the differences of weather and climate not yet having been solved.

Nine days after the *Endeavour* arrived home, on Friday 21 June 1771, tragedy struck Kew. 'In the night' says the *Gentleman's Magazine*, 'some villains got into the garden of the Princess Dowager of Wales at Kew and destroyed all the greenhouse plants, which were deemed a very curious collection.' This may well have been a malicious attack springing from political motives, Augusta being identified in the public mind with the unpopular Bute.

In February 1772 Princess Augusta died. With her passing, there passed whatever residual influence Bute had on the botanic garden. It was natural for George III, himself young, to turn to the young Banks, returned from his long voyage with such honour and glory, with first-hand knowledge of many plants growing in their natural habitat. Bute faded from the scene to pursue his botany in retirement.

The botanic garden at Kew, set in an ornamental garden, now became the interest of the highest in the land, the King himself. Botany had come a long way from William Turner and his 'sekyng of herbes' in the fields and lanes around Kew, and gardening from the 'hortyard' of the mediaeval castle which, someone has said, 'might almost be called a backyard'. The great new empire recently acquired opened up enormous vistas of opportunity for botanical exploration and economic exploitation of the plant resources it contained. The time and the men were ripe to take advantage of the situation, and the King's garden at Kew was there to facilitate their labours.

[84]

IX

THE

GARDEN

PROSPERS

'... O might I wander there
Among the flowers, which in that heavenly air,
Bloom the year long.'

Robert Bridges

On 14 May 1772 George III, Queen Charlotte and their eight children moved from Richmond Lodge to the White House. At the same time Queen Charlotte acquired the nearby Kew Palace, giving the expanding family the extra space they so badly needed. Old Richmond Lodge was already doomed but the need for the new building which George had begun to erect near the old Lodge now also vanished and work on that was abandoned. They had not long moved into their new home when a further attack was made in its gardens, not this time on the plants, but on George himself. According to the *Gentleman's Magazine* of 11 June 1772:

the madman who formerly cut the trees in Kew Gardens made an attempt, as it is supposed, to assassinate His Majesty in his way from one garden to another at Kew. He was, however, fortunately discovered by a treasonable paper he had put into the keyhole of the garden door; and being apprehended, three loaded pistols were found on him, and a cheap knife, with which he wounded one of the Keepers of the madhouse, from whence he made his escape, in the belly.

Even before he took up residence in the White House George indicated that he intended to continue and expand the work of his mother there. Cook's second voyage had begun with the sailing of the *Resolution* from Deptford on 9 April 1772. On that vessel sailed Francis Masson, bound for South Africa, the first plant collector formally commissioned and sent out from Kew. Banks' enthusiasm was infectious and he had little difficulty in persuading the King that a professional gardener should be sent out to the Cape to collect seeds and plants for the royal garden.

Born at Aberdeen in 1741, Masson had been working under Aiton in the Kew botanic garden for some time. He was academically not very well educated, but he had mastered a fair knowledge of botany and was a competent draughtsman so that his lack of book learning did not prove a handicap. The *Resolution* reached Table Bay on 30 October 1772 and it did not take Masson long to organise his first trip. On 10 December 1772 he set off from Cape Town with a wagon and eight oxen accompanied by a Swede named Oldenburg and a Hottentot driver. He travelled north-east and then east from Cape Town via the Paardeburg, the Drakenstein valley, Paarl, Stellenbosch, Hottentots Holland and the Zonder End River until they reached Swellendam, where they stayed two days, and then returned to the Cape by the same route, arriving on 18 January 1773. He was much impressed with the Hottentots Holland mountains, of which he said that they 'abound in a great number of curious plants'. He collected on this journey the seed of a number of South African heaths, which are still among the attractions of Kew, though not derived from his seed but from much later introductions.

While Masson was acclimatising himself in South Africa, George III's alterations to the gardens of Richmond Lodge and the White House were coming in for criticism. The blame for what was being done was put on Brown. The Rev W Mason, in his *Heroic Epistle to Sir William Chambers* wrote:

> Come then, prolific Art, and with thee bring
> The charms that rise from thy exhaustless spring;
> To Richmond come, for see, untutor'd Brown
> Destroys those wonders which were once thy own.
> Lo! from his melon ground the peasant slave
> Has rudely rushed and level'd Merlin's Cave,
> Knocked down the waxen wizzard, seized his wand,

[86]

> Transformed to lawns what late was fairy land
> And marred with impious hand each sweet design
> Of Stephen Duck and good Queen Caroline!

Similar criticism appeared in the *London Magazine*.

In 1773 Kew Palace was ready to take the overflow of the royal family from the White House and the Prince of Wales and Prince Frederick, aged eleven and ten respectively, were moved into it. With them went their governor, Mr Smelt, a friend of Fanny Burney the novelist, the sub-governors and three daughters of Stephen Duck who acted as housekeepers. It was only a question of time before something more would have to be done to relieve the congestion in the White House but this move gave some relief for the time being.

One day in June 1773 a small, dusty and rather bizarrely-dressed figure came toiling up the road from Richmond to Kew, clutching a book in its hand. Obscure then, this figure was later to make a great stir in the world, and to become a character in history and literature. The great William Cobbett had been employed as a boy-gardener in his home town of Farnham and had there heard of Kew Gardens, which he conceived a desire to see. He can tell his own story much better than I can:

> At eleven years of age my employment was clipping of box-edges and weeding beds of flowers in the gardens of the bishop of Winchester, at the castle of Farnham, my native town. I had always been fond of beautiful gardens; and a gardener, who had just come from the King's Gardens at Kew, gave me such a description of them as made me instantly resolve to work in these gardens. The next morning, without saying a word to anyone, off I set, with no clothes except those upon my back, and with thirteen halfpence in my pocket. I found that I must go to Richmond, and I accordingly went on from place to place, enquiring my way thither. A long day (it was in June) brought me to Richmond in the afternoon. Two-pennyworth of bread and cheese and a pennyworth of small beer, which I had on the road, and one halfpenny which I had lost somehow or other, left threepence in my pocket.

Cobbett continues:

> With this for my whole fortune, I was trudging through Richmond, in my blue smock-frock, and my red garters tied under my knees, when, staring about me, my eyes fell on a little book in a bookseller's window, on the outside of which was

[87]

written '*Tale of a Tub*; price 3d'. The title was so odd that my curiosity was excited. I had 3d, but then, I could have no supper. I went in, and got the little book, which I was so impatient to read, I got over into a field, at the upper corner of the Kew garden, where there stood a haystack. On the shady side of this I sat down to read.

His purchase enthralled him:

The book was so different from anything I had read before, it was something so new to my mind, that, although I could not at all understand some of it, it delighted me beyond description; and it produced what I have always considered a sort of birth of intellect. I read on until it was dark, without any thought about supper or bed. When I could see no longer, I put my little book in my pocket, and tumbled down by the side of the stack, where I slept until the birds in Kew Gardens awakened me in the morning, when I started off to Kew reading my little book. The singularity of my dress, the simplicity of my manner, my confident and lively air and, doubtless, his own compassion besides, induced the gardener, who was a Scotsman, to give me victuals, find me a lodging, and set me to work.

The 'Scotsman' can be no other than William Aiton, who shows up in this incident as a man of great kindliness, prepared to give a penniless but likely lad a helping hand. Cobbett had more to say about his stay at Kew:

And it was during the period I was at Kew that the present King William IV and two of his brothers laughed at the oddness of my dress while I was sweeping the grass-plot round the foot of the Pagoda. The gardener, seeing me fond of books, lent me some gardening books to read, but these I could not relish after my *Tale of a Tub*, which I carried about with me wherever I went; and when I, at about twenty years old, lost it in a box that fell overboard in the Bay of Fundy in North America, the loss gave me greater pain than I have ever felt at losing thousands of pounds. This circumstance, trifling as it is, has always endeared the recollection of Kew to me.

Cobbett probably never knew that Swift, the author of the book that gave him so much pleasure, had once lived, as Sir William Temple's secretary, in a house in the old village of West Sheen, not much more than a stone's throw from where that small boy had flung himself down beside the haystack.

[88]

As William Cobbett was settling himself down in his new job at Kew, Francis Masson, away in South Africa, was preparing for a new and longer journey, this time in company with the Swedish botanist C P Thunberg, who seems to have planned the trip. They were again accompanied by Oldenburg and, with four Hottentots, left Cape Town on 11 September 1773. They made their way at first parallel to the western coast until they came to Saldanha Bay, where they found a great variety of interesting plants, including *Buphane disticha*, the Cape Poison Bulb, used by the old colonists as an antiseptic and by the Hottentots to poison their arrows.

They continued on from Saldanha Bay via Witte Klip. Masson commented on this section of the journey that 'the whole country affords a fine field for botany, being enamelled with the greatest number of flowers I ever saw, of exquisite beauty and fragrance. . . .' They turned east from here along the Great Berg River and then along the Olifants River and tried to cross the Cold Bokkeveld Mountains but without success. Sending their wagons by a different route to Roodezand, Masson and Thunberg themselves went south-east through Eland's Kloof, in the Cold Bokkeveld Mountains, where they saw few plants, into the Cold Bokkeveld, and by a steep path descended into the Warm Bokkeveld, a fertile grassland where there were many plants. Crossing the upper course of the Breede River several times with great difficulty because of the large stones in its bed which had rolled down from the mountains, they were heartened by the discovery of numerous hitherto unknown species, the banks of the river being covered with 'a great variety of evergreen trees . . . and the precipices . . . ornamented with *Ericae* (heaths) and many other mountain plants never described before'. They reached Roodezand, rejoined their wagons and, after climbing the Great Winterhoek Mountain, disappointingly devoid of interesting plants at the top, continued their journey down the Breede River, collecting 'many remarkably fine flowers' on the way, being particularly impressed with *Ixia viridis*. As they crossed the Goree River on 31 October, they found more new plants, particularly 'gerania and stapeliae', and arrived at Swellendam on 5 November.

Thunberg was nearly drowned in the Duivenhoeks River on 11 November, falling with his horse into a hippopotamus-hole as he was fording the river. They continued their journey across the Kafferkuils River, noting the large clumps of *Aloe succotrina* on the slopes of the low hills through which they passed, and on 15 November reached the Gouritz River. Here Masson noted:

On each side of this river lies an extraordinary track (tract) of land, which in the Hottentot language is called Carro (part of the Little Karroo). It is dry burning

[89]

soil, of a reddish colour, intermixed with rotten rock, and entirely divested of grass; but enriched with an infinite number of evergreen shrubs ... we found many new species of crassula, cotyledon, euphorbia, portulaca and mesembryanthemum.

Their course took them down to Mossel Bay on the coast, where they turned northward to the mountains again, passing through Hartiqua's Kloof by 19 December. Travelling via the Great Thorn River, Lange Kloof and Crooked River they reached, on 1 December, 'fine, level country bordering on the eastern ocean'.

On the evening of the day they reached the level country they came to the Seekoe River where they stayed for eight days at the house of Johannus Jacobus Kok, a German from Hesse. Here they saw for the first time a plant of special interest. Masson says:

We found here a new palm, the pith of which the Dutchman told us the Hottentots make bread; but we could get no satisfactory account of their method of making it. We observed two species; one about a foot and a half diameter in the stem, and about twelve feet high, with entire leaves; they appeared to be very old and seldom bore fruit. The other sort had no stem.

The twelve feet high species was undoubtedly *Encephalartos longifolius*, a member of the *Cycadaceae*, a primitive cone-bearing order ranking lower in the evolutionary scale than pine and fir trees. This species still grows in the coastal region where Masson saw it.

The plant derives its special significance in the Kew story because in 1775 Masson introduced a specimen of it into the Royal Botanic Gardens. John Smith I found it still alive when he joined the staff of Kew in 1820 and records that 'in 1819 it produced a male cone, which, being considered remarkable, led Sir Joseph Banks to come and see it, such being his last visit to the Garden.' In 1822 'it had a nearly globose stem, about a foot in height' and in 1848 was removed to the newly constructed Palm House where it formed 'a conspicuous object opposite the south door'. It still stands in the southern wing of the Palm House but owing to its size now occupies a place some way in from the door with smaller plants in front of it.

By the time John Smith I wrote in the late 1870s the plant had attained 'a height of 3 feet 8 inches, with a girth of 3 feet 11 inches, and a spread of leaves 10 feet!' In 1908 W J Bean observed that 'even now the stem is but eight feet high'. It is now upwards of eleven feet in height and must be roughly of the same age as the original specimen that Masson saw on the Seekoe River.

Leaving the pleasant home of Johannus Kok, Masson and Thunberg continued their journey across the Gamtoos, Lory's and Van Staaden's Rivers until 12 December, when the finding of a good area for new plants slowed down their progress. Here buffalo, which kept to the woods during the day, made collecting very hazardous. On 17 December they reached Sunday's River, where their servants refused to go further as they were 'on the borders of a powerful nation of Hottentots, called Caffers' who, the servants said, would kill them to get the iron from their wagons. By 29 December they were beyond the Kamanassie Mountains on their return journey westward. The country was level and very dry but productive of 'many rare species of crassula, mesembryanthemum and other succulent plants'. Climbing the Great Zwartberg Mountains, they saw the extensive and desolate Great Karroo, getting lost for a night in early January when exploring part of it. They continued their journey homeward without anything further of note to report and arrived back in Cape Town on 29 January 1774, after a journey of four months and fourteen days. Masson's two journeys were very productive, bringing several hundred new species to the notice of science.

The advent of Sir Joseph Banks as virtual controller of the botanic garden introduced somewhat more system into the arrangements for dealing with the intake of plants and recording the contents of the garden. Lists were compiled of the various species and the labelling improved. The *London Gazette* for 1773 carried the report that 'orders have been given to the Head-Gardener at Kew that instead of placing numbers as references to a printed catalogue upon the different plants and flowers in the garden, they shall be inscribed with their names at full length.' William Aiton remarks, in the dedication to his *Hortus Kewensis*, that the composition of it 'cost him a large portion of the leisure allowed him by the daily duties of his station, during more than sixteen years.' As it was published in 1789, this indicates that he began it in 1772–3, not long after Banks returned, and it may well be that both the relabelling and Aiton's work were undertaken as an immediate result of suggestions made to the King by Sir Joseph Banks.

One of the interesting plants whose introduction is referred to the year 1773 is *Strelitzia reginae*, the Bird of Paradise Flower, which almost certainly preserves an unbroken descent at Kew. It was figured in the third volume of *Curtis's Botanical Magazine*, which commenced publication in 1786, and William Curtis says of it:

It is well-known to many botanists and others, who have experienced Sir Joseph Banks' well-known liberality, that previous to the publication of the *Hortus Kewensis* he made a new genus of this plant, which had before been considered a

[91]

species of *Heliconia*, and named it *Strelitzia* in honour of our most gracious Queen Charlotte . . . this plant was introduced to the Royal Garden at Kew, by Sir Joseph Banks, Bart, in the year 1773, where it lately flowered.

Although its introduction was attributed to Sir Joseph Banks, the *Strelitzia* had doubtless been sent over by Francis Masson.

According to Thunberg, Francis Masson was not too keen on making another long trip but he did, in fact, decide to participate and set off again with two Hottentot servants on 26 September 1774. He traversed the Cape Flats and passed along the foot of the Stellenbosch mountains to Paarl, where Thunberg joined him. On the Paarl Mountains, the Paardeberg, and on Riebeck Castell they found 'a treasure of new plants'. The last of these gave up 'a hyacinth, with flowers of a pale gold colour', which particularly attracted them. Crossing the Great Berg River on 12 October they arrived at the foot of the Piquetberg where they also found 'a great variety of beautiful plants', especially species of *Aspalanthus*. Climbing the Piquetberg, they travelled via the Verloren Vlei River to the mouth of the Olifants River, which they reached on 25 October. The country here was desolate, but rich in new succulent plants, mesembryanthemums, euphorbias and stapelias.

Moving northward through Karroo country they climbed the Bokkeveld mountain on 4 November where they found 'a new species of aloe (*Aloe dichotoma*) called by the Dutch 'Koker Boom', of which the Hottentots make quivers to hold their arrows'. From here they moved northwards through dry barren country and then on 6 November turned south-east through uninhabited country to the Rhinoceros River which they reached on 14 November. Two days later they arrived at the Rogge Veld where they found no trees and few other plants, descending on 3 December into Karroo country. In the Hex River valley, which they reached on 15 December, they found many new plants on the sides of the lofty mountains which enclose it. They returned to Cape Town via the Breede River, Roodezand and Paardeberg, reaching it on 29 December 1774. In March 1775 Masson sailed for home. A memorandum by Sir Joseph Banks, probably written in 1782–3, speaks highly of Masson's achievement:

In the course of this voyage, Mr Masson collected and sent home a profusion of plants, unknown till that time to the Botanical Gardens in Europe . . . by means of these Kew Gardens has in great measure attain'd to that acknowledged superiority which it now holds over every similar Establishment. . . . So far as I am able to judge, his Majestie's appointment of Mr Masson is to be accounted among the few Royal bounties which have not been in any degree misapplied.

Francis Masson had, indeed, given a great send-off to the line of official plant collectors who were to serve Kew in the next hundred years.

Mrs Papendiek's memoirs contain some vivid stories of the precautions necessary at this time on visits to London because of the ever-present necessity to guard against highwaymen and footpads. The position became so bad in the Kew area that in 1776 it was decided to build 'a watch-house for the confinement of rogues and vagabonds, and to erect a pair of stocks in the most convenient part' of the parish 'as may be thought fit'. These were accordingly built in 1777 adjoining the 'Chapple Yard'. A cage was also provided on the north side of the church. Lloyd Sanders, in his *Old Kew, Chiswick and Kensington* has a note of one villain who apparently escaped scot-free, but then he was a kindly rogue who recognised an obligation to friends who harboured him and in return eschewed violence:

> ...an esteemed visitor to Kew was Mr Frame, burglar and footpad, whose father had married the widow of the farmer who supplied the Green with milk, eggs and bacon. 'Blows and murder belong not to my gang', said that amiable gentleman, 'and if I am allowed to take my beer on the Green, and sit with my neighbours without being insulted, I shall take care that no harm happens here.' He was always greeted as a friend, and was never refused a trifle.

The area was undoubtedly a lucrative patch for robbers. Most of the houses on the south side of the Green were now occupied by the royal family or persons attached to the court, and they and their visitors probably carried more wealth about with them in the form of money and jewellery than the average run of traveller.

At this time Kew had become a place of considerable pleasure for many, the public being admitted to the Richmond Lodge gardens on Sundays and to Kew Gardens on Thursdays. The Green on these days was covered with carriages, more than £300 often being taken in tolls at Kew Bridge on Sundays. The ait (island) opposite Kew Palace, now silent and deserted against the background of industrial Brentford, was then a centre of festivity, being a resort of parties which came up by water, bands playing and flags flying. The visitors were often rewarded with a glimpse of the King and Queen or the royal children.

The outbreak of the American War of Independence in 1775 did not prevent Francis Masson or Captain James Cook from embarking on further expeditions. Masson sailed for Madeira on 19 May 1776 and, after a year there, went on to the

Canary Islands and the Azores and then to the West Indies, where he lost his collections and most of his possessions in the war and a terrible hurricane on 14 October 1780. He returned to England in 1780. Cook set off on his third voyage to the South Sea on 12 July 1776, taking with him as Kew plant collector David Nelson, a botanist recommended to Banks by James Lee, the nurseryman. Cook's objective on this voyage was to try to find a northern passage between the Pacific and the Atlantic. Unfortunately, he lost his life at the hands of natives in Hawaii in February 1779. David Nelson completed the voyage safely.

As the 1770s drew to a close, George III began to worry about his eldest son. Repressed in childhood, there was a natural reaction as the Prince grew out of his adolescence. After various amorous adventures he saw, at Drury Lane Theatre, the actress Mrs Mary Robinson, and, for the first time in his life, fell really in love. He saw her first as Perdita in *A Winter's Tale*, and to him Perdita she remained, to his Florizel. On the promise of £20,000 as soon as he commanded such a sum, she consented to meet him at Kew.

Lord Malden was the go-between in the affair. He brought Perdita to an inn which formerly existed on the ait between Kew and Brentford and, at the signal of a handkerchief waved from the Kew shore, landed at the iron gates of 'old Kew Palace' (the Dutch House) where she met the Prince of Wales and his brother Frederick. The first meeting was short as they were startled by the noise of people approaching, but many subsequent meetings took place and their walks along the towpath lasted until past midnight. Where National Car Parks Limited now ply their prosaic trade on Queen Elizabeth's Lawn, these young lovers wandered and acted out their romance, no doubt lingering under 'Queen Elizabeth's Elm', then in the prime of its life. But Mrs Papendiek introduces a sordid note: she maintains that innocence was conspicuously lacking in the affair, and that two of the servants who had been about the princes since childhood smuggled Perdita into the Palace, which at that time was their residence. If so, this is a chapter in the history of the old house hardly in keeping with the rest of its blameless career. In two years, however, the affair was over, the bond of £20,000 was redeemed by George III for £5,000 and a pension of £400, the royal heir was free again, and the Kew towpath heard no more the murmur of the royal voice in the still of the dusk.

Sir Joseph Banks was shocked and saddened on 16 May 1782 by the death of his librarian and keeper of his herbarium, Daniel Solander, who had been a faithful friend and companion for nearly twenty years. Fortunately another Swedish naturalist, Jonas Dryander, who had come to England with Solander but was some twelve years younger, was available to fill the gap and he became Banks' librarian, and carried on Solander's work.

[94]

About this time the freehold of the White House and Kew Gardens was purchased from the Dowager Countess of Essex. As part of the manor of Richmond, both Richmond Lodge and Kew Gardens had in mediaeval times belonged to the royal family, so that 'the King shall have his own again' came literally true in this case. The same year saw another change at Kew. The first Kew Bridge was financially a failure, the seven central arches of the eleven of which it was composed being made of wood, and needing constant repair. There was no help for it, the bridge either had to be replaced or fall into ruin. The proprietor decided on the first course, and in 1782 obtained an Act of Parliament which authorised him to build, at his own expense, a stone bridge of seven arches. It took six years to complete the work.

The ending of the war saw Francis Masson on the move again and in 1783 he went to Portugal, visiting also Spain and Gibraltar, the latter recovering at the time from the long siege to which it had been subjected. In the same year he crossed over to the African continent, sending Banks plants from Tangier and Sallee. He then returned to Portugal and went for a second time to Madeira, returning to England in 1785.

Up to 1784 William Aiton had had charge of the botanic garden section of the White House estate only, the pleasure ground area being under the control of John Haverfield, who had charge of the Richmond Lodge gardens. When the latter died in that year, however, William Aiton took over the White House pleasure ground and became responsible for the whole of the White House estate, that is, all that part of modern Kew which lies to the east of Holly Walk. The separation of Richmond Lodge gardens and the gardens of the White House seem to have ceased from this time. Love Lane which divided them had fallen into disuse after the building of Kew Bridge in 1757 and the improvement to the Kew to Richmond road which the King had effected in the 1760s. An Act of Parliament was passed in 1785 which empowered the King to close the Lane, but this does not seem to have been put fully into operation until later, possibly because there were still some residents who used it. From this time on, however, the name Richmond Gardens seems to have dropped out of currency, and the name Kew Gardens to have been adopted for the whole of the area north of the Old Deer Park.

[95]

X

MERINOS
AND
MADNESS

'I had a sort of conference
with His Majesty, or rather I
was the object to whom he
spoke, with a manner so
uncommon, that a high fever
alone could account for it; a
rapidity, a hoarseness of
voice, a volubility, and
earnestness – a vehemence,
rather – it startled me
inexpressibly.'

Fanny Burney

On 16 October 1785 Masson left again for the Cape, arriving at Cape Town on 10
January 1786. He found things very different there from the time of his first visit:
he had been able to travel about on the earlier occasion without hindrance but the
Dutch authorities were now much more difficult because of the activities of a
soldier, William Paterson, who had travelled in the Cape before the war and used
his knowledge to assist the British Navy in an attack on Dutch shipping in
Saldanha Bay in 1781. He was allowed to collect only on condition that he stayed
away from the coast.

In June 1786 Fanny Burney, afterwards Madame Frances D'Arblay, who wrote
Evelina and *Cecilia*, two novels which enjoyed much popularity in their day, was

The Tropical Water-Lily House, showing the flamboyant red inflorescences of *Acalypha hispida*.

The Temperate House from the air.

invited to attend Queen Charlotte. Although she liked the Queen she accepted only with reluctance because it meant the loss of much freedom, and the society of her friends, which she valued greatly. She took up her duty at Windsor on 17 July 1786, making her first visit to Kew on the 25 July. The accommodation allocated to her in the White House was satisfactory: she had two rooms, 'both small and up two pair of stairs; but tidy and comfortable enough'. All the apartments but the King and Queen's and one other were 'small, dark and old-fashioned': there were 'staircases in every passage, and passages to every closet'. Even in passing from her own room to the Queen's, she lost herself. Just as she was getting to her own room she heard the King's voice. She tried to avoid him but he saw her and said 'What! Is Miss Burney taking possession?' He walked round her room, as if to see whether it was comfortable enough for her and then, 'smiling very good-humouredly' walked out again.

Fanny observes that 'the Kew life ... is very different from Windsor':

> As there are no early prayers, the Queen rises later; and there is no form of ceremony here of any sort, her dress is plain, and the hour for the second toilette extremely uncertain. The Royal family are here always in so very retired a way, that they live as the simplest country gentlefolks. The King has not even an equerry with him, nor the Queen any lady to attend her when she goes her airings.

Because the King and Queen lived in such an unreserved way, 'running about from one end of the house to the other', it was difficult for those who served them to have visits from their friends and this made Kew very irksome for Fanny.

Visits to Kew took place from Tuesday to Friday in every other week during the summer. Sundays were rarely passed at Kew as there was no private chapel there and the damp and draughty old house was almost uninhabitable in the winter. At the beginning of August there was an attempt on the life of the King, who fortunately escaped without injury. On 8 August the family made its usual visit, to be met on Kew Green with such an enthusiastic reception, expressing loyal satisfaction in the King's safe return after the attempted assassination, that, according to Fanny, it 'affected the Queen to tears; nor were they shed alone; for almost everybody's flowed that had witnessed the scene. The Queen, in speaking of it afterwards said "I shall always love little Kew for this!"'

On 5 January Fanny records the arrival at Windsor for a tour of duty as Equerry to the King, of 'Col Wellbred', this being her name for Col the Hon Robert Fulke Greville. By great good fortune Robert kept a diary for part of the time he was with the King. He appears to us first, however, in Fanny's diary, as the relevant part of his own does not begin until November 1788.

In the second half of the 1780s the botanist William Curtis conceived the idea of starting a new magazine, *The Botanical Magazine: or Flower Garden Displayed*, the aim of which was to describe and illustrate 'the most Ornamental Foreign Plants, cultivated in the Open Ground, the Greenhouse and Stove'. The first part, which contained three plates only, was published on 1 February 1787, at one shilling per part. Three thousand copies were sold. Curtis drew heavily on the collections at Kew for his material, and the magazine prospered. Many famous botanical artists have contributed to this work, which has been published continuously since it began and is still issued. The association with Kew has become closer as the years have passed and the magazine is now published by the Bentham-Moxon Trustees, a Kew-based body.

While this was in course of preparation Banks was giving instructions to a second official Kew plant collector to collect plants in India. The new man was a Polish doctor named Anthony Pantaleon Hove, which seems to be an anglicised version of a Polish name which defeated his English contemporaries. He had already sent seeds to Banks from South Africa. He set out for India on 14 April 1787, spending his first two months in Bombay. A notable event occurred in the glasshouses at Kew about this time. Although exotic orchids had reached Great Britain in the past, attempts to grow and flower them had failed. John Smith I records, quoting Sir J E Smith, that in 1787 *Epidendrum cochleatum* flowered at Kew and in October 1788 this success was followed by the flowering of *Epidendrum fragrans*.

In the account of their voyage to the South Seas, Cook and Banks had drawn attention again to a tropical food plant, the breadfruit, of great potentialities, which had first been brought to notice by William Dampier, the seventeenth century pirate-cum-naturalist. Several West Indian planters had realised how useful this tree might be to them. Their negro slaves needed a lot of food and relied heavily on the banana for nourishment. Unfortunately the frequent high winds in the West Indies damaged the banana plant very easily and there was need for a food plant which would stand up more robustly to the conditions and obviate the necessity for expensive imports when the banana crop was reduced. Various efforts were made and inducements offered to anyone who managed to introduce the breadfruit tree to the West Indies but no one made the effort before the American War of Independence broke out. Pressure was renewed when peace returned and eventually Banks submitted a petition to the King.

The project appealed to George III and on 5 May 1787 he instructed the

[98]

Admiralty to despatch a ship to Tahiti to collect breadfruit cuttings and take them to the West Indies. At the same time the first members of the crew were selected, David Nelson, the botanist who had sailed with Cook on his last voyage, and William Brown, one of the gardeners at Kew. Less than three weeks later, on 23 May, a suitable ship was found and the work of adaptation for a voyage which was likely to last at least two years was put in hand. Special provision was made for upwards of six hundred pots containing the breadfruit plants to be housed in the main cabin in the stern. By the end of July so much progress had been made that a captain was selected for the ship, which had been named *Bounty*. The man chosen was Captain William Bligh, who had sailed with Cook on his third voyage as sailing master on the *Resolution*, and was well acquainted with the breadfruit and the South Sea. Since the voyage with Cook he had commanded merchant vessels on the West Indian run, and thus also knew the West Indies well.

After several abortive attempts frustrated by bad weather the *Bounty* sailed on 23 December 1787, but was so buffeted by storms in the first few days that it had to put into Teneriffe to refit on 6 January 1788. The vessel then set off on the long haul towards Cape Horn, Bligh's instructions being to follow this route if he could. The *Bounty* had been no more than a few days on its voyage when, on the other side of the world, another vessel, which had been making its way along the south-eastern coast of Australia, arrived at the point which Cook and Banks, in 1772, had named Botany Bay. This ship, which carried 700 convicts and a guard of 200 marines, was the first ship sent out to settle in the new territory. When the first boatload went ashore, the history of the Australian nation began. By another quirk of Providence, almost at the same moment a development took place back in England which was to have great influence on the future of that nation.

The practice of mixing fine wool imported from Spain with English wool to produce finer cloth than could be made from English wool alone had existed for many years and the notion of producing the finer wool in England had been mooted. Some merino sheep had found their way out of Spain and Sir Joseph Banks had a pair which were French-bred. According to Col Fulke Greville, he put the notion in the King's head that merino sheep could be imported direct from Spain and that, if anyone could arrange this, Sir Joseph Banks would be the man. Two months after the landing in Australia the first three sheep to be imported from Spain itself arrived at Kew and were seen by the King for the first time on 4 April. From this beginning the King's flock of merinos was established which later played an important part in the foundation of the great sheep-rearing industry of Australia.

While these events were taking place Anthony Hove, the new Kew collector, had been having a more than eventful time in India. He had set out on 1 October 1787, on a tour of cotton-growing centres, starting at Surat, but on his first attempt could not get further than plantations near Broach and was robbed on the way back to Surat. On another attempt he was also robbed. Finally, as he tried again he was set on twice by Grassia tribesmen and lost nearly everything, including his clothes, but even this did not deter him. He continued northward eventually reaching Mittimpur on the River Sabernati on 21 December. He was back in Bombay by 19 January 1788. He made two further trips over the same territory but was recalled by Banks who complained about his expenses, but was unable to get a ship until February 1789. The vessel called at Cape Town and Hove met Francis Masson, who gave him some seeds to bring home.

Although Captain Bligh had done his best to carry out his instructions to proceed to Tahiti via Cape Horn he had found it impossible to do so and had turned east to make his way via the Cape of Good Hope. On 21 August 1788 he reached Tasmania. In the autumn of that year, however, a very serious and unexpected development occurred at home: the King began to exhibit some alarming symptoms of illness. Fanny Burney first mentions George III's condition on 17 October 1788, saying that he had not been quite well for some time. On 20 October she records that he was very ill in the night but five days later had so far recovered that he could travel to Windsor. On that day, says Fanny:

> I had a sort of conference with His Majesty, or rather I was the object to whom he spoke, with a manner so uncommon, that a high fever alone would account for it; a rapidity, a hoarseness of voice, a volubility, and earnestness – a vehemence, rather – it startled me inexpressibly. ...

As Fanny was undergoing this daunting experience, the *Bounty*, eleven thousand miles away, was approaching Point Venus in Tahiti, the end of its outward run. Bligh dropped anchor there on 26 October 1788. He soon found an opportunity to make known his desire for breadfruit trees. In conversation with the chieftain Tinah, he mentioned that out of goodwill King George had sent many presents for him and his people and suggested that Tinah should send something in return. Tinah, eagerly enough, listed breadfruit among possible gifts which gave Bligh the opening he wanted to say that 'breadfruit trees were what King George would like', upon which Tinah promised that 'a great many should be put on board, and seemed much delighted to find it so easily in his power to send anything that would be well received by King George'. The collection of the breadfruit plants accordingly began.

[100]

Back at Windsor the King's condition had deteriorated. The symptoms exhibited to Fanny had greatly increased and the whole establishment was put in disorder as the King could not sleep properly and had periods when he had to be forcibly restrained. Fulke Greville, who was in attendance on him the whole time, gives a clear picture of the confusion which reigned and Fanny's account shows the gloom and distress which afflicted everyone about the King and Queen during this period. Towards the end of November it was decided to remove him to Kew, as that was more secluded than Windsor, but on the day chosen he would not get up: even Mr Pitt could not persuade him and it was quarter to four in the afternoon before the carriage moved off with the King inside it. For the first few days at Kew he was very bad, at times being almost unmanageable, but the specialist Dr Willis from Lincolnshire, and the two sons and attendants he brought with him, exercised a much firmer control and the situation became easier. Fanny's part was an unenviable one: she had to go down at seven in the morning and hang about in the cold, draughty and damp passages to get, for the Queen, a bulletin on the state of the King during the night.

An extraordinary incident occurred on 19 January 1789. Arrangements had been made for the King to go for a walk and Fulke Greville was expecting to be asked to go with him but found that the King had gone without him. 'As the day was very fine', he says:

> ... I proposed to General Gordon that we should sit close to the House, rather than to sit longer in the Library. This met his wishes as well as mine and we walked before the Green House, keeping a good look out towards Kew Gardens for the King.
>
> At length I espied Dr John Willis returning, and soon after I saw a Cluster of People following. These stopped behind some shrubs, which for some little time intercepted Them from my View, until they moved on.
>
> As they advanced I thought they were holding the King as they all walked so close together, but on a nearer approach great was my Astonishment when I saw the King extended on his back, and thus carried upon the shoulders of some of his attendants. As soon as he was brought to his apartment he asked to be allowed to sitt down to play at cards, but he was carried directly to the couch and there confined in the Waistcoat (straitjacket).

'From the details I collected afterwards,' continued Greville:

> ... it seems that on first going out His Majesty made some hesitation. This

occurred at the Little Garden Gate, leading out of Kew Gardens into Richmond Gardens. He there made a halt and said if he did go there he would not walk.

Upon this Dr John Willis with firmness told him he must walk, and where they chose. The King hesitated, but the party being firm, he at last suddenly gave way, and walked on saying 'To enjoy is to obey'.

After this he continued his walk and got as far as the Pagoda, up to which he went, and when there, was desirous to go up it. To divert him from this, he was told they had not got the key, upon which he told them that the key of the house would open it. Spicer, one of Dr Willis's men, who heard this conversation, answered that he had opened the house door to let His Majesty out, and that he left the key in the door.

All was now settling quickly when one of the Pages incautiously produced the key. The King got hold of it, but it was immediately but not easily taken from him by Mr Thos Willis.

On this he said he would go no further. He was desired, and then told, that he must walk on. To prevent this he sat down and afterwards lay extended on the grass, from whence, on his continued refusal to get up and walk, he was taken up by force, and carried about a mile on his attendants' shoulders.

When His Majesty found that he was unable to resist he said it was pleasanter to be carried than to walk, and that he liked it vastly. Whatever might have been his real opinion as to this change, he was thus brought home.

This incident had some consequences. The *Morning Post* which reported it on 11 February 1789 said that the lying down of the King on the grass 'was seen over the wall by a passenger, who supposed that His Majestie's calamities had concluded in the most fatal way and a report to this purpose was soon spread over Kew and its neighbourhood!'

Fanny Burney had a most harassing experience at Kew on Monday 2 February which, though her account is long, she must be allowed to tell in her own words. 'What an adventure had I this morning!' she begins her diary entry:

... One that has occasioned me the severest personal terror I ever experienced in my life. Sir Lucas Pepys still persisting that exercise and air were absolutely necessary to save me from illness, I have continued my walks, varying my gardens from Richmond to Kew, according to the accounts I received of the movements of the King. ... This morning when I received my intelligence of the King from Dr John Willis, I begged to know where I might walk in safety? 'In Kew Gardens' he said, 'as the King would be in Richmond.'

'Should any unfortunate circumstance' I cried, 'at any time, occasion me being seen by His Majesty, do not mention my name, but let me run off without call or notice.' This he promised. Everybody, indeed, is ordered to keep out of sight. Taking, therefore, the time I had most at command, I strolled into the Gardens. I had proceeded, in my quick way, nearly half the round, when I suddenly perceived, through some trees, two or three figures. Relying on the instructions of Dr John, I concluded them to be workmen or gardeners; yet tried to look sharp, and in so doing, as they were less shaded, I thought I saw the person of His Majesty!

Alarmed past all possible expression, I waited not to know more, but turning back, ran off with all my might. But what was my terror to hear myself pursued! To hear the voice of the King himself loudly and hoarsely calling after me 'Miss Burney! Miss Burney!' I protest I was ready to die. I knew not what state he might be in at the time; I only knew that the orders to keep out of his way were universal; that the Queen would highly disapprove of any unauthorised meeting, and that the very action of running away might deeply, in his present irritable state, offend him. Nevertheless, on I ran, too terrified to stop, and in search of some short passage, for the garden is full of little labyrinths, by which I might escape.

The steps still pursued me, and still the poor hoarse and altered voice rang in my ears. More and more footsteps resounded frightfully behind me: the attendants all running, to catch their eager master, and the voices of the two Dr Willis's loudly exhorting him not to heat himself so unmercifully. Heavens, how I ran! I do not think I should have felt the hot lava from Vesuvius, at least, not the hot cinders, had I so run during its eruption. My feet were not sensible that they even touched the ground.

Soon after, I heard other voices, shriller, though less nervous, call out 'Stop! Stop! Stop!' I could by no means consent: I knew not what was purposed, but I recollected fully my agreement with Dr John that very morning, that I should decamp if surprised, and not be named. My own fears and repugnance also, after a flight and disobedience like this, were doubled in the thought of not escaping; I knew not to what I might be exposed, should the malady be then high, and take the turn of my resentment.

Still, therefore, on I flew; and such was my speed, so almost incredible to relate or recollect, that I fairly believe no one of the whole party could have overtaken me, if these words, from one of the attendants, had not reached me 'Dr Willis begs you to stop!' 'I cannot! I cannot!' I answered, still flying on, when he called out 'You must, ma'am; it hurts the King to run'.

[103]

Then, indeed, I stopped, in a state of fear really amounting to agony. I turned round, I saw the two doctors had got the King between them, and three attendants of Dr Willis's were hovering about. They all slackened their pace, as they saw me stand still; but such was the excess of my alarm, that I was wholly insensible to the effects of a race which, at any other time, would have required an hour's recruit. As they approached, some little presence of mind happily came to my command; it occurred to me that, to appease the wrath of my flight, I must now show some confidence. I therefore faced them as undauntedly as I was able, only charging the nearest of the attendants to stand by my side.

When they were within a few yards of me, the King called out 'Why did you run away?' Shocked at a question impossible to answer, yet a little assured by the mild tone of his voice, I instantly forced myself forward to meet him, though the internal sensation which satisfied that this was a step the most proper to appease his suspicions and displeasure, was so violently combated by the tremor of my nerves, that I fairly think I may reckon it the greatest effort of personal courage I have ever made.

The effort answered: I looked up and met all his wonted benignity of countenance, though something still of wildness in his eyes. Think, however, of my surprise, to feel him put both his hands round my two shoulders, and then kiss my cheek! I wonder I did not sink, so exquisite was my affright when I saw him spread out his arms! Involuntarily, I concluded he meant to crush me: but the Willis's, who have never seen him till this fatal illness, not knowing how very extraordinary an action this was from him, simply smiled and looked pleased, supposing, perhaps, it was his customary salutation.

Fanny soon recovered her composure, but afterwards took her walks along the Kew Road, outside the wall of the Gardens. By 21 February the King had returned almost to normal and on 14 March the royal household resumed its usual life at Windsor.

Having taken on board more than a thousand breadfruit plants the *Bounty* set sail from Tahiti on Friday 3 April. Three weeks later, on the 24 April, Bligh and Nelson went ashore on Annamooka in the Friendly Islands to get a few replacements for plants which were sickly or dead. Then, on 28 April, just before sunrise, Bligh was seized by Fletcher Christian in his cabin, and the notorious mutiny commenced. Among those put into the boat with Bligh was David Nelson, while William Brown, ex-Kew gardener, stayed with the mutineers. The story of the voyage in the open boat, which sailed 3,618 miles in 41 days, has so often been told that it need not be repeated. The occupants suffered great deprivation and hardship, Nelson among them. His specialist knowledge was a help at times. When for example, they were struggling around the north-eastern tip of Australia, he identified a species of *Dolichos*, from which a small edible bean could be obtained, but later some who had eaten a large quantity uncooked felt some ill-effects.

On 1 June, David Nelson fell ill with 'a loss of sight, much drought and an inability to walk', which Bligh attributed to sunstroke. He had somewhat recovered by the next day. On 14 June they arrived at the Dutch settlement of Coepang in Timor, and their troubles were over. Not, alas, for poor Nelson. He, says Bligh, 'who since we left New Holland (Australia) had been but in a weak condition . . . was taken ill in consequence of a cold caused by imprudently leaving off warm clothing.' On 20 July 1789 he died 'of an inflammatory fever'. Of him, Bligh wrote:

> The loss of this honest man I very much lamented. He had with great care and diligence attended to the object for which he was sent, and had always been ready to forward every plan that was proposed for the good of the service in which we were engaged. He was not less useful in our voyage hither in the open boat, in the course of which he gave me great satisfaction by the patience and fortitude with which he conducted himself.

Thus died, in pain and agony in what were then the uttermost parts of the earth, the first Kew-trained man to lose his life overseas in the course of his duty. This man, 'one of the quietest fellows in nature', will be remembered by the noble epitaph of Bligh's words, so long as Kew endures.

According to the testimony at the subsequent court-martial, William Brown was seen by several people on deck with a musket and without doubt was a mutineer. One witness says, indeed, that he was among those who were 'publicly insulting' Captain Bligh when the boat was being loaded. He is described by Bligh as 'aged twenty-seven years, five feet eight inches high, fair complexion, dark brown hair, slender made; a remarkable scar on one of his cheeks, which contracts the eyelid and runs down to his throat, occasioned by the King's evil; and is tattooed.' Whether he suffered any pangs of conscience when the breadfruit plants were dumped overboard immediately after the mutiny is not recorded, but in any case the mutineers had irrevocably committed themselves, and there was no turning back. To follow them further is outside our story, except to say that Brown was one of the party that settled on Pitcairn Island, that he located the principal water-supply, which became known as 'Brown's Well', and perished in the murders that after a few years reduced the members of the original *Bounty* crew on Pitcairn to one survivor.

XI

THE NEW

LANDS

'So sits enthroned in vegetable pride
Imperial Kew by Thames's glittering side ...'

Erasmus Darwin

There were some notable introductions to the Botanic Garden during 1788–9. Frederick Scheer, who in 1840 published a book on the Gardens, wrote that he would like to have seen:

> ...a pictorial representation of the scene of Sir Joseph Banks introducing the first *Hydrangea hortensis* to Kew, about the beginning of 1789, for the inspection of the curious. It had begun to flower in the Custom House, and its green petals were a puzzle to the botanists of the day. The next day he exhibited it in his house at Soho Square, from whence it was returned, and lived in Kew, the parent of its numerous progeny now spread all over Europe, till within these few years. This year also saw the *Paeonia moutan* introduced from China, and it is in the Gardens to this day, alive and well, a venerable monument of happier times. The common fuchsia also became then first known, and we are told that

Lee sold small plants at five guineas each.

The Moutan or Tree Paeony was obtained for Banks by a Dr Duncan of the Hon East India Company. By 1829 this shrub, whose flowers were said to be very double, magenta at the centre fading to a lighter tint at the outside, was reported as being eight feet high and ten feet across. There is a fascinating but probably apocryphal story about the fuchsia.

James Lee the elder, of the famous nursery firm Lee and Kennedy which flourished in the second half of the eighteenth century, holding a leading position in the trade for more than sixty years, was showing a friend round his nursery when the friend mentioned that he had seen a marvellous plant in the front window of a cottage in Wapping, and described it. James Lee, suspecting something new and good, posted immediately down to Wapping and bought the plant from the sailor's wife who owned it. When he got back he straightaway turned it into cuttings and propagated numbers of it as fast as he could. When the first plants came into flower they were snapped up by society ladies eager to get something with which to impress their friends. By the end of the season Lee is supposed to have made three hundred guineas from the plant.

There are a number of versions of the story and how much Lee paid for the plant or made out of it, but the truth is probably more prosaic. The *Hortus Kewensis* records the introducion in 1788 of *Fuchsia coccinea* from Chile, brought in by a Captain Firth. Sir J E Smith wrote a letter on 2 July 1789 reporting that:

> . . . at Kew the beautiful *Fuchsia* is multiplied without end and Lee has plenty of it; it will soon be very common.

This implies that the Kew plant and those of Lee had a common origin and it seems likely that Captain Firth supplied Lee with a specimen at the same time as he introduced another to Kew.

According to John Smith I the hydrangea, the Moutan and the *Fuchsia* were given special treatment. Before his time 'the original plants . . . occupied a bed of earth in a small lean-to house 12 feet in length and 6 feet in width, with a low roof'. In 1823, just after Smith started at Kew, this building, which had become very dilapidated, was removed, the plants being protected thereafter in winter by a covering of dry fern and mats. In 1842, the site being required for another purpose, the plants had to be removed after having occupied the spot for fifty years.

The late summer of 1789 saw William Aiton's labour over sixteen years come to fruition with the publication of his *Hortus Kewensis*. The work was issued in three volumes and contains 5,500 species arranged according to the Linnean system. Aiton took great pains to insert where he could both the probable date of introduction of each species and the name of the person who introduced it, and only in a very small proportion of cases failed to do so. The botanical descriptions were supplied by the botanists Solander, Dryander, and L'Héritier.

Francis Masson was getting very frustrated by the restrictions imposed by the South African authorities on his movements and it was not until 1790 that he was able to make a journey to the Olifants River, 200 miles from Cape Town and on to the Kamiesberg in Namaqualand. It is possible to deduce from the *Hortus Kewensis* that he found many new species on this trip.

John Sibthorp, Sherardian professor of botany at Oxford, and Baron Nicolas Joseph von Jacquin of Vienna were instrumental in the introduction to Kew at this time of an individual whose superlative standard of work over a long lifetime has remained an everlasting source of gratification to the Royal Botanic Gardens. In 1784 Sibthorp travelled to Vienna and during his visit was introduced by von Jacquin to the botanical artist Ferdinand Bauer and induced him to accompany him to Greece. When he returned Ferdinand persuaded his brother Francis to visit England with von Jacquin the younger. Here he met Sir Joseph Banks who at once realised that he had found the man he had been looking for to fulfil the much-needed role of permanent botanical artist at Kew. Francis settled at Kew in 1790 on a salary provided by Banks and remained there until his death fifty years later. He worked away steadily year after year at his botanical paintings and microscope drawings, for he was a highly skilled botanist, and gave lessons to Queen Charlotte and her princesses. Wilfred Blunt, in his *Botanical Illustration*, has the highest praise for him, saying that 'it must, perhaps for ever, remain an open question as to who is the greatest botanical artist of all time . . . I would myself unhesitatingly give the first place to Francis Bauer.'

The Gardens at Kew have in their time stirred many people to poetry. Not least among them is Charles Darwin's grandfather, Erasmus Darwin, a successful physician who practised at Lichfield where in 1778 he bought eight acres of ground on which he established a botanic garden. In 1789, inspired by this garden, he published *Loves of the Plants* which, although issued first, was the second part of a long poem called the *Botanic Garden*. The first part, entitled *The Economy of*

Opposite: An *Agave* in flower in the Orangery, reaching a height of more than 26 feet. The top of the spike had to be cut off to avoid damage to the ceiling.

Vegetation, followed in 1791. Lines 561 to 586 of Canto IV of *The Economy of Vegetation* are concerned with Kew:

> So sits enthroned in vegetable pride
> Imperial Kew by Thames's glittering side;
> Obedient sails from realms unfurrow'd bring
> For her the unnam'd progeny of spring;
> Attendant Nymphs her dulcet mandates hear,
> And nurse in fostering arms the tender year,
> Plant the young bulb, inhume the living seed,
> Prop the weak stem, the erring tendril lead;
> Or fan in glass-built fanes the stranger flowers
> With milder gales; and steep with warmer showers.
>
> Delighted Thames through tropic umbrage glides,
> And flowers antarctic, bending o'er his tides;
> Drinks the new tints, the sweets unknown inhales,
> And calls the sons of science to his vales.
> In one bright point admiring Nature eyes
> The fruits and foliage of discordant skies,
> Twines the gay floret with the fragrant bough
> And bends the wreath round George's royal brow.
>
> Sometimes retiring, from the public weal
> One tranquil hour the Royal Partners steal;
> Through glades exotic pass with step sublime,
> Or mark the growths of Britain's happier clime;
> With beauty blossom'd, and with virtue blaz'd,
> Mark the fair scions, that themselves have rais'd;
> Sweet blooms the Rose, the towering Oak expands,
> The Grace and Guard of Britain's golden lands.

Although it enjoyed some popularity for a time the poem was not really successful. To the average person of the present day the poetic style of that era, in which the Romantic movement was just beginning to gain momentum, seems so highly forced and artificial as to be almost comical, and far removed from natural expression. The verdict of the critics as time went on resolved itself into the view that, while Darwin had great facility of language, the effort to give an interest to scientific didacticism in verse by elaborate rhetoric and forced personification was too artificial to succeed.

Archibald Menzies took a degree in medicine in 1781 and developed an interest in exotic plants. He entered the Navy, serving first under Rodney in the West Indies and then for four years on the Halifax station, where he made himself familiar with the vegetation of eastern coastal America. He sent seeds to Banks and later on the latter was instrumental in getting him appointed to the *Prince of Wales* which circumnavigated the world between 1786 and 1789. On his return Banks got him posted as naturalist on the *Discovery*, commanded by Captain Vancouver, which sailed for the north-west Pacific coast of America on 1 April 1791 and arrived in sight of California on 17 April 1792.

Most people are acquainted with the *Bounty* mutiny but few know that when this affair was cleared up Captain Bligh was given another ship, the *Providence*, and asked to return to Tahiti to carry out the task which the *Bounty* had failed to complete. Four months after Vancouver and Menzies set out Bligh's new command set sail for Tahiti carrying two men from Kew, Christopher Smith and James Wiles, to do the work Nelson and Brown had undertaken on the *Bounty*. By the time the *Providence* had reached Tahiti, Vancouver and Menzies were exploring the intricacies of Puget Sound and the waterways surrounding Vancouver Island. They were in this area from April until October 1792 and Menzies saw and recorded many trees and shrubs but unfortunately rarely noted the localities exactly. The vessel spent some time in California and then returned to Hawaii, reaching there on 1 March 1793.

Masson had not been idle while Bligh and Menzies were on their voyages. His very successful trip to Namaqualand in 1790 had whetted his appetite for further long journeys and in 1792 he made a trip of five months' duration to Klein Roggeveld and the Zwarteberg, again with considerable success. So great had been the volume of his introductions since 1786 that two new glasshouses had had to be built, one in 1788 and another in 1792.

Bligh had completed his second mission to Tahiti in 1792 and safely delivered the breadfruit trees to the West Indies, where he left James Wiles in Jamaica to look after and distribute the bulk of them. They were successfully established but the effort appeared at first to be abortive as the slaves preferred their staple yams and plantains, consigning the breadfruit to the pigs, but after emancipation in the middle of the nineteenth century they began to be more eaten as human food. Bligh arrived back in England in 1793 carrying a large number of other plants, having faithfully carried out his orders that he was to collect and bring home as many specimens as he could accommodate in addition to the breadfruit, the carrying of which was his main task. A substantial number of hitherto unknown

A Pitcher Plant (*Nepenthes*)

species were among the consignment. The burden of cultivating these new plants fell, however, not on William Aiton, who died on 2 February 1793, but on his son, William Townsend Aiton, who succeeded him in charge of the Botanic Garden at Kew.

When the *Providence* arrived home, the *Discovery* had still two years to serve. At the end of March 1793 the vessel sailed for Nootka and spent the summer exploring north from there as far as Wrangel, Alaska. Menzies was able to collect little during this period, the exploration of the narrow channels and long inlets being an arduous matter in the incessant heavy rains. In the autumn they returned to Nootka and sailed for California. After further exploration southwards the *Discovery* returned to Hawaii.

While Menzies was north of Nootka, Masson was making a third trip, once again to the north, going again to Namaqualand, taking in the Seekoe Valley and

A South American Pitcher Plant (*Heliamphora nutans*)

the Kamiesberg, the Groen River north-west of Kamiesberg, and returning via Meerhof Casteel and the Olifants River, having again had a very fruitful journey. Later in the year a development took place in India which was greatly to affect the work at Kew. In 1787 Lt Col Robert Kyd had proposed to the Hon East India Company that a garden should be established at Calcutta to grow plants of possible economic value. The proposal was accepted and such a garden formed, with Kyd as Director. Kyd died on 26 March 1793 and William Roxburgh took over in November. He immediately began that fruitful association of the Calcutta Botanic Garden, for such Kyd's foundation became, with the Royal Botanic Gardens at Kew which has lasted ever since.

In February 1794 Menzies was climbing Mauna Loa in Hawaii, the first ascent of that mountain. Later, the *Discovery* returned to the north-west coast of America and explored further north, ascertaining that Cook's Inlet was not a river, as Cook had thought it, and establishing almost certainly that there was no north-west passage or waterway into the interior of America. Turning south, the vessel made its way again to California and then began its long journey home. When it called at Valparaiso, Vancouver and Menzies were entertained by the Captain-General of Chile, the famous Irish immigrant whose son Bernardo O'Higgins won independence from Spain for Chile. They were served at dessert with some nuts unfamiliar to Menzies, who pocketed a few. On the way home on the ship he managed to germinate these and arrived in England with five seedling trees. The seeds were those of that remarkable tree of the southern hemisphere the Monkey-Puzzle (*Araucaria araucana*). This story sounds apocryphal but H J Elwes vouched for its truth, Sir Joseph Hooker having heard it from Menzies himself when an old man. Although it takes the story on further in date than the period now being described, it is worthwhile following up the history of these trees, as the Monkey-Puzzle remained comparatively rare for fifty years after Menzies introduced it: it was not until William Lobb collected it in South America for Messrs Veitch in the 1840s that seed became available generally.

One of the seedlings was planted out in Sir Joseph Banks' garden at Spring Grove, Hounslow and the remainder went to Kew, three of them being kept under glass and the other planted outside. This plant, and the one at Spring Grove did not survive. The three left at Kew continued under glass until, about 1807, it was decided to try one outside again. Owing to the loss of the two originally planted out, the hardiness of the seedlings, now sizable young trees, was still doubted, and it was customary to protect this one in the winter for a number of years with a frame covered with mats.

According to Frederick Scheer this tree became 'the lion of the Gardens', which William IV 'delighted to point out to strangers' whom he brought into the Gardens on his frequent visits. It was twelve feet high in 1836 and grew on sturdily for many years, surviving until 1892. It was for a long time known as 'Sir Joseph Banks' Pine'. One of the other two specimens received a setback. Sent up to a gala at Carlton House, the servants unwisely attached lanterns to its branches, the heat from which caused considerable damage. It was not, however, killed, but both this and the remaining specimen were later removed from Kew. One of them, five feet high, was presented by William IV to Lady Grenville in 1833 for her collection at Dropmore. This tree, while it grew into a fine specimen sixty feet high in 1880, was inferior to another at Dropmore, said to have been reared from a cutting stolen by a lady from a plant at Kew in the 1820s. There is an illustration of the latter tree in Veitch's *Manual of Coniferae* showing that it truly was an exceptionally fine specimen. The other tree was taken to Windsor in 1841 at the request of the Prince

Consort and planted in the Castle garden but, according to John Smith I, when he wrote in 1880, it had 'not grown much'. Long after Menzies was dead these trees reared their trim but bizarre shapes towards the sky as a reminder of that impulse of botanical curiosity which led him to ignore good table manners and pocket his dessert on that day in Valparaiso in 1795.

Although Menzies' collections in the hitherto unexplored area of the north-west coast of America led to a considerable advancement of botanical knowledge, the number of living plants he was able to introduce to the King's garden was far smaller than the consignments sent in by Masson from South Africa. In his eleven years in that country he sent back nearly nine hundred plants which were new to science. But that was not all: his impact on the gardens of England and, in particular, the plant population of British glasshouses was set out by Sir James Smith in an article in *Rees Cyclopaedia* of 1819:

> The writer of this well recollects the pleasure which the novel sight of an African geranium (*Pelargonium*), in Yorkshire and Norfolk, gave him about forty years ago. Now every garret and cottage-window is filled with numerous species of that beautiful tribe, and every greenhouse glows with the innumerable bulbous plants and splendid heaths of the Cape. For all these we are principally indebted to Mr Masson, besides a multitude of rarities, more difficult of preservation or propagation, confined to the more curious collections. Many of these have perhaps survived to bloom only once or twice within the walls to which they were first consigned; to be defined and named by the skill of a Solander, a Dryander, or of the younger Linnaeus in his transient visit among us.

Truly, as Banks had written earlier to the King, the royal bounty to Masson had not been misapplied.

On 7 March 1795 a young man of twenty-five named George Caley wrote to Banks sending him some specimens he had collected during botanical excursions and indicating his desire to increase his botanical knowledge. Banks replied that if Caley had bodily health and strength and understood the business of a garden labourer, working as such among exotic plants was in his view the only sound method of getting instruction. 'We have,' he said:

> ... several foreigners who every year enter that capacity in the King's garden and some of them persons of property. They receive about ten shillings a week upon which they can maintain themselves, and if they behave well they have great opportunities, not only of studying the culture of plants, but also exotic botany.

[115]

Caley came to London and worked for a time under William Curtis in the Chelsea Physic Garden and then reluctantly for a short time at Kew but this did not suit him and he returned to the north again complaining that Banks had treated him badly. He wanted to go out as a plant collector to New South Wales but Banks would not send him. Banks dealt with him very patiently, pointing out that the 'school' in which he had placed him was 'the very school in which the elder Aiton, Lee (the nurseryman), Mr Dickson (also a famous nurseryman) and several other respectable botanists' had 'laid the foundation of their knowledge'. There, for a time, the matter rested.

XII

FAR

SOUTHERN

SHORES

'I travelled among unknown men
In lands beyond the sea . . .'

William Wordsworth

In 1797 Masson was off again, this time to North America. Whether it was his own enthusiasm which led him to this adventure in a cold continent after many years in warmer climates or whether he was dragooned into it by Banks we shall never know. Perhaps the question of his ability to stand the climate after his long sojourn in the warm was discussed. If it was, the decision was made to risk it, and he set off. He had a most exhausting voyage, which he describes in a letter from New York dated 1 January 1798:

> We experienced many difficulties. Near the Western Isles we were stopped by two French privateers, one of which boarded us, examined our papers and let us pass. Nothing happened afterwards till the eighth of November.
> Towards night we saw 3 sail bearing down upon us, one of which was a French pirate belonging to San Domingo who fired several shots and volley of small arms into our ship and soon after boarded and took possession of us. Next morning we were desired to prepare ourselves to go on board a Bremen vessel

bound to Baltimore which they had detained on purpose.

We were accordingly all together with the crew of another vessel bound to Philadelphia put on board the said vessel with only about 4 days allowance of water and provisions. We thought ourselves very fortunate by being released from such savages but was in great hopes of soon seeing the coast of America but two days after a violent gale damped our hopes and our vessel being a bad sailer and a lazy timid crew of Dutchmen we found ourselves in a most dreadful situation.

Being about fifty three in all we found it necessary to put ourselves to the allowance of half a pound of black bread made of the husks of wheat and rye and 3 half pints of bad water each per diem and we were obliged to lay upon the cables at night with the common men.

We beat about in the Gulph Stream for 28 days without making one degree of westing and was bearing away for the West Indies when a schooner from the West Indies bound to New York came up with us and agreed to take the crew and passengers of the Ellice. We with great danger and difficulty got on board the schooner and after 4 days saw Long Island. ...

Their troubles were not yet over:

... the wind being westerly and blowing strong we were obliged to bear away for the Sound and two days after all the vessels were frozen up and we were obliged to make the best of our way overland a distance of 88 miles. ... We suffered much from the intensiveness of the cold.

After recuperating from the voyage Masson set off for Canada. On 18 October 1798 he reported progress to Banks from Montreal:

I arrived at Niagara about the beginning of July after a very disagreeable passage of five weeks from New York. According to your desire I took the route by the Mohawk River and Wood Creek to Oswego and then coasted along the south shore of Lake Ontario. I had frequent opportunities of going on shore and collected many beautiful specimens but very few in seed. From Niagara I proceeded up to Queenston where I met a most friendly reception from Mr Hamilton who took me to his house and gave me the use of two elegant rooms. Had I not had so good a recommendation I should have been in great distress, as being a new place there was no decent lodging to be got.

As soon as I recovered from the fatigues of the voyage I resolved to visit

[118]

Detroit and proceeded as far as Fort Erie where several vessels bound up the lakes lay but I remained 15 days wind-bound. Finding the season far advanced I returned to Niagara without accomplishing the voyage. I after visited York and other adjacent places and two days ago I arrived here to spend the winter. My intention is to attempt an expedition up the Grand Rivers to Lake Superior with the traders and return again to Niagara where I expect to be at the end of next summer.

Masson did his best, but the results were very meagre compared with what he had been able to find in South Africa.

Among those who began contributing to the Kew collections in 1800 was George Caley. Much to his joy and surprise Banks had sent him a letter out of the blue offering him a post of collector in New South Wales and he had arrived at Port Jackson on 15 April 1800. He was given lodgings at Paramatta and the Governor told Banks that a site had been marked out for a botanic garden and Caley would be allowed to use Government House at Paramatta to dry out his specimens. Banks had no illusions about Caley, saying in a letter to the Governor, 'He is a wild man, but I have no doubt will answer my patience if he is left to do just as his fancy leads him'. Caley's prickly personality soon led to difficulties with others and complaints to the Governor and to Banks, but he settled down and, as Banks had foreseen, began to do a good job.

On 17 December 1800 Banks offered the post of naturalist and collector on another expedition which was being fitted out to explore the unknown parts of Australia to Robert Brown, a young army officer. Like Caley, Brown was overjoyed at receiving the offer, accepted at once, and came to London. He set about equipping himself for the task with great thoroughness. His diary for 22 December 1800 reads:

Attend Sir Joseph's library every forenoon in order to form a herbarium of New Holland plants from the specimens brought by different collectors from Botany Bay, but chiefly from Sir Joseph's own collection. This occupied Mr Dryander and myself nearly a fortnight. I then employ my time in extracting information relative to New Holland plants consisting of four thin 8vo volumes altogether containing 620 pages ... went once to Kew. ...

The vessel on which Brown sailed was the *Investigator*, under the command of Captain Matthew Flinders, and with him Banks sent Ferdinand Bauer as artist, and Peter Good, an experienced foreman who had already been out to India for

Kew in 1796. The voyage commenced on 18 July 1801.

Round about the time that Brown visited Kew the King suffered a setback. For twelve years he had been free from serious attacks of his malady, porphyria, but at the beginning of 1801 his mind was again affected. On 20 April the royal family moved to Kew, the King being well enough to ride on horseback and being accompanied on the journey by four of his sons. His condition soon deteriorated, however, and the services of the Drs Willis were once again called upon, it being necessary, as before, to put the King under restraint. He could not be kept in the White House with the Queen and Princesses, and had to be removed to Kew Palace, where he was accommodated in a wing which has since been demolished. After a few weeks he recovered and resumed normal life again.

Caley, at Paramatta, continued his collecting during 1801, making a local coasting voyage and short trips inland, but progress away from the coast was always brought to a halt by the ridges and precipitous valleys of the Blue Mountains, which presented a formidable obstacle. Caley must have often looked at these mountains and speculated on what lay beyond but at this stage an attempted crossing was not feasible. Money and other resources were not in plentiful supply and in a land populated by rum-soaked convicts kept under control by threat of flogging and living 'on the stores', with as yet virtually no free settlers and natives whose ideas were far removed from those of Europeans, suitable comrades and support to organise even a modest expedition just did not exist, particularly for a man of Caley's somewhat awkward personality. Local collecting trips were difficult enough, but Caley did manage to train one aborigine, Moowat'tin, to assist him and, indeed, became attached to him. From time to time he was able to send consignments home to Banks, although even the supply of suitable boxes caused difficulty which resulted in some acrimony between Caley and the Governor.

In the meantime, the *Investigator* was making its way out from England. The vessel touched at Madeira and spent three weeks at Cape Town, during which Robert Brown collected orchids around Table Bay. On 8 December 1801 they anchored at King George Sound on the south-western tip of Australia. In the 24 days the ship remained in the Sound Brown and Good collected 500 species of plants. Continuing its way along the southern coast, the *Investigator* stopped at sixteen different points, at each of which Brown and Good added to their collection. By the time they reached Sydney on 8 May 1802 they had accumulated 750 species, 300 of which were new to science.

By 1801 the old White House had become so ramshackle, damp and draughty that the King decided to have it demolished and this was done during 1802. Kew

George III's proposed new Gothic Palace which was intended to replace the White House but which, although building was commenced in 1802, was never finished, and was demolished in the 1820s.

Palace was refurbished to provide temporary accommodation and George laid plans for a replacement for the White House to be built by the riverside on the land next to Kew Palace now called the Lower Nursery. The building was designed by James Wyatt, Surveyor-General of His Majesty's Works: several pictures of it have been preserved, which show it to be, in Lloyd Sanders' words in *Old Kew, Chiswick and Kensington*, 'a most astonishing edifice, castellated, turreted, loopholed, machicolated and crenellated'. The bizarre nature of the edifice, which had upwards of thirty towers or turrets, cannot, however, be entirely laid at Wyatt's door. He was working under orders from the King, who wanted a mediaeval castle, which would necessarily have a number of towers, though perhaps not as many as he got! In the end, however, it did not matter. The building, although started, was never finished.

Caley and Brown joined forces in 1802, soon after the latter's arrival, and made several botanical excursions into the foothills of the Blue Mountains, conceiving in the process a high respect for one another. The *Investigator* then continued up the east coast of Australia, touching at a number of points, which gave Brown and Good opportunities to collect, of which they took full advantage. The vessel was, however, becoming increasingly unseaworthy and, after calling at Coepang on 31 March 1803 came back to Port Jackson for a refit via the west coast of Australia. Repair was becoming so urgent that this journey was made without any intermediate calls. Unfortunately dysentery broke out on the voyage and among the victims was Peter Good, who died shortly after the return. An able and experienced collector and cultivator of exotic plants, he was a considerable loss. He was the second Kew collector to lose his life in the course of his duty.

The *Investigator* being no longer fit for sea, other arrangements had to be made. The *Porpoise* was available and on 10 August sailed for England, carrying Flinders but not Brown or Bauer, the arrangement being that they should remain in the colony until Flinders returned with another ship or until eighteen months had expired. The *Porpoise* had on board living plants housed in a glasshouse on the quarter-deck, and the better half of Brown's dried specimens. By the greatest mischance, the vessel was wrecked on 17 August on Wreck Reef and the whole of these collections lost. Brown said of this misfortune that: 'The loss of the garden and specimens is to my department irreparable, for altho' I possess duplicates of almost all the specimens, yet those sent were far the best, belonging to the south coast, and in consequence the most valuable that have been collected during the voyage.' Flinders continued his journey in another ship but was captured by the French and detained in Mauritius for a number of years. Brown, of course, could not know the turn events were going to take and continued collecting.

During 1803 Banks commissioned another collector to furnish material for the King's garden. The new man, William Kerr, was a foreman gardener at Kew. He took ship for China, his primary station being Canton, but he also visited Java and the Philippines. Caley, in Australia, set off in 1804 to explore an area called the 'Cow Pastures', where escaped cattle were running wild, but found it a relatively unprofitable expedition. Brown meanwhile had moved to Tasmania, where he climbed Mount Wellington twice but found only a small number of plants hitherto unknown to him. He was present at the inauguration of some of the first Tasmanian settlements and thus played a minor part in general history.

The King's flock of merino sheep had prospered and it had become evident by 1804 that the most useful way of disposing of surplus animals would be by public auction. The date of the first sale was fixed for Wednesday 15 August. The place of sale was originally to have been the barn on Marsh Gate Farm across Kew Lane opposite the Pagoda and this was printed on the sale particulars but it probably took place 'in a paddock . . . by the side of Kew Foot Lane, not far from the Pagoda' or in 'a field south of the Pagoda'. H B Carter sets the scene for us:

> The fine harvest weather that had been so general seemed to have withdrawn. From the eighty dragons on the Pagoda . . . rain had splashed in fitful streams for some days. The morning of Wednesday 15 August also dawned under low clouds and incessant showers, but as the morning advanced the sun at last cut through to bring rainbow glitters from the varnished iron plates of the ornate tower. High above the Royal parkland it now cast a beckoning gleam to the approaching carriages. Almost at right-angles to the water-filled ditch of the ha-ha which bounded the Old Deer Park along the Kew Road from Richmond ran a pleasant avenue of trees under which the show pens for the Spanish sheep were now arranged. Nearby on the damp pasture from eleven in the morning the horses and carriages of 'a number of intelligent gentlemen' collected, about fifty 'amateurs and breeders' intent upon examining minutely the strange animals of which so much had been surmised but so little seen in public.

In truth, the 'strange animals' were not very impressive, some being in poor condition and temporarily blind. One onlooker commented that had they been sold 'in a country market and unknown, they would scarcely have fetched five shillings a head.' According to the *Agricultural Magazine* for August 1804:

> Mr Fairbairn, the auctioneer, of Richmond, opened the business by a short but neat speech on His Majesty's gracious views in promoting the breed of excellent sheep before them, and read the printed conditions of sale. The first twenty-three lots consisted each of a single shearling ram. Lot 1 was . . . labouring under a temporary privation of sight, which Sir Joseph Banks and Richard Stanford, the King's shepherd, stated not to be uncommon with these sheep at this season, but from which there is no doubt he will perfectly recover. . . . He was knocked down to Capt MacArthur at £6–15s. . . .

but not until some small stir had been caused because Sir Joseph Banks:

> apprised him that an old act of Parliament stood in the way of exporting sheep from this country, the captain's object being to take the sheep which he was then purchasing to New South Wales in about three weeks' time to add to the flock

[123]

which he is rearing near Botany Bay with a degree of success which promises to be of the greatest national importance.

It seems possible that there was some bad feeling between Banks and MacArthur, who had differing views on the suitability of Australian pastures for the rearing of sheep but, whatever their relationship, MacArthur succeeded in shipping sheep to Australia: six of those he purchased survived to be landed at Sydney on 7 July 1805 and scampered ashore to fulfil their magnificent destiny among the founders of Australia's prosperity.

The King had not been very well during the spring of 1804 and had remained quietly at Buckingham Palace, but on 17 May he was sufficiently recovered to come out to Kew to enjoy the country air. On 16 June the royal family came for a longer stay. The Kew Green residents made much of the occasion, the landlord of one of the inns firing a salute of twenty-one guns from a small cannon at the top of his house. By November the King was well enough to go hunting at Windsor. During that month Caley took his longest and most arduous journey. He wrote to Banks on 1 November 1804 announcing his intention and admitting quite openly that botany was not his primary object. The mountains to the west were to him a constant challenge. Previous efforts to penetrate them had always petered out in a chaos of tangled ridges, deep valleys and precipices. Caley had the urge of the genuine explorer. 'You must excuse me from saying', he wrote, 'that botany is not the prime object, but there is an enthusiastic pride in going further than any person has yet been.'

On Saturday 2 November with some companions, he began to approach the mountains from Richmond at the junction of the Hawkesbury and Grose Rivers. On Sunday they climbed the Kurrajon Heights, inexperience leading his companions to start a bush fire inadvertently when they camped. Moving on through very difficult country they eventually reached the height now called Mount King George, but which Caley named Mount Banks. This was their furthest point: they were six miles only in a direct line from Mount Victoria, from whose summit it would have been possible for them to have seen the 'promised land' to the westward. But the extra distance was not attempted and the party turned back. J E B Currey comments that 'it is probably no exaggeration to say that if Caley had managed to penetrate those few extra miles the history of the colony would have been changed.' Caley missed his niche in general history and the crossing of the divide had to wait another nine years.

At this time Brown had gone up the north branch of the Hunter River and on 12 December reported to Banks that since his return from Tasmania he had examined all the branches of that river as far up as a small boat could reach and had added 50 species to his collection. In the same letter he mentioned that he had found 540 species in all in Tasmania, of which he expected about 100 to be new. After some other journeys Brown decided that it was time he returned to England. Leaving his collection of living plants with Caley to be forwarded by a later vessel, he sailed on the *Investigator*, now repaired, reaching home on 13 October 1805. The measure of the success of Brown and Good as collectors may be judged by the number of species Brown brought home: these amounted to 3,200, estimated to be a quarter of the total of the whole flora of Australia, a fantastic number for one voyage.

In the summer of 1805 the King had trouble with his eyes and it was necessary for him to see a specialist in London. Banks organised a second sheep sale in the field by the Pagoda but there was trouble over this one. Banks, anxious to interest the most prominent agriculturists, sold some of the merinos privately to Coke of Holkham, breaking the instruction given by the King that all his merinos were to be made available generally, so as to spread the breed widely. When he heard of the deal the King lost his temper and expressed great displeasure with Banks. The latter, on hearing of this, relinquished management of the flock. It was the first real breach between these two, but both were now old men and physically sick, Banks with persistent attacks of gout and the King with porphyria and the ailments of old age, and friction between them was perhaps inevitable. The sheep sales were held annually until 1810 in the same place, but Banks never resumed management of the flock.

Across the Atlantic in Canada Masson was writing on 14 May 1805 that although the winter had been 'dreadful severe and ... scarce any spring yet but constant fog and rain ...', he had 'been in very good health for some time'. He wrote again saying that he was coming home in the spring but apologised for not sending a collection of aquatic plants he had promised but explaining that he had not been able to search for them owing to 'excessive rains'. Alas, the Canadian weather was too much for him. He died in Montreal in December, an exile from those hot and sunny lands in which he had spent his prime and vigour. James Lee, the nurseryman, who was a friend of Masson's, thought he had not been well-treated. He wrote to Sir James Smith on 11 March 1806 telling him of Masson's death and saying:

> We lament his fate most sincerely. He was hardly dealt with, in being exposed to the bitter cold of Canada in the decline of life, after twenty-five years service in a hot climate, and all for a pittance. He has done much for botany and science and

deserves to have some lasting memorial given of his extreme modesty, good temper, generosity and usefulness.

Seven years later Lee reiterated that he thought that Masson:

...had been ill-paid, considering what he had done for the science of botany....
He was of a mild temper, persevering in his pursuits even to a great enthusiasm, of great industry, which his specimens and drawings of fish, animals, insects, plants and views of the countries he passed through, evince; and though he passed a solitary life in distant countries far from society, his love of natural history never forsook him.

The King and his family spent a month at Kew in the autumn of 1805. The *St James Chronicle* recorded at this time that the Queen's Cottage had 'undergone considerable alteration and improvement under the directions of the Princess Elizabeth'. It seems very probable that the decoration simulating a tent and the bamboo and climbing plant motifs in the upstairs apartment was designed by the Princess and perhaps even painted by her. She devoted much of her time to painting and some of her work was reproduced. Though she favoured figure subjects, she also painted flowers. An article in 1808 on poly-autography, an early name for lithography, refers to flower pictures by her. The passage in the *St James Chronicle* mentions incidentally that 'several of the rooms have been hung with the principal originals of Hogarth, and a number of paintings valued at several thousand pounds.'

If the royal family had but known it, this stay was to be the last occasion on which they were to be together at Kew. The long association of George III with Kew was almost at an end. He visited there on 9 January 1806 for a walk in the Gardens on his way from Windsor to London, dined there and went on to his destination, but afterwards was seen there no more. From 1807 onwards the King became increasingly infirm, and while he fulfilled some formal obligations and held levées the family remained quietly at Windsor or in London.

The cessation of the royal visits to Kew must necessarily have entailed some decline in interest in the botanic garden, at least among those formerly drawn to it because it was a source of pride and pleasure to the King. For the moment, however, the collectors abroad continued their work and material continued to arrive. William Kerr, the collector based on Canton, who had gone to the Philippines in 1804 because the activities of pirates prevented him from collecting in the waterways around Macao, experienced special difficulties because of the long voyage his plants had to endure which led to many losses. Banks persuaded the East India Company to send a Chinese gardener with the plants, a move which reduced the losses greatly.

Growing up in Norfolk in the past twenty years had been a young man destined to make a great mark in the botanical world. William Jackson Hooker had inherited a love for plants from his father and artistic talent from his mother's family. In 1805 botany had not yet seized his imagination to the exclusion of other biological disciplines, but a find as he was wandering through a fir plantation at Sprowston brought him into contact with botanists and steered him on to his life's work. He found in the plantation a small moss which he did not know, and taking it in December 1805 to Sir James Edward Smith, founder of the Linnean Society, at his house in London, learnt that it was the first specimen of *Buxbaumia aphylla* to be found in Britain. Advised to send a specimen to Dawson Turner of Yarmouth, the leading cryptogamist of the time, he wrote on 29 December 1805 making the contact that was not only to help him as a naturalist, but also to provide him with a wife: he eventually married Maria Turner, one of Dawson Turner's daughters. In the early spring of 1806 he went to Soho Square to see Sir Joseph Banks, was shown his collections and library, and met those who were working there. He came home a dedicated botanist, 'determined', as he wrote in a memorandum, 'to give up everything for botany'.

XIII
WAR
AND
PEACE

'O! Wither'd is the garland of the war ...'

Shakespeare: *Anthony and Cleopatra*

The crisis in New South Wales affairs which occurred in 1808 when, during what is known as the 'rum' rebellion, the governor, our old friend Captain Bligh, now an Admiral, was removed from his office and imprisoned by the Army, seems to have worried George Caley greatly. He appears to have done little during this period of his stay but remain at his home at Paramatta brooding over the melancholy state of the colony, yet the old urge was still gnawing him like a persistent toothache, as may be seen from a letter he wrote to Banks in which he said, 'I oftentime occupy my thoughts, what plants there are in some parts of the Blue Mountains undiscovered and lament that I am deprived of the means of going thither'. Presumably his inability to mount an expedition arose from lack of support from the Governorship, impossible to obtain in the troubled state of the times.

Caley became worried when he did not hear from Banks for three years, but in a letter dated 6 August 1808 Banks broke the long silence. He offered Caley a pension of £50 a year for life and the option to continue farming in Australia or return home. The letter contains the following revealing comment: 'I cannot say that Botany continues to be quite as fashionable as it used to be. The immense

The sunken garden, which is part of the Queen's garden, filled with medicinal plants and showing the wrought-iron obelisk and gazebo to the right.

Crab-apple trees in flower on Crab Mound.

number of new plants that have every year accumulated seems to deter people from making collections as they have little hope of making them perfect in any branch.'

On 12 May 1810 Caley left Australia, bringing with him extensive collections. When the immediate fuss of his arrival back in England was over, the old yearning began to pull at him again, a feeling that he expressed in a letter he wrote on 10 August 1812 in which he said, 'It's those damned mountains after all my sufferings that I am enraptured with. . . .' Caley's unquiet spirit could not rest, but he never returned to Australia: the further trials awaiting him were experienced elsewhere. One of the plants he introduced, *Livistona australis*, was for long one of the most striking ornaments of the Gardens, surviving in the Palm House, not built until some forty years after it was introduced, until 1876.

For a number of years W T Aiton had had in mind the republication, updated, of his father's *Hortus Kewensis* and in April 1803 he took the first steps towards this end. The labour of compilation was devolved upon Richard Cunningham. A part of the manuscript which has survived is in his hand and consists of a transcript of the first edition with numerous additions, with intercalated slips of further additions, probably by a clerk under the botanist Dryander's directions, and occasional interlineations by Dryander himself. There are also numerous additions as to the introducers of certain plants in the hand of W T Aiton. In the Kew Records Book for 1793–1809 there are further corrections by Aiton, doubtless for the use of Cunningham, and it is clear that Aiton played the dominating role in the preparation of this edition. Jonas Dryander died as the first volume was being issued in 1810 and Robert Brown, who succeeded him as Banks' librarian, continued the work through the remaining volumes, the fifth and final volume appearing in 1813.

The revised work is dedicated to the King, but it is doubtful whether the King ever opened it. The long illness of Princess Amelia had worried him and in September 1810 his reason finally broke down. When the Princess died in November he had already entered that final phase from which he never recovered. The Prince of Wales assumed the Regency on 5 February 1811. Work on the castellated palace was stopped, but the botanic garden continued, although the war had brought about a catastrophic decline in the number of new species coming in from 203 in 1803 to an all-time low of 3 in 1811.

After Peter Good's death his collection of seeds was sent home and from these W T Aiton raised no less than 104 new species recorded under Good's name in the *Hortus Kewensis*. Collections also came in from Caley, Brown, from a captured French vessel and, notably, from William Kerr in Canton who sent, among other things, quantities of Chinese garden varieties of trees and shrubs. The new species included *Rosa banksiae*, *Pieris japonica*, *Lilium tigrinum* (the Tiger Lily) and *Lilium japonicum*. W T Aiton found the Tiger Lily so easy to grow that in a very short time he had raised and distributed some ten thousand bulbs of this popular plant.

After a period of retirement when the King became ill, Queen Charlotte resumed her customary duties. In August 1813 she paid her first visit to Kew for eight years, accompanied by the Princesses Elizabeth and Mary. They would probably have seen the change in progress in the extensive area of water which was in process of being reduced from the original ten and a half acres to the two and half acres of which the Palm House lake is at present comprised.

The five volumes of the second edition of the *Hortus Kewensis* were unwieldy for general use and W T Aiton produced in 1814 an *Epitome* for practical gardeners, adding to the text a list of fruits and vegetables grown at Kew. Once again, the work of compilation fell upon Richard Cunningham. Two new collectors, Richard Cunningham's brother, Allan, and James Bowie, both of whom had been working at Kew, were now selected and sailed for Brazil on 29 October 1814. While waiting for permission to travel into the interior they collected around Rio but set off for São Paulo on 3 April 1815, where they arrived on 2 May, having experienced very bad weather on the way. There they stayed for three months, arriving back in Rio on 28 September, having collected some 700 species. During the next twelve months they made a number of similar journeys.

William Roxburgh of the Calcutta Botanic Garden retired in 1813. His regime had been noteworthy for the great flood of botanical drawings poured out year after year by native artists, more than 2,000 in all, which are preserved at Kew and a selection of which was published by Banks in *Plants of the Coast of Coromandel*. Roxburgh did not himself travel or collect, his introductions being all glasshouse plants, but his successor, Dr Nathaniel B Wallich, became a collector of considerable importance.

One of the first ventures launched by the British government on the advent of peace in 1815 was an attempt to penetrate the interior of tropical Africa. An expedition comprising 54 persons under the command of Captain J K Tuckey was formed with the intention of doing for the Congo River what Mungo Park had done for the Niger. A Swedish botanist, Christen Smith, not to be confused with Christopher Smith who sailed with Bligh, was selected at the recommendation of Banks to accompany the expedition. He was given the assistance of David Lockhart, a native of Cumberland. The expedition sailed in February 1816, the river was reached on 6 July, and the journey began. All went well at first as the party pushed upstream but then member after member began to fall ill and die.

The expedition reached Sangala, the highest rapid, and a group which included David Lockhart explored above the falls but the results were disastrous: everyone in this party perished except Lockhart. As the commander himself, Captain Tuckey, was one of those who lost their lives, there was no alternative but to abandon the expedition. Of the orginal 54, only 33 survived. Christen Smith was among those who perished, but Lockhart reached England safely, bringing with him seeds and specimens. On 30 January 1818 he was appointed Superintendent of the Trinidad Botanic Garden.

George Caley was appointed Curator of the St Vincent Botanic Garden, and on 1 August 1816 arrived in the island. Cunningham and Bowie were now coming to the end of their stay in Brazil and on 26 September 1816 Bowie embarked for South Africa and Cunningham for Australia. Bowie arrived at Table Bay on 1 November 1816 and was at first put off by what he called a 'supercilious' reception by the Governor, but matters were soon resolved in a way satisfactory to him. He was given four negro slaves and a plot of land on which to grow plants.

Cunningham's rather longer journey to Sydney took until 21 December. His reception by Governor Macquarie was somewhat better than Bowie's: he was invited to dine and the Governor immediately began to talk about the possibility of his participation in a forthcoming expedition which intended to follow up the hitherto unexplored Lachlan and Macquarie Rivers. Cunningham found himself a cottage at Paramatta, which he used as a base throughout his time in Australia, and settled himself in preparatory to carrying out his task.

Another new man was on the move in the winter of 1816. With the ending of the war it had become possible to fill Kerr's place in the botanic garden in Sri Lanka. The man chosen to do so was another Kew-trained gardener, Alexander Moon. Bowie says in his journal that Moon called to see him at Cape Town on 7 January 1817 and re-embarked on 14 January. Moon wrote to Aiton on 28 May 1817, saying:

> At the Cape of Good Hope I fell in with Mr Bowie who had arrived from the Brazils some months before whom I accompanied to the top of Table Mountain where we had the pleasure of drinking the good health of Sir Joseph and yourself and afterwards collected a variety of orchids and other plants several of which I brought alive to Ceylon and are now in a thriving state.

Sir Richard Phillips recorded a striking sight which was to be seen at Kew during the latter years of the war and some years after it. He walked from London to Kew and published an account of the walk in 1817. Approaching the end of his journey, he wrote:

> Another quarter of a mile, along a dead flat, brought me to Kew Green. As I
> approached it, the woods of Kew and Richmond Gardens presented a varied
> and magnificent foliage, and the pagoda of ten stories rose in splendour out of
> the woods. . . . As I quitted the lane I beheld, on my left, the long boundary wall
> of Kew Gardens, on which a disabled sailor has drawn in chalk the effigies of the
> whole British navy, and over each representation appears the name of the vessel,
> and the number of her guns. He has in this way depicted about 800 vessels, each
> five or six feet long, and extending with intervening distances about a mile and a
> half. As the labour of one man the whole is an extraordinary performance, and I
> was told the decrepit draughtsman derives a competency from passing
> travellers.

John Evans had also seen this apparently as early as 1810, as he dates a letter
recounting an excursion to Windsor in which he mentions seeing it in July of that
year, although an *Excursion to Windsor* in which he included the account was not
published until 1817. In *Richmond and its Vicinity*, published in 1825, he says that
the drawings were 'nearly obliterated.'

A quiet walk in the suburbs of London was to be far from the lot of Allan
Cunningham in the next few months. He was to do much walking, but in territory
never yet trodden by the foot of European man. In the early months of 1817 the
expedition mentioned by the Governor was being formed under the leadership of
John Oxley to explore and trace the courses of the Lachlan and Macquarie Rivers.
It was a good opportunity for Cunningham to begin his work and on 4 April 1817
he set out for Bathurst, reaching there on 14 April. On the way he passed the pile of
stones which was for long called 'Caley's Repulse', being believed to mark the
farthest point that George Caley had reached, but it is thought now not to have
been built by Caley.

On 20 April the expedition proper began. They left Bathurst for a camp on the
Lachlan and on 25 April began to descend the river by boat. It was not long before
it began spreading out and on 12 May they reached a point where it was lost in
swamps. Leaving the boats, they pushed overland in a south-westerly direction
thinking that they might eventually reach Cape Northumberland but had to give
up this notion because of the arid nature of the scrubby country through which
they passed. This did not prevent Cunningham 'planting the seeds of quinces and
the stones of peach and apricot trees . . . with the hope rather than the expectation
that they would grow and serve to commemorate the day and situation, should

[132]

these desolate plains be ever again visited by civilized man', of which Oxley thought there was 'very little probability'. When they turned north-west again to regain the Lachlan they were within twenty miles of the Murrumbidgee, which would have relieved their wants, but the discovery of this had to wait until later. On 23 June they were back again on the Lachlan, which they followed westward until they lost it again in swamps and creeks. Turning again and keeping near the river, they crossed to the northern bank by a raft, spent a few more days in arid country and then, after a journey northwards of 150 miles from the Lachlan reached the Macquarie in Wellington valley, and Bathurst on 29 August.

George Caley in St Vincent had become so exasperated with difficulties which he was experiencing that he had appealed to higher authority. The planters whose property adjoined the botanic garden appropriated land from it and the natives stole plants and sabotaged the administration. He received the support he requested from no less a personage that Lord Palmerston, who wrote from the War Office to Banks on 5 December 1817:

> I have requested Lord Bathurst to give strict instructions to the Governor of St Vincent to exert his utmost authority in supporting Mr Caley in protecting this part of the property of the Crown entrusted to his care from all trespass whatsoever and to repress any attempts on the part of individuals to encroach upon the garden and molest the superintendent.

On the back of Lord Palmerston's letter is a draft by Banks which shows clearly that he thought Caley brought some of the trouble upon himself and that he ought to be 'more amiable' and not excite opposition.

On his return to Paramatta Cunningham had found instructions from Banks to join Lieutenant P P King in the *Mermaid* to survey and explore the north and north-west coasts of Australia. The expedition sailed on 22 December 1817 and arrived at King George's Sound on 21 January 1818. Cunningham, like Menzies and Brown before him, found this a happy hunting ground. Moving on they explored Exmouth Gulf, Curlew River and Dampier's Archipelago: here Cunningham found Sturt's Desert Pea (*Clianthus dampieri*) perhaps, with its vivid red, the most striking of all Australian plants. The expedition moved on to the Goulborn Islands on the north coast, from there sailed on to Coepang in Timor to replenish stores and then returned to Port Jackson, which they reached on 29 July.

For the whole of 1817 and the first months of 1818 Bowie continued collecting in the area around Cape Town, getting no further afield than Paarl. But at the end of 1817 he acquired a wagon and oxen, together with a Hottentot 'coachman', and on 23 March 1818 set off on a longer trip. Going first to Hottentots Holland, he moved on to Caledon, Zonder End River and Swellendam, arriving at Groote Vader Bosch on 5 May. There he stayed a month collecting in the mountains before he moved on again across the Duivenhoeks, Gouritz and Great Brak Rivers to George, Knysna and Plettenberg's Bay. He had great difficulty with some of the rivers and with the terrain, but he had learnt much about travelling over difficult country in Brazil and was not deterred by hardship.

The Queen's health had been giving cause for worry and she moved to Kew on 21 June, with the intention of going on after a rest in the country air to join her husband at Windsor. For the first fortnight she was able to take airings in the Gardens in a small chaise, but eventually even this became too much for her. When Princess Charlotte, the daughter of the Prince Regent and heir to the throne, died at Claremont on 6 November 1817, the succession was put in jeopardy and the Royal Princes were required, as a matter of state policy, to marry. The Queen's presence was essential at these marriages and as she could not be moved elsewhere, they had to be solemnized at Kew Palace and were duly performed in mid-July, 1818. The Duke of Clarence married Adelaide, eldest daughter of George, Duke of Saxe-Coburg-Meiningen and the Duke of Kent married Victoria Mary Louisa of Saxe-Saalfield-Coburg. The Duke of Cumberland was, of course, already married, having, to the great scandal of his mother, who would not receive her, espoused in 1815 the divorced Princess Frederica, daughter of the Duke of Mecklenburg-Strelitz. The Duke of Cambridge, who lived at Kew, was also, of course, already married. After the marriages of Clarence and Kent the Queen continued to decline until 17 November 1818 when she died, sitting in her chair, surrounded by her children, holding the hand of the Prince Regent. She lay in state in Kew Palace and was buried at the beginnning of December 1818.

Bowie had remained in the area of Plettenberg's Bay during the whole time of the Queen's illness. He followed the same road back as he had taken on the way out, arriving at Caledon on 10 December, where he remained for a month. On 6 January 1819 he moved on to Swellendam, arriving back at Cape Town on 11 January. In the meantime, Cunningham had been on another trip. After spending a period sorting out his collections and arranging for the loan of a horse, a packsaddle and cart from Governor Macquarie, with whom he was not on the best of terms, he set out on 18 October 1818 to visit the Illawarra, a narrow strip of country just south of Sydney between an escarpment and the sea. Leaving his cart at the top of the Bulli Pass he scrambled down the scarp and established a base near the present Port Kembla:

Working from this base, mainly in dark gullies overgrown with ferns, abounding in the orchids which so interested him and alive with the sounds of the invisible bell-birds, he hardly noticed the passing of a fortnight and the accumulation of so many specimens that he had to spend several backbreaking days getting them up the mountain.

Although Cunningham enjoyed himself, he did not find very much that was new, most of what he collected having been first found by Brown in the Hunter's River area.

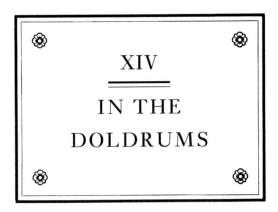

XIV

IN THE

DOLDRUMS

'The light of other days is faded,
And all their glory past.'

Alfred Bunn

The death of Queen Charlotte reduced Kew Palace to the care and maintenance basis on which it had operated before her illness. This was virtually the end of the old house as a royal residence. John Heneage Jesse, who visited the Palace before the death of William IV, described it:

> When many years since the author wandered through the forsaken apartments of the old palace at Kew, he found it apparently in precisely the same condition as when George III had made it his summer residence and when Queen Charlotte had expired within its walls. There was still to be seen, distinguished by their simple furniture and bedcurtains of white dimity, the different sleeping-rooms of the unmarried princesses, with their several names inscribed over the doors of each.
>
> There was still pointed out to him the easy chair in which Queen Charlotte had breathed her last; the old harpsichord which had once belonged to Handel, and on which George III occasionally amused himself with playing; his walking

stick; his accustomed chair; the backgammon board on which he used to play with his equerries; and, lastly, the small apartment in which the pious monarch was accustomed to offer up his prayers and thanksgivings.

In that apartment was formerly to be seen a relic of no small interest, the private prayer-book of George III. In the prayer which is used during the session of Parliament, the King with his own hand had obliterated the words 'our most religious and gracious King' and substituted for them 'a most miserable sinner.'

There was a danger for a time that the old house might share the fate of the White House and be pulled down to make way for George IV's plans for other developments, but this idea was abandoned. To enable it to be carried out, however, the Prince Regent bought in 1818 the eight acres of land between Kew Palace and the modern Herbarium site. He also bought the three houses facing over Kew Green which adjoined this land to the east, the first of which was Hunter House, around which the Herbarium was afterwards built. According to John Smith these were to be converted into an occasional summer retreat which was to be called 'King's Lodge'. For the moment, however, no further progress could be made as an Act of Parliament was required to enclose the portion of Kew Green, which was common land, which the Prince wished to add to his new abode.

Before resuming his main task, Captain King made a short trip to Tasmania, staying there during most of January 1819, during which time Cunningham studied the Huon pine, a useful timber tree. Returning to Sydney in February the *Mermaid* sailed again at the beginning of May. Turning north up the east coast of Australia to the Endeavour River, calling at several spots en route. From then onwards bad luck dogged them. Failing to find a suitable anchorage in the Torres Straits they crossed the Gulf of Carpentaria and anchored on the Liverpool River, then moved on to Goulburn Island, where poor Cunningham fell ill with jaundice and had to cease collecting for a time. At Cape Voltaire it was decided to turn to Timor to revictual but they were blown far westward and did not reach Coepang until 1 November. There was no further opportunity to collect as Captain King decided to return straight back to Port Jackson around the western coast of Australia. They reached port on 12 January 1820.

Bowie had also been on the move in 1819, making a journey eastward from Cape Town to Tulbagh, southward down the Breede River, and then being forced by bad weather to return to the Cape via Swellendam. This journey occupied him from May to August. He set off again in the same direction on 18 September following much the same route but in better conditions, this time getting as far as

[137]

An artist's impression of John Smith I, the first Curator of Kew.

Plettenberg's Bay. He arrived back in Cape Town on 22 January.

A week after Bowie returned, on the evening of Saturday 29 January 1820, the body of the tired old King, from which his mind had long been absent, slowly ran down like an unwound clock, and his long reign ended. Vast changes had come about since that time long ago when he had waited in Kew Palace for the great Chatham to come to tell him that his grandfather was dead and he was King of England. Small part though it was of the great affairs with which he had been concerned, the little exotic garden, formally established by his mother, had played as the years went on an increasingly important part in the investigation of the vegetation of the world and now possessed, in addition to a full range of plants from more familiar countries, collections from the southern hemisphere unequalled elsewhere.

Bowie stayed at the Cape only five days before returning to his host's house at Plettenberg's Bay, where he remained for the next six months. About the time

[138]

Bowie reached his destination Cunningham took a Russian party on a short trip into the Blue Mountains. In early June the *Mermaid* was damaged by foul weather. While it was still in harbour, on 19 June 1820, Sir Joseph Banks died at his house, Spring Grove, at Isleworth, bringing to an end the first period of the Royal Botanic Gardens, which had been dominated by his drive, inexhaustible energy and enthusiasm.

By a coincidence, a young man who was to do much, albeit on a lower level, to hold the garden together in the bad times that were coming, and to serve on beyond those times into the new Kew which was to arise, joined W T Aiton's staff in 1820 at Kensington, and was thus a link between the old and the new. The newcomer was John Smith, whose manuscript and printed works, although not free from error and bias, carry the authority of an eye-witness for much of what they record and are thus of immense value, in the paucity of other records, for the early history of the Gardens.

On the higher level Banks, just before his death, had taken the step which was eventually to bring to birth his cherished dream of Kew as the botanical centre of the British Empire: in the last months of his life he was instrumental in arranging the appointment of William Jackson Hooker to the Professorship of Botany at Glasgow, a post which he was to fill with distinction and which was to mark him out for preferment.

Banks left an annuity of £300 to enable Francis Bauer to continue his work at Kew and George IV seems to have agreed that accommodation should be set aside for him as the small room at the right of the front entrance of Hunter House was fitted out with bookshelves to take the botanical books in the King's library.

John Smith throws some light on the treatment of young gardeners who came to Kew in his earlier days. When a theft occurred of some of the rare specimens they were immediately suspected and were 'kept in close confinement in a shed' for four or five days. 'There was no special means in use,' he says, for teaching them, 'books being beyond their reach'. Their wages were only twelve shillings a week and it is not surprising that, in these circumstances, they could be tempted by an unscrupulous nurseryman to steal likely plants. They had to obtain their knowledge of plants from direct observation and study, and what information they could get from the foreman. 'I,' says John Smith, 'on first coming to Kew was considered wonderful in possessing three books, viz. Mawe's *Gardener's Calendar*, Lee's *Introduction to Botany* and Smith's *Compendium Flora Britannica*'. When they completed their training they became head-gardeners on the great estates of the land. At Kew in the 1820s was John Gould the famous ornithologist who worked for several years as a gardener and whose illustrated bird books now sell for immense sums at auction. As part of their duties the gardeners were required to look after visitors. Although their work was hindered, and the plants often suffered, the gardeners did not find the visitors a nuisance. Taking tips from them was forbidden on pain of dismissal but ways were found of getting round the ban.

Bowie terminated his stay at Plettenberg's Bay on 12 September, setting off east and breaking new ground. On 14 October he arrived at Uitenhage and then moved on to Algoa Bay. Travelling via the Sunday River, Addo Heights and the Bushman River, he turned west in the Bathurst district to Grahamstown, returning then to Algoa Bay. Not being very well, he sailed on 15 January on the *Mary* brig to Cape Town, remaining there for five months. The *Mermaid* had become so crazy that, although it made an attempt to begin another voyage it had to return and was scrapped. Cunningham set off on his fourth voyage with King in the *Bathurst*. On reaching Point Adieu on 26 August King decided to make for Mauritius for a refit, Cunningham being ill again, this time with an ulcerated throat.

Bowie reached Algoa Bay on 5 June and launched off from Bathurst northward into new territory. The sight of a burned farmhouse scared his driver and there was general reluctance on the part of his 'boys' to push on further into border country where they might be set on and murdered by 'Caffers'. There was an abundance of wild life in these regions: he noted on 8 July that:

> ...numbers of quaggas and a few ostriches were feeding in sight of the wagon and a troop of upwards of 50 elephants passed at a short distance; traces of these animals as well as buffaloes were in every direction, making it rather unsafe to go far among the bushes. Tigers (?) and wild dogs appear plentiful.

By 9 July he had reached the Great Fish River at a place he called Trumpeter's Drift. On 16 July he had arrived at a point near Grahamstown and set out on the return journey, arriving back at Uitenhage on 24 July. He applied to the governor for permission to go into Caffraria in spite of the dangers, but it was refused and, changing his plan, he went along the Sunday River to Graaf Reinet and then on to the Orange River. On the way back he became worried by the lack of water and decided to wait for rain before pushing on. He was still there when Cunningham left Mauritius in the *Bathurst* on 15 November, having been ill again with liver trouble. By 23 December the *Bathurst* was back in King George's Sound. Bowie had become impatient. There had been a little rain, but not enough. In spite of this, he left Graaf Reinet on 19 December and almost at once regretted it. There was little pasture and no water for the oxen and on 23 December one fell and had to be left behind. Then some of the spokes broke on one of the wheels but near enough to Uitenhage to obtain a substitute wagon, which brought him back to Algoa Bay on 30 December.

The *Bathurst* did not move from King George's Sound until 6 January but a few days later ran into bad weather in which Cunningham was nearly lost in a storm which sprang up when he was out in the cutter. The weather continued stormy and King made for Port Jackson, arriving there on 25 April 1822. This was Cunningham's last voyage with King. On these journeys he had collected some 1,300 species. Although almost all were of established genera, and descriptions of over a third had already been published, this was still a fine achievement.

In 1822 the piece of land on which the Pagoda stands, which had not been part of the Essex estate and was still held on lease, was purchased from William Selwyn. In this year also the King, in advance of Parliamentary authority, began enclosing that part of Kew Green that was to be brought within the Royal grounds. Other changes were also made anticipating the greater use of Kew Palace. Work was also going on at Windsor which affected Kew. 'For several years', says John Smith, 'it was Mr Aiton's custom to drive in a gig almost daily from Kew to Windsor, for if from any inadvertent cause he was prevented for two or three days, a mounted dragoon carrying a message from the King was sure to be seen early in the morning at his house at Kew.' Aiton did not, however, allow this to interfere with his Kew work: he was still very conscious of his botanic garden responsibilities, and the need to record accurately what was grown and flowered in the garden. As plants were added to the collection and named they were entered in an interleaved copy of the *Epitome*, a task no doubt falling on Richard Cunningham. At the same time specimens of the plants were preserved and, after Banks' death, drawn by one of the gardeners, Thomas Duncanson, who had been found to have a talent for this work.

Aiton's heavy involvement elsewhere probably led to the transfer of the able young garderner John Smith from Kensington to Kew in 1822. He was made foreman in 1823, there being only two in this grade, the other being Robert Begbie, and from then onwards played a prominent part in the care of the collections. A native of Aberdour, he had taken steps before he came to Kew to acquire a horticultural education above the average, and stood out among the other young gardeners. Three things surprised him when he took up duty, the lack of labels of on the plants, the use of green glass for the glasshouses, and the weight of the heavy mats which were used for shading, which often broke panes of glass. The first of these faults he rectified over the years, the second was phased out as opportunity offered and he effected an immediate improvement in the third by substituting home-made canvas roller blinds of his own invention – possibly the first time such were used for greenhouse shading.

Bowie stayed around Uitenhage for the first two months of 1822 and then in March made another sortie out towards the Cowie River and Port Alfred, arriving back in early April. Back in Plettenberg's Bay by 2 June he was laid low by illness for three months. By this time Cunningham had returned from another visit to the Illawarra and set out again on 27 September on a journey which was to take him into new territory. Furnished by the governor with two horses and a cart and an extra convict, he arrived at Bathurst on 14 October, made several sorties in the neighbourhood and then on 18 November left for the Cudgegong River with the intention of going on to the Liverpool Plains. A mishap in which one of his horses escaped and was lost was somewhat of a deterrent and he limited his efforts to the Cudgegong and around Bathurst, arriving back in Paramatta on 4 January 1823.

While Bowie and Cunningham were collecting so industriously, George Caley's efforts were brought to an end, the Treasury abolishing his post in St Vincent. He arrived home in 1822, to live in retirement until he died in 1829. His faults were considerable, but he worked long and hard for Kew, being described by Robert Brown as '*Botanicus peritus et accuratus*' (a skilful and experienced botanist). George Suttor wrote of him that:

> ...his friendship and conversation were to us, in the early days of the (Australian) colony, a great treasure and a shining light. His mind was rich in nature and much cultivated (when he finally retired he spent much of his small income on books). ... He was one of the most sincere and kindest friends we ever had.

Bowie arrived back at Cape Town on 4 December but in January the axe that had fallen on Caley fell on him also, and he was ordered home. At St Helena on the way back he was given some twigs of the willow that hung over Napoleon's grave. Whether or not it was these twigs that were involved or those, as John Smith avers, brought in by Thomas Frazer in 1825, the acquisition by Kew of Napoleon's willow caused some excitement. It created 'such interest' says John Smith, that:

> ...a great number of people came to Kew to see it, the crowd on one Sunday being so great that the gates (then folding doors) were by the pressure of the crowd burst open, the result being bruises and flattened hats and bonnets. For a time the twig had to be nursed under a bell-glass.

[142]

It was planted out near the then public entrance of the garden, not far from the large specimen of the Corsican pine which still stands a little distance inside the present Main Gate, but which was at that time a mere slip of a tree, having been brought by the botanist R A Salisbury from the south of France in 1814. This spot, continues John Smith, Napoleon's Willow:

> ...occupied for 40 years, having attained at its death a height of 40 feet, the circumference a little above the ground measuring $7\frac{1}{2}$ feet. French visitors paid reverence to it by taking off their hats, some even kneeling to it.

Bowie arrived at Kew on 19 August 1823. His collections while abroad were considerable. The succulents were written up by Haworth and it seems probable that he contributed towards the work of Francis Bauer, published in 1818, on *Strelitzia*, as he seems to have made a special effort to collect this genus. John Smith notes that, when he returned, he 'brought back with him many plants of the fine cycad *Encephalartos horridus*' and Kew records show an entry of seeds of 1,018 species against his name for 1824 which he must also have brought back with him. His contribution of succulents to the collection was so substantial that a low lean-to stove house 40 feet long had to be remodelled in 1825 to take it.

In the Orange River area Bowie discovered a beautiful plant which gave rise to an unfortunate botanical contretemps. It was received at Kew in 1823 and having flowered was figured by W J Hooker in the *Botanical Magazine* as *Imantophyllum aitoni*. Surreptitiously, however, a bulb had been smuggled over to Sion House, where it also flowered and was figured by Dr John Lindley in the *Botanical Register* under the name of *Clivia nobilis*!

Cunningham, after another trip to the Illawarra, suggested to the Governor that he might make another sortie towards the Liverpool Plains which Oxley had first seen. The Governor, who by now regarded Cunningham as explorer first and plant-collector second, gave his consent and help and on 31 March 1823 he set off from Paramatta with five men and five packhorses, reaching the Cudgegong on 18 April. Proceeding west, north and then north-east, Cunningham reached the Goulburn River and could see, 25 miles away, the mountains between himself and the Liverpool Plains. Pushing on into increasingly broken country he arrived at the range, scrambled to the top and saw the plain beyond covered with brown grass. It took him some time and several abortive attempts before he found a way through. He had almost given up hope in an apparently closed valley when he spotted a way round a spur on the western side which led him eventually through other valleys to the Plains. He named the way he had found 'Pandora's Pass'. It

The Orchid House at Kew showing epiphytic orchids, i.e. those which grow on a support such as a branch but merely use it as a perching place, without their roots actually drawing sustenance from it.

served as a way in for colonists to the Plains until a better was discovered and 'played an important part in the extension of grazing and settlement in the large area he had crossed'.

The King's need for money caused him to sell Hunter House to the nation in 1823. The Commissioners of Woods and Forests reported it in good order and valued it at £18,250. Although no deeds have been produced, a receipt for the money is extant, so that there is no doubt that the sale went through. The receipt, which is in the Library of the Royal Botanic Gardens in box file No KEW 276, is dated 3 July 1823 and signed by S Hulse on paper bearing the crest of H M Office

The interior of House No. 4, the Conservatory, devoted to decorative conservatory plants.

The interior of the large fern house.

of Works at 12, Whitehall Place SW. A few days after this sale Parliament passed the Act which gave effect to the enclosure of part of Kew Green by the King. This added a large triangle in front of the present Main Gate through the centre of the long side of which was made an imposing entrance flanked on each side by a lodge, one of which bore the effigy of a lion which now adorns the Lion Gate of the Gardens at the south end and the other an effigy of a unicorn which may be seen on top of a small private gate to the Gardens on the Kew Road. A new entrance to the botanic garden was provided next to the present Director's Office, which was then a private house.

The amount of money made available for the botanic garden was reduced and, little by little, it began to slide away from its original standards. W T Aiton was away much of the time and a great deal was left to John Smith, who did his best under increasing difficulties. He left an invaluable description of the botanic garden as he found it. 'When the Arboretum came under my charge in 1823,' he says:

> ...the general collection was about forty or sixty years old, the average size of the trees being from 40 to 50 feet high: while others such as *Ailanthus*, *Platanus*, *Gleditschia* and *Populus alba*, were at least 60 to 70 feet high: on the latter was a large bunch of mistletoe, which could be seen from various points for a considerable distance round.

A few special trees grew in the Herbaceous Ground, of which he lists *Pyrus baccata*, *Robinia viscosa*, two fine flowering trees, a beautiful pendulous birch, *Magnolia glauca*, *M. acuminata*, *Ostrya vulgaris* and *Sophora japonica*, the last previously mentioned as still surviving. Some also stood in a place called the 'experimental ground'. These included the *Araucaria araucana* (the 'Monkey Puzzle' – 'Sir Joseph Banks' Pine'), *Cupressus disticha*, *Broussonetia papyrifera*, *Koelreuteria paniculata*, one of the first plants of *Pyrus japonica*, and *Aucuba japonica*. John Smith continues:

> ...with the exception of the more tender species planted against the wall, there were to be found in the Arboretum examples of nearly all the 630 species of hardy trees and shrubs (excluding *Rosa* and *Salix* which were planted elsewhere) enumerated in the second edition of the *Hortus Kewensis*. ...

Although the area was small, the Arboretum was a remarkable spot. As one entered, the scene conveyed the idea of being in a large forest with underwood. It was 'the resort of hundreds of birds'.

In November 1823 Cunningham began to explore a new route over the Blue Mountains, finding some orchids in the rain forests. Although there had been some success in flowering orchids, the secret of the successful cultivation of the epiphytic species had not been mastered when John Smith took over. He found those which had been received from Cunningham and Bowie in a deplorable state, most of them being dead or dying. In December 1823 he tried another consignment from Cunningham in 'loose turfy soil interspersed with small portions of stems'. They liked this better and 'many of them grew freely'. The full breakthrough, however, was not achieved until a year or two later. 'Between the years 1823 and 1825 a considerable number of species was received from Trinidad, forwarded by Mr David Lockhart ... all of which were epiphytal.' Many of them were sent 'growing on portions of branches as cut from the trees' and were 'accompanied by instructions from Lockhart as to how they should be treated.' The instructions were followed and success achieved, a notable advance for Smith and Lockhart and the Royal Botanic Gardens.

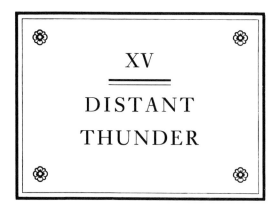

XV
═══
DISTANT
THUNDER

'Now is the time, when all the lights wax dim ...'

Robert Herrick

During the first half of 1824 Cunningham made journeys to new country south of Paramatta and to the Illawarra rain forest. One of the 'remarkable plants collected on this occasion was the lofty tree-nettle of that district (*Urtica gigas*), a tree measuring 80 or 90 feet in height, with a diameter of 3 feet, and also having violent stinging propensities, producing great irritation on the part affected for 24 hours.' This plant arrived at Kew in 1826, but John Smith records that, although it 'attained a height of 5 feet ... its powerful stinging properties ... led it to meet with general ill-will from the men, and as it died suddenly, it is supposed to have been wilfully killed. It has not (1880) since been introduced.'

A government decision had been made to explore the Moreton Bay hinterland and the Brisbane River to see whether it was fit for settlement, and Cunningham jumped at the chance to join Oxley on this venture. The expedition reached Moreton Bay on 11 September 1824 and while Oxley fixed the site for the settlement, Cunningham pursued his task of collecting. They were on the look-out for a gap in the Dividing Range but Oxley's ill-health prevented any progress on this, Cunningham's chief profit from the journey being greater knowledge of the

[147]

hoop pine, *Araucaria cunninghamii*, and the Norfolk Island Pine, *Araucaria excelsa*, which he was able to distinguish from it. He was back in Paramatta on 14 October. Further work was hampered by a severe drought in the summer of 1824–5. He made an abortive attempt to reach the Liverpool Plains but was driven back by heavy and continual rain.

John Smith was now beginning to get a grip on the collections and to make changes to improve their cultivation. While his work with the orchids was going on he was also concerning himself with other groups. The 20 species of aroids mentioned in the *Hortus Kewensis* had increased to 44 in the second edition and Bowie and Cunningham had added a dozen more. John Smith writes:

> In 1825 I began to take a special interest in this (the Arum Lily) family and found them, like the ferns, dispersed in different hothouses. I brought them together, forming a group of them at the west end of the hothouse, then a lean-to ... while the small collection of ferns numbering about 25 species occupied the east end. ... In order to show their natural mode of growth, I placed the epiphytal ones on portions of tree stems to which their roots clung and thus they remained for a number of years.

In the early summer of 1825–6 Cunningham made a sweep of about 150 miles each side of the Macquarie finding, among other things, 25 species of terrestrial orchid. He was back by the end of 1825 but his health gave cause for concern. He was very ill with a recurrence of his old liver trouble and it seemed likely that he had contracted tuberculosis. He recovered sufficiently, however, to collect in the Blue Mountains in March and a convict he had trained brought more material back from the Illawarra. He spent three weeks in the region himself searching for still more from that prolific forest.

In 1826 J C Loudon founded the *Gardener's Magazine*, a journal for professional gardeners. For a number of years he visited Kew regularly and reported on its affairs at length. Almost from the beginning the magazine reveals that there was a great deal of public dissatisfaction with the state of affairs at Kew. Aiton was thought to have reversed the policy of sharing new plants with other collections, which was considered to have been directly responsible for the thefts from Kew. The restriction of funds which did not, for example, allow the results of the voyage of the *Investigator* to be published, so that the work of Robert Brown and Ferdinand Bauer remained largely unseen, was also heavily criticised, as was the starving of the Gardens themselves of funds, leading to an inevitable decline in standards. No changes were made, however, and matters drifted on with the

[148]

dissatisfaction steadily growing.

The young gardener Thomas Duncanson, whom Aiton had employed since 1822 to make drawings of the plants as they flowered, succumbed to mental illness in 1826 and had to give up the work , but not before he had completed in all some 300 valuable drawings. By a lucky chance there was another young gardener already at Kew, George Bond, who had shown similar talent, and was able to take over the task. Aiton was away at Windsor so much the selection of subjects devolved largely upon Richard Cunningham and himself.

For some years Cunningham had toyed with the notion of visiting New Zealand but this was still a wild and savage place and it needed considerable courage to resolve, as Cunningham did, to make a visit to collect plants as this is a pursuit which takes the collector away from the protection of his fellows. Nevertheless, he was not deterred, and took a ship for the Bay of Islands, arriving at Paihia on 9 September 1826. After spending a week in the vicinity of the settlement he followed rough tracks across the peninsula to Hokianga Harbour. He had to return by the same route and the hardships of the journeys affected his health again so that he had to take things quietly for a time. On 17 October he journeyed to the headwaters of the Kawa Kawa River where he found much to collect. He spent a month at Whangaroa 'working mainly among the high ridges among great stands of the fascinating Nikau palm, *Rhopalostylis sapida*'. He then took the opportunity of the mission steamer to go to the Bay of Plenty, 200 miles to the south, but found the botany very little different from what he had seen. He arrived back in Sydney on 19 January 1827.

When, a few days after his return, Cunningham called on the Governor, a discussion arose about the need for further exploration of Australia. In the course of this, Cunningham revealed 'a plan of a journey he had long had in contemplation', namely, 'to explore a portion of the totally unknown country lying north from the Liverpool Plains between the meridian of 150°E and the coastline.' He suggested to the Governor that he might travel north from the point where Oxley had crossed the Peel River in 1818 to latitude 29°S. From there, depending upon the season and the condition of his expedition he would either go west to assess the extent of the marshes seen by Oxley or east to reach the headwaters of the Brisbane River. The plan was accepted and he was lent enough convicts and horses to provide him with a total of six men and eleven pack animals, rations for fourteen weeks and a good set of surveying instruments.

The expedition set out from a station called 'Segenhoe' on the Page River near the Liverpool range on 26 April 1827. Two days of 'slogging hard work' over very steep territory took them over the shoulder of Towarri Mountain and they then went down into the country of the headwaters of the Mooki River, heading for the Peel River. After crossing Currabubula Creek, just west of where Oxley had reached the Peel, Cunningham found himself separated from the latter by a ridge, and rather than attempt to cross this he continued north down the valley of the Mooki, and on 12 May crossed the Namoi near the site of the modern township of Carroll.

Cunningham was now in country which Oxley had not seen but was at first disappointed by what he found, nothing but deep stony gullies and ridges ending in the 'poverty-stricken hills' of the Nandewar Range. From this territory, however, he suddenly descended into Stoddart's Valley, a place of lush grass and tall eucalypts, populated by emus and kangaroos. Here he was astonished to find traces of cattle and later, on his return, a temporary shelter. Although he was the first officially to see this territory, others had clearly preceded him, almost certainly cattle thieves.

Following Bingara Creek down to the Gaydir and crossing the latter, he was disappointed to find the fertile country in the grip of drought, with all the watercourses, including one fifty yards wide which he crossed on 26 May, absolutely dry. He was now near the 29th parallel and had to decide whether to go east or west. The drought gave him no real alternative. By sticking to the higher ground to the east he would be more certain of fodder for his horses and this route would also enable him to connect the parts through which he had already travelled with known landmarks in the vicinity of Moreton Bay.

A few miles on his way brought him to the MacIntyre River, which he forded near Yetman a few miles upstream. Almost immediately the drought broke and travelling became more difficult, a path having to be hacked through tangled thickets to another stream, the Dumaresq. Here he found 'a richer and more luxuriant growth of grass than had been met with in any stage of the journey from Hunter's River.' Pushing on through more dense scrub he saw, on 5 June 1827, the sight of his life. Stretched out in front of him, as he looked ENE from the Herries Range across the Condamine River, he saw an expanse of wonderful country. What he was looking at was the valley of Glengallan Creek and the hills, 'downs of a rich black and dry soil, clothed with an abundance of grass', the Darling Downs. What he had at first seen was a tiny part only of a much larger fertile area. Cunningham was the first European to look upon this territory and his name, already in the books because of his discovery of Pandora's Pass, became on that day a part of Australian history. The name 'Darling Downs' is today applied to some 3,600,000 acres. Following this discovery an attempt was made to find a gap in the Dividing Range which would permit access from Moreton Bay, but the party was forced to turn back without achieving its aim.

For a brief moment, in Samuel Molyneux's time, Kew had been caught up in the history of astronomy. Now, also for a brief moment, it was caught up in the history of photography. In May 1816 the French inventor Nicéphore Niepcé had been partly successful in fixing images on paper coated with silver chloride, but, because the results were imperfect, he went on to experiment with other substances. In 1826 he coated a plate with a solution of bitumen of Judaea and, after exposing the plate for eight hours, obtained the first permanent photograph. The next year he brought his invention to England, and, according to Scheer:

... resided about the year 1827 in Kew, and induced Mr Bauer to submit his discoveries to the Royal Society; which, however, took but little notice of them. Niepcé returned to France, but left a brother at Kew, who died shortly afterwards, and was buried in our churchyard. Some of the earliest specimens of Niepcé's art are now in possession of Mr Bauer, and there are others to be met with at Richmond.

After some local trips Cunningham sailed again for Moreton Bay on 7 June 1828. He had a stormy journey during which one of his horses was killed by rough seas. Learning that the Commandant, Captain Patrick Logan, was about to make a trip in three weeks' time in a south-westerly direction he decided to wait and go with him. They set off on 24 July, soon reaching the Logan River, which they could not follow because of the difficulty of getting through the 'viney brush', so they crossed it, climbed the Birnam Range, and joined the Logan on the other side. They were now able to follow it for a time. Climbing a high point they saw the McPherson Ranges ahead, descended and continued south until they reached another high point, now known as Mount Barney, which was Logan's objective.

On 5 August they turned to look for a gap in the Dividing Range which had been seen as a possible way through the year before. Heading north-west they found they had to turn north and then north-east for a time to get round Flinders Peak at the end of the Teviot Range before they could approach the Dividing Range itself. Logan's party broke off and headed back to Moreton Bay on 11 August, leaving Cunningham with his own two men and one lent by Logan to rest and stock up at Limestone station (now called Ipswich) before tackling the rest of the journey.

On 18 August they set off in a south-westerly direction. They found the going hard and took four days to cover the thirty miles to the foot of the divide, camping on the fourth day about four miles from what Cunningham took to be the gap. He sent one of his men to reconnoitre, but he found the way blocked by cliffs. Moving further north, Cunningham sent two men to climb as high as they could but they still could not descry the gap. He therefore decided that his first guess was more likely to be right and, moving south again to a place about a mile beyond his original point, he sent one of his men who had seen the Downs the previous year to make a further reconnaissance. By now it was early in the afternoon of 24 August and Cunningham could not have been very hopeful of making much progress that day as the way towards what he called the 'hollowback' of the range seemed to lie over forest ridges. To his great delight, however, the man returned at dark 'having traced the ridge two and a half miles to the foot of the Dividing Range, whence he ascended into the pass and, from a grassy head immediately above it, beheld the extensive country lying west of the main range', which he recognised as the Darling Downs. The next day Cunningham climbed the pass himself and verified that it provided a feasible route for a road across the mountains. He had found a way by which settlers could pass through to exploit that vast area of fertile country which lay beyond the Dividing Range and by so doing had rendered a signal service to his fellow men.

Before he returned to Brisbane, Cunningham made a short journey along the Brisbane River which did no more than whet his appetite to explore further, and then sailed for Sydney, arriving on 4 November 1828. At the end of the year he spent some time in the Blue Mountains, being hampered again by heat and drought. In 1829 he made another visit to Moreton Bay, concerned this time primarily with botany, although he again got into new territory. Arriving in May, he spent a month collecting near Brisbane and then attempted to make his way up the eastern bank of the Brisbane River, but floods prevented his crossing and difficult bush country forced him westwards before he could turn north. Near the modern Gatton he crossed Lockyer Creek and climbed Mount Davidson to obtain a view, but this did not disclose any gap in the Dividing Range. He turned east to the junction of the Lockyer and Brisbane Rivers and then followed the latter to its junction with the Stanley River. Still following the Brisbane River he reached on 6 July the furthest point yet attained by any traveller. Further progress was impeded by the aborigines, the only time Cunningham had serious trouble with them in all his journeyings.

The going was rough and some of the salt meat had got spoiled, but Cunningham nevertheless pressed on for a few days longer and on 12 July climbed Lister's Peak, near the modern Linville. He saw that the Dividing Range stretched north for at least thirty miles and that the river, by now nothing more than a series of pools, must clearly rise not far away on the west side of the divide and was thus a comparatively short stream. He turned back to the junction of the Brisbane and

Stanley Rivers and, still being harassed by aborigines, followed the Stanley River for a short distance, but was soon compelled by dwindling provisions to return to Moreton Bay, where he spent another six weeks, troubled this time with 'a most painful rheumatic infection.' He returned to Sydney in September, making a short trip to Broken Bay and another to the Illawarra in the last months of 1829.

Although provision had been made for hardy aquatic plants at Kew, there had never been any place to house tender water plants. Advantage was taken in 1826 of the need to repair a lean-to house, 60 feet long, to do something for these. The house contained a bark bed, at the end of which a small oval tank about 8 feet long and 4 wide was constructed, in which were grown '*Nelumbium*, Water Lilies, *Pontederia caerulea*, *Papyrus antiquorum* and a few other rarities'. Two years later W T Aiton allowed John Smith to rearrange the grass collection on condition that he took responsibility for the names, which he agreed to do. He remodelled the old circular beds and edged them with brick, bringing in about 100 loads of fresh soil and allocating the centre area and inner circle to *Cyperaceae*. Cast iron labels in the form of a letter T were used, painted white with the letters in black. These lasted for many years. In 1828 the house used for the palm collection was heightened by four feet because of the rapidly-increasing size of some of the plants.

In mid-1830 Cunningham visited Norfolk Island and Philip Island, having a terrifying experience on the latter from escaped convicts who robbed him of practically everything he possessed. He was rescued by a boat sent to look for the convicts. A week after this calamity there were developments at home. On 26 June 1830 George IV died and the Duke of Clarence came to the throne as William IV at the age of 64. The new King was fond of Kew, having spent his childhood there. One of his first acts was to present the house known as Royal Lodge, formerly Hunter House, to the Duchess of Cumberland for her life: this despite the fact that it had been sold to the nation in 1823! On the same day he gave orders that the iron railings and lodges put up by George IV should be removed and all other changes he had made obliterated.

Cunningham heard during 1830 that he would not be paid after 1 April 1831 and after a final visit to the Illawarra rain forest and another over the Blue Mountains to Cox's River left for home on 1 February 1831. On arrival he settled down quietly at Strand-on-the-Green across the river from Kew to work with Aiton and Brown on the vast mass of specimens he had accumulated. In quietness and serenity, so far as he was able to achieve it with his broken health, far from the land of vast and lonely distances vanishing into sunbaked horizons which he had opened up for millions to settle, his few remaining years slipped away.

Professor S P Rigaud, nephew of the Rev Stephen Demainbray, who was

[153]

The Tompion sundial on the Palace Lawn which marks the site of the White House and was placed in position in William IV's time to commemorate the astronomical discoveries which were made in that house.

Superintendent of the Kew Observatory, used to act for him during the Oxford vacation. His interest in James Bradley's discoveries led him to suggest to the King that they should be commemorated at Kew. A Tompion sundial was brought from Hampton Court, where a similar one still remains. The gnomon of the sundial is highly ornamented. It was put in place on a marble pedestal in 1832 with an inscription as follows:

> On this spot
> in 1725
> The Rev James Bradley
> made the first observations
> which led to his two great discoveries
> the aberration of light
> and the nutation of the earth's axis.
> The telescope which he used
> had been erected by Samuel Molyneux esq.
> in a house which afterwards became a royal residence,
> and was taken down in 1803
> To perpetuate the memory of so important a station
> this dial was placed on it in 1832
> by command of his most gracious Majesty
> King William IV

Although William IV was well disposed towards Kew Gardens he disliked W T Aiton personally because he associated him with George IV's changes which he had reversed. He now restricted Aiton's responsibilities, which for a time had covered all the royal gardens, to Kew Gardens only.

In 1832 Allan Cunningham was offered an appointment as Superintendent of the Sydney Botanic Garden but did not accept it, recommending his brother Richard instead, whose workload had declined with Aiton now present full-time, and Richard duly set off for Australia, perhaps with dreams of emulating his brother.

As the 1830s progressed, public dissatisfaction with arrangements at Kew continued to simmer. Pressure was gradually building up but had not yet reached danger point. There are, indeed, still some events to record before that happened.

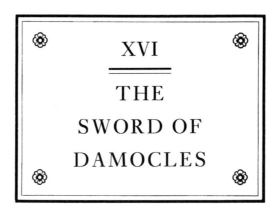

XVI

THE

SWORD OF

DAMOCLES

'... What hell it is, in suing long to bide:
To lose good days, that might be better spent ...'

Edmund Spenser

In the autumn of 1832 another tragic blow struck the unfortunate Cumberlands: their son George, who had already lost the sight of his left eye, was playing with his cousin, Prince George of Cambridge, in the garden of Royal Lodge (Hunter House) when he was the victim of an accident which destroyed the sight of his other eye. Swinging a long green silk purse in the air, one of the large gold acorn-shaped tassels struck him in the face, with tragic results.

The King continued his alterations at Kew, taking down several of the garden walls that separated properties at the north end of the Gardens. This, however, had one unfortunate consequence; it gave free play to the wind and from time to time trees were blown down. The area between Hunter House and the precincts of the Palace, and the grounds of the Palace itself, were shortly afterwards cut off from the public by a wire fence.

Professor William Jackson Hooker resolved as early as 1833 to obtain the Directorship of Kew Gardens if it could be managed, and enlisted on his behalf the sixth Duke of Bedford. As the 1830s progressed he wrote a number of letters both to the Duke and others advancing his claims, endeavouring to ensure that, if the

Sir William Jackson Hooker, the first Director of the Royal Botanic Gardens after they were taken over by the state in 1840 and on whose vision of those Gardens as a world centre of economic botany and botanical research the modern Gardens were largely built.

[157]

post did become available, his qualifications for it would be well known.

In 1835, at the request of Robert Brown, a young man named George Barclay was appointed collector on HMS *Sulphur* which, under the command of Captain Beechy, was sent out to western South America on a survey. He was disappointed to find that the accommodation afforded him on board was far from adequate and the captain quite unco-operative. The vessel reached Rio de Janeiro on 15 February 1836.

William Jackson Hooker's merits and achievements for botany were recognised in 1836 by the award of a knighthood. The year was not lucky, however, for Allan Cunningham. His brother Richard had joined Thomas Mitchell's expedition to look for the source of the Darling River. Wandering away from the party in search of specimens he fell in with aborigines who somehow conceived the notion that he would do them harm and murdered him during the night. When news of this tragedy reached Allan Cunningham he offered to replace Richard and took up duty as Superintendent of the Sydney Botanic Garden on 1 March 1837.

In 1836 a small house was set aside for the cultivation of tropical species of orchid, the Australian and Cape species being housed elsewhere. Action was also taken to provide accommodation for the palms. A glasshouse which at Buckingham Palace was too much in the shade was moved to Kew to a site just inside the Main Gate, where it still stands, though it does not now contain palms. The cylindrical pillars at each end of this house came from Carlton House, Pall Mall, a town residence of George IV's which occupied the site on which the Duke of York's column now stands.

Although the *Sulphur* called at Santo Catarina and Montevideo Barclay had little opportunity to collect until the vessel rounded the Horn and reached Valparaiso, where he was able to make a trip inland to Santiago. Leaving on 13 June 1836 he arrived at the Cuesta Del Prado mountains two days later, crossed the 'great plain of Maypo' and reached his destination soon after. He would have liked to cross the Andes but the snow was too deep. Moving on to Guayaquil via Callao, he was able to make substantial collections while the survey of the Guayaquil River and the island of Puna was being undertaken. By May 1837 the vessel was at San Blas in Mexico, moving on from there to the Sandwich Islands and then proceeding northward to Port Etches and Sitka, then a Russian colony. At all these places Barclay was able to collect. Turning south, the *Sulphur* arrived at San Francisco on 19 October and stayed until 30 November, giving Barclay time to make two journeys, each 60 miles in length and in different directions. From San Francisco the vessel returned to San Blas, from whence they had set out seven months before.

[158]

Apart from those already mentioned, the King commissioned Sir Geoffrey Wyatville to carry out other works for him in the Gardens, the principal of these being the 'Temple of Military Fame', now known as King William's Temple, which is located on a slight eminence in the southern part of the Gardens. It seems to have been the King's intention to commemorate the battles fought by British soldiers from 1760 to 1815 and in a sense, therefore, the new building complemented the Temple of Victory which had been erected in 1759 to celebrate the battle of Minden. At the same time as he built the new temple the King did, in fact, have a bust of Prince Ferdinand of Brunswick, who had driven the French out of Hanover on 1 August 1759 put in the Temple of Victory and had emblazoned on the wall the arms of Lord Waldegrave, who had distinguished himself in the battle.

The new Temple, which was of classical design, bore eighteen tablets on its side walls recalling the feats of British arms and was embellished with busts of George III, George IV, William IV and the Duke of Wellington by Chantrey. The principal ornament, however, was a large marble tablet placed on the wall opposite the entrance. This had been brought from Egypt by Lord Hill who presented it to the King. It bore an inscription recording the defeat of Bonaparte's navy at Aboukir Bay in Egypt by Nelson and the defeats on land which Abercrombie inflicted on the French.

The King also contemplated some improvements to the Orangery. At this time the two ends of the building were entirely of brickwork against which there was originally a shrubbery, and it was suggested to the King that the house would be greatly improved by making a glass door at each end in the same style as the front. The King approved the notion, says John Smith, and the doors were chalked out on the brickwork. The work was not, however, carried out in the King's lifetime.

All these efforts to improve the estate, particularly those which directly benefited visitors to the Royal Gardens, contributed greatly to William IV's popularity. There is a print of Kew Green in 1837, at the time of his last visit, showing a triumphal arch which had been erected across the road near the east end of the church to welcome him. This was, however, merely the flaring of a guttering candle about to go out. On 20 June 1837 William IV died, and his young niece Victoria came to the throne.

An early result of the change of monarch was the return of one royal resident to Kew and the departure of another. Because of the operation of the Salic Law Victoria could not inherit the throne of Hanover, which passed to the Duke of Cumberland, but although he had to go and live in that country, he did not relinquish his house at Kew, which became known as the King of Hanover's House. The arrival of a King in Hanover removed the need for a Governor-

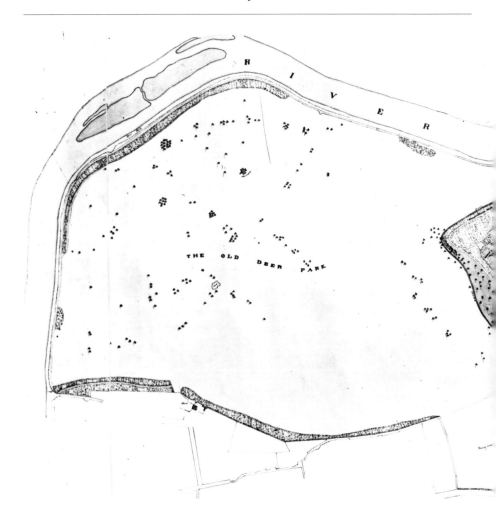

Plan of Kew and the Old Deer Park in 1837, drawn just before Kew became a state garden, showing the small oval botanic garden with its entrance off Kew Green at the north end, the King of Hanover's Game Preserve, the large area at the southern end called Cottage Wood and the field marked 'Stanford's Piece' in the unshaded portion beyond the southern end which is probably the field where the historic auction of the King's merino sheep took place.

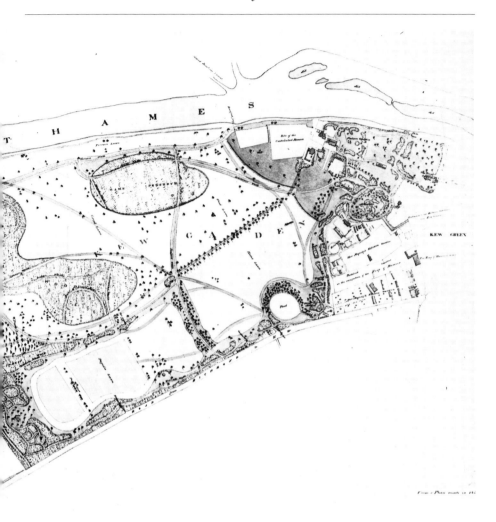

General and Adolphus, Duke of Cambridge, George III's youngest son, who had
held this position since 1814, was recalled to England and returned in July. He
occupied the house on the south side of Kew Green which had been the home of
the Earl of Bute, which became known as Cambridge Cottage and still bears that
name.

In 1837 the first detailed news of a wonderful new plant that was eventually to
be one of the permanent attractions of Kew was received in England. Something

was already known in France about the giant water-lily of South America, but it was not until Sir Robert Schomburgk, who had been exploring the Berbice River on behalf of the Geographical Society, sent in a description of it and its enormous leaves, which were 'from five to six feet in diameter, salver shaped with a broad rim of light green above and a vivid crimson below', that interest was aroused here. Sir Robert's observations were expanded by John Lindley into a memoir of 'Atlas folio size' illustrated with 'a splendid figure'. Only 25 copies were printed for private distribution, one of which Lindley sent to Sir William Hooker.

During 1837 the Admiralty appointed another botanical collector, John Armstrong, to accompany Captain Bremer in the *Alligator* which was being sent out to establish a colony at Port Essington on the north-west coast of Australia. The vessel left Portsmouth in January 1838. By this time Barclay had left San Blas. He had been able to travel into the interior of Mexico as far as Tepic, where he stayed four days. The *Sulphur* sailed for Acupulco on 3 January, reaching Realejo in Nicaragua on 5 February. Barclay went ashore the next day but succumbed to fever and was not able to rejoin the ship until 17 March. In the meantime noteworthy events had been occurring at Kew.

Attacks on the botanic garden had come to a head in the autumn of 1837. Brickbats flew in articles and letters in the *Gardener's Gazette*, the *Morning Chronicle*, the *Horticultural Journal* and the *Gardener's Magazine*. To the old charge that W T Aiton was too parsimonious in his distribution of new species and that he followed Banks who had been the real dog-in-the-manger, was coupled the accusation that you could get them if you were a foreigner or member of the aristocracy, that the Gardens were ill-managed, and that the plants were badly cultivated. Aiton, however, had his defenders, who did their best to rebut these charges, pointing out that the botanic garden was for specialist study, and was not an ornamental garden maintained solely for the admiration of uninstructed visitors.

A more informed anonymous letter signed 'C C', dated December 1837 and published in the *Gardener's Magazine* early in 1838, took a less captious view. It recommended that the Parliament now assembling, the first in Victoria's reign, should take control of the botanic garden from the Lord Steward and accept it as a state liability to be developed into a national institution concerned with botanical and medical research and the exploitation of the world's plant resources.

'C C' had not long to wait. During January 1838 the government made up its mind that an enquiry was needed to lay out future policy for all the royal gardens. Informal approaches were made by the Parliamentary Committee charged with looking into the matter, and Dr John Lindley of the Horticultural Society was

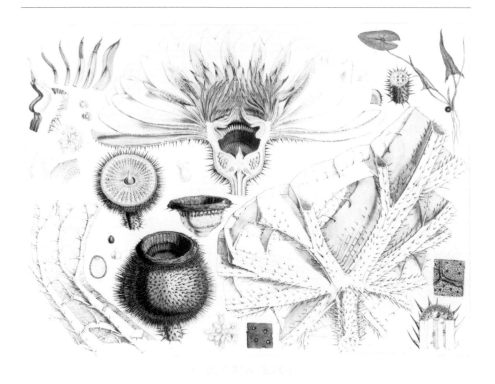

The Giant Water-Lily flower dissected to show its structure and parts.

chosen to head the enquiry. Sir Joseph Paxton and Mr Wilson, gardener to the Earl of Surrey, were associated with him. Lindley was requested to take upon himself the examination of 'the state and condition of the different Royal Gardens', which were listed in the margin of his instructions as Kensington, Hampton Court, Kew, Windsor and Buckingham Palace. This included, of course, the supply of fruit, vegetables and flowers for all the royal needs as well as the botanic garden. Specific questions relating to the latter covered the vexed question of distribution of surplus material.

The members of the enquiry met first at Lindley's house at Turnham Green on 12 February and visited the kitchen garden at Kew on Friday 16 February, looking

[163]

Sir Joseph Paxton, gardener to the Duke of Devonshire and the designer of the Crystal Palace, was the first man who flowered the Giant Water-Lily in Britain and was a member of the government enquiry which recommended that Kew should become a state garden.

[164]

at the botanic garden on the following Monday 19 February. The weather was appallingly cold and snowy during this period. According to J C Loudon, 'the severe weather of January 1838 ... killed, or greatly injured, almost all the half-hardy ligneous plants in the neighbourhood of London. The foliage of the trees on the walls of the Botanic Garden at Kew ... is quite black ... so much damage has scarcely been done to evergreen shrubs within the memory of any gardener living.' Hardly the best time, as John Smith later pointed out, to make an inspection of a living collection, and liable to give an entirely erroneous impression of it. He took pains later to set out his criticism in detail. The team were, however, otherwise very thorough in their examination of the books and records and their quizzing of Aiton on his tasks and views.

Aiton began by explaining the terms under which he and John Smith were employed and also James Templeton, who was arboretum foreman and 'accountant, also acting as clerk'. There were ten labourers who received twelve shillings a week which had been the standard wage since at least 1820. Six of the gardeners were what would be called today 'student gardeners': they were at Kew 'for improvement' and went through all the departments of the Gardens.

Aiton made no bones about his opinion of the financial provision for the botanic garden. He did not consider it 'at all adequate' but 'miserably insufficient'. He had taken the matter up strongly with the Board of Green Cloth in 1830 and produced copies of letters he had written to the Board in the autumn of that year appealing in vain against successive annual cuts in the allowance. He produced statements of the annual expenditure of the botanic garden over the years 1824 to 1837 which showed clearly the niggardly policy which had been followed and amply proved his point. Expenditure between 1824 and 1827 had averaged £1,900 per annum, between 1828 and 1831 £1,460 per annum, and between 1832 and 1837 £1,280 per annum, a reduction of a third in the money made available over the years. In his opinion more glasshouses were required. Those which existed were all heated by flues, the smoke from so many fires close together causing a great deal of inconvenience from the amount of soot which discoloured the walks and disfigured the plants.

The evidence recorded with regard to the admission of the public to the botanic and pleasure garden revealed that, although Aiton chose to regard it as a royal private garden from the point of view of dispensing specimens, it had, in fact, become semi-public. Visitors were admitted daily except Sundays from 1 pm to 6 pm in the summer and till dark in the winter. There was no admission charge and no restriction provided the people appeared respectable and decently dressed. They were attended by Gardens men and the expense of this duty formed part of

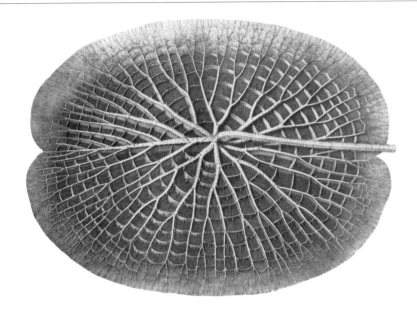

A Giant Water-Lily leaf showing the ribbed cellular pattern of the underside which gives it strength and buoyancy.

the charge for garden labour. No injury to the Garden had resulted from the admission of the public and they were allowed everywhere without reserve. They obtained information about the plants from the men or from the labels. No general classification scheme was followed, the foreman John Smith being responsible for naming the plants and answerable for the names. There was no general catalogue for the Garden, but many lists.

On 28 February Lindley sent the report of the enquiry to the Treasury for consideration by the Parliamentary Committee which had set up his investigation. The kitchen garden they found well run and said, of the various parts of the botanic garden, that the Arboretum contained fine specimens, but the collection was not very extensive, and the plants too crowded. The collection of herbaceous plants was, in their view, inconsiderable, and some were unnamed. The plants in the houses were also excessively crowded but most, especially those from New Holland, were 'in excellent health, clean and well attended to; the general

The leaves of the Giant Water-Lily being sponged to remove deposits from the river water used for watering.

appearance was ... very creditable'.

The report severely castigated Aiton for the lack of a system of classification and incomplete naming, which fell short of what should be expected of a garden provided for scientific study. They castigated him even more for thrusting responsibility for naming onto the foreman, although they gave John Smith great praise for shouldering the task so well. They considered that this work could 'only be executed properly by a man of high scientific attainments, aided by an extensive herbarium and considerable library'. Criticism was also directed at the relations with the Colonies, which looked in vain for the initiative they had a right to expect from the home country. On the accusation that Aiton had been too restrictive in the distribution of plants they concluded that 'it really does seem impossible to say that' distribution had 'been conducted with that liberality or anxiety to promote the ends of science, and to render it useful to the country, which it is usual to meet with similar institutions elsewhere'. The report then went on to consider what

[167]

ought to be done, recommending that the botanic garden should be removed from the control of the Lord Steward and either taken for public purposes by the state or abandoned altogether. It was a waste of money to continue it in its present state. The report then enumerated the reasons why a national botanic garden was needed.

First, the rather doubtful proposition that Britain should have such a garden because every other country had one, which amounts to no more than saying that we were bound 'to keep up with the Jones's'. The second argument had rather more substance. There were now many students in the London area to which 'such a means of instruction as a botanical garden affords' was indispensable. The third argument rested on the need which the members of the enquiry felt for central co-ordination and direction of the botanic gardens in the Empire overseas and here, of course, they were on a point of the utmost importance. Such a centre was required so that the immense plant resources of the Colonies could be organised and exploited in an orderly and advantageous manner. Kew could exercise this function admirably but would have to be expanded and take in at least 30 acres of the Pleasure Grounds. Considerable additions would also have to be made to the glasshouses. On the vexed question of disposal of specimens from the Garden within Britain, they recognised that there was no perfect solution, but laid down some rules which they thought might improve arrangements in the future. They concluded with a firm recommendation that the Garden should be transferred to the control of the Commissioners of Woods and Forests.

The Parliamentary committee deliberated on Lindley's report and accepted it and the Treasury wrote off to the Commissioners of Woods and Forests to ascertain the views of that body on the proposals. Those interested expected an early decision but month succeeded month and nothing was heard of the Government's intentions. The Garden continued on its old lines and, except for a few who concerned themselves with the matter, the momentary stir of interest died down and was forgotten.

In the meantime, oblivious to all this, George Barclay had moved on from Realejo to Port Culebra, Cocos Island and Callao. From here, he said 'my first excursion was to the Sierra of Guamantang, a ridge of the Andes ... about 20 leagues distant from Lima.' He reached 12,000 feet above sea level but unfortunately 'had the misfortune to be attacked ... by robbers upon the road to Cavillaro ... who robbed me of an ounce in gold and 2 rials of silver ... which ... put me in an unpleasant position as it was all I had to defray the expense of the journey. ... In the affray I received a musket-ball through the thigh but the bone was not injured and the wound does not appear to be troublesome.' He made a second trip, this time to Lariga, 'a ridge of the Cordilleras 70 miles east of Lima'. After a virtual mutiny as a result of which a number of petty officers were flogged and discharged, the *Sulphur* moved on to Panama, but things did not go at all well for Barclay, who found Captain Belcher, Beechy's replacement, unduly restrictive with regard to visits ashore, the friction finally blowing up into a tremendous row, in which Belcher thoroughly berated Barclay for laziness, claiming that he had neglected his employer's interests. Barclay poured it all out in a letter to John Smith which, of course, he did not receive until long afterwards.

John Smith was notified in October 1838 of the arrival of the New Zealand ship the *Buffalo*. Robert Brown saw the plants brought by this vessel first and then John Smith went to collect them. They were worth the effort, being, as John Smith noted on the letter, Kew's 'first real set-up with New Zealand plants'. The plants in the three Wardian cases (one of the first uses of this newly-invented method of transporting plants, the cases being like small portable greenhouses, preserving the plants much better than any method previously used) were in good condition and included 'the famous Kauri pine, *Dammara australis, Dacrydium cupressinum, Podocarpus totara, Vitex littoralis, Phyllocladus trichomanoides* and *Laurustoma*'. John Smith adds to his note twenty years later (1858) that 'the two Dammaras now 20 feet high are of this lot'.

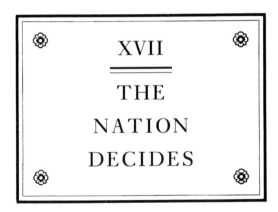

XVII

THE

NATION

DECIDES

'I charge you by the law,
... proceed to judgement.'

Shakespeare: *The Merchant of Venice*

A year after the Treasury had written to them, almost to the day, on 24 April 1839 the Commissioners of Woods and Forests broke their long silence on the Lindley report. Their reaction was simple: they could cope with the practical task of carrying out the works required for the expansion envisaged by the report, but had no expertise within their Department on which they could call to control the scientific policy. In effect, they bounced the ball back firmly into the Treasury's court. Once again there was a long silence while the Treasury considered the matter further.

Three months before this, the *Sulphur* had sailed from Realejo and had been surveying first in the Gulf of Nicoya, then on the coast of New Grenada, and then in the province of Veraguas and at Baya Honda. From the Panama the *Sulphur* returned to the Friendly Islands, arriving on 31 May 1839 after a passage of 62 days during which Barclay was ill most of the time with fever. Collections were sent home to Kew from all these places.

The summer of 1839 passed and there was still no word from the Treasury. One of the difficulties was the position of the botanic garden in relation to the rest of the Kew demesne. Some of the Pleasure Grounds was needed to provide adequate room for Kew's proposed new role, thus interfering with the amenities of the Palace, should it ever be used again. There was also the question of the money required and the selection of someone to run the place and the conditions under which he should operate. The Duke of Bedford, Sir William Hooker's patron, continued to mention his name in the right places, so that, when the time came, his successful candidature for any post which might be created in connection with the garden would be assured.

Allan Cunningham's latter years in Australia had not been particularly happy due to difficulties over the use of the Sydney Botanic Garden and his health finally gave way. He died on 27 June 1839. It is invidious, in a company which includes such men as Francis Masson and Robert Brown, to claim pre-eminence for any Kew collector, but Allan Cunningham was certainly among the greatest and, moreover, by his geographical discoveries, which were of immense economic importance, he earned himself a place in general history. His death at a comparatively early age was accelerated by the hardships he endured on his many journeys and he thus deserves to rank also with those others who gave their lives for Kew.

By September 1839 Barclay was again in north-western America. On the way from the Sandwich Islands the *Sulphur* had called at Kodiak and Sitka and was now, on 3 September, lying off Port George. He had been for a time on the schooner *Starling* and able to get ashore every day. He was greatly impressed with the flora, particularly the conifers, which he saw. The *Sulphur* then returned to San Blas. Armstrong had a different story. Every obstacle had been put in his way at Port Essington, where he was regarded not as a plant collector, but gardener to the colony. It was Barclay's story all over again and seemed to show that there was a failure of communication between Kew, the Admiralty and the captains of their vessels with regard to these collectors, who had not been allowed to carry out the tasks for which they had been appointed.

At Kew an ominous development now occurred. Lord Surrey, the Lord Steward, visited the Garden and it became known that 'it was his intention to convert' the glasshouses in the botanic and kitchen gardens into 'vineries and pine stoves, and that the plants had been offered to the Horticultural Society' and the Botanical Garden 'at Regent's Park; but the offer in both cases was declined.' All the protagonists of a new and expanded Kew were scandalised at these proposals but Lord Surrey was not to be deterred. On 18 February 1840 the kitchen gardener was instructed to take possession of the Botany Bay House and 'convert it as soon as possible into a vinery, and that the Cape House was to follow, and to enable him to do so he was to destroy the plants.'

The Lord Steward's action in issuing these instructions seemed to confirm without doubt that the botanic garden was to be broken up, and precipitated immediately a widespread reaction against this. What caused particular offence was the persistent assertion, which was alleged to be true by some in a position to know, that the plants had been offered to the Horticultural Society and other bodies but refused by them, an offer that was held to prove that the government intended to abandon the Garden. Nevertheless, a statement emanating from official sources denying that the government had any such intention was published in the *Times* on 24 February. Similarly, when Lord Aberdeen challenged Lord Duncannon in the House of Lords on the matter on 3 March he replied that 'he could assure the noble earl that there was not only not the least intention now to break up those gardens, but there never had been any such intention'. Later he repeated the denial, saying that 'though the care of the gardens was not in his department, he had the authority of the Lord Steward for stating that no intention of breaking up the gardens now existed.' There is a document in the archives of the Royal Botanic Gardens which seems to prove that these statements are not in accordance with the facts.

There seems no reason to doubt the genuineness of this document. It is in Lindley's handwriting, signed by him, and seems later to have been handed over to Sir Joseph Hooker as it is inscribed in pencil on one side 'For Dr Hooker', having possibly been passed to him on Lindley's death. It is entitled 'Minute of a conversation at the Treasury with Mr R G, 11 February 1840'. Above the heading is written 'corrected and authenticated by Mr Robert Gordon, 12 February 1840'. There are some pencil amendments to the document which are presumably the corrections to which this note refers. The very first paragraph which, it may be noted, has not been amended and was therefore clearly understood by both parties to the conversation, indicates that both the denial in the *Times* and Lord Duncannon's statement in the Lords on 3 March that 'there had never been any ... intention' of breaking up the gardens was a lie, since it states categorically that 'It is the intention of HM's Government to abolish the Botanical Gardens at Kew, to pull down the houses and disperse the plants' and Gordon, who was Secretary to the Treasury, is hardly likely to have made and agreed such a statement unless he was absolutely certain that such an intention was a fact. The second part of the document states that 'It is proposed to offer a part, or the whole, of them' (the plants) 'to the Horticultural Society (altered in pencil to 'some public body') upon the condition that the public shall have free access to them, gratuitously, on two

Drosera capensis, a member of the Sundew family which traps and digests small insects in the sticky hairs on its leaves which may be seen in the picture.

days in the week.' The third and fourth paragraphs outline the conditions under which the Society would obtain the contents of the Garden. The alteration of 'Horticultural Society' to 'some public body' may well have been made because it became obvious to Gordon that the Society, from the attitude of Lindley, was unlikely to accept the offer, and he would have to try elsewhere.

The document refutes the story put about by the government and shows it up in an exceedingly poor light. Lindley had no doubt about its meaning. On the day Robert Gordon corrected his note of the meeting Lindley wrote to him telling him that he intended to have the matter raised in Parliament. In pursuance of this he wrote on the same day to Sir Robert Peel to enlist his help in the matter and also Joseph Hume, the Middlesex MP. A few days later he received a letter from Lord Aberdeen asking for information, to which he immediately replied, with the result that Aberdeen asked the question in the House of Lords which elicited from Duncannon the disgraceful denial that there had been any intention of abandoning

Kew. Elsewhere, some part in inducing the government to drop its proposal has been attributed to others, but there is no doubt that the responsibility for stopping it rests almost solely on Lindley's prompt action, which had already caused the government to go into reverse before anyone else entered the picture.

The tide now turned strongly in favour of the defenders of Kew, helped by the excellently written historical pamphlet *Kew and Its Gardens* produced by Frederick Scheer, an independent botanist who lived at Kew, which appeared at about this time and from which quotations have already been made. Lord Surrey, the Lord Steward, whose plans for disposing of the garden had been proceeding unhindered up to 18 February, had clearly been told unequivocally that he had got to stop, and the instruction must have emanated from a level which brooked no argument, since he himself disappeared from the scene with some celerity. Driven into a corner, the government had to do something and on 11 March removed the botanic garden from the charge of the Lord Steward and placed it under the Commissioners of Woods and Forests. The hand-over document was signed by Lord Erroll, indicating that Surrey had already been replaced, although barely a week had elapsed since Aberdeen had asked his question.

While this was going on Barclay was making his way over to the other side of the world. He was at Otaheite in April 1840, doing some collecting there, and then moved on to Singapore. Here there was a sudden change of plan because of the Opium War with China. The *Sulphur* was ordered to the China station and as a plant collector obviously could not go ashore on an enemy coast Barclay was discharged and sailed for home on the barque *Culnare*.

The handing over of the botanic garden to the Commissioners of Woods and Forests was followed on 12 May by the publication of Lindley's report and there, once again, the matter rested. As 1840 wore on it became apparent that the turmoil over Kew must be resolved soon. On 19 November W T Aiton, whether by persuasion or his own volition, but probably the latter because of demands likely to be made on him by his new employers, decided to retire at the end of the year. Lord John Russell, whose aid had been enlisted by his brother the Duke of Bedford on Sir William's behalf, now began to advance his claims to have charge of the garden.

On 11 December 1840 the great botanical artist Francis Bauer died. A marble tablet in Kew church records what his contemporaries thought of him, saying that 'in the delineation of plants he united the accuracy of the professional naturalist with the skill of the accomplished artist' and 'in microscopical drawing he was altogether unrivalled.' Posterity has endorsed this verdict.

On 24 January 1841 Sir William Hooker was summoned to see Lord John Russell in Downing Street, who quizzed him on what money he thought might be required to run the garden and what new ground would be needed. Sir William's astute reply resolved itself into no more than a request for an additional £1,000 to meet Aiton's allowance and a determination to get on without any new ground, which meant that the Pleasure Grounds would be untouched. He was told to see Lord Duncannon, which he could not do for more than a month, but the result when it came was all that he could wish. He was officially informed of his appointment as Director of the Royal Botanic Gardens at a salary of £300 per annum with £200 allowance in lieu of a house. On 26 March 1841 W T Aiton transferred the charge of the Gardens to the new Director, but retained all the books and drawings as his private property and all journals, accounts, correspondence and other documents as not being the property of the Commissioners. On 1 April Sir William took up duty as the first Director of Kew in its new guise as a state garden for which the government was solely responsible. It therefore ceased from that time to be 'Royal' Kew in its full sense as a personal property of the monarch, but the glamour and interest of royalty remained as, instead of that intimate relationship, it now took on the wider role of serving the countries of the Empire over which the descendant of its founder reigned as Empress.

XVIII

WIND OF

CHANGE

'Her plot hath many changes; every day
Speaks a new scene. . . .'

Francis Quarles

Sir William soon found a house at Kew which met his requirements and moved
into 'a very pretty place within ten minutes walk of Kew called Brick Farm,' also
known as West Park, which had adequate accommodation for his herbarium,
totalling when packed up for removal '60 great packages'. He had other troubles at
this time, a daughter dying in Jersey, an aged father not in good health, and the
absence of his son Joseph, who would have been some support, in the Antarctic
with the *Erebus* and *Terror* expedition.

Towards the end of February 1841 George Barclay had arrived back, bringing,
among other things, a cone of *Pinus coulteri* from which were raised the fine
specimens of this species noted as growing at Kew by John Smith in the 1880s. A
very early act of Sir William after his arrival was to abolish the rule that visitors
while in the Gardens must be accompanied by a member of the Gardens staff. He
also initiated steps immediately to augment the collections, buying collections of
Erica and orchids, and some *Banksia*, *Grevillea* and *Hakea* plants. During August

1841 he sent John Smith on a tour of botanic and other gardens in the north of England to see what was available for purchase or exchange, or by gift. The Duke of Bedford gave 50 cacti and 141 plants came from the Horticultural Society's garden at Chiswick. 50 ferns were received from the Berlin Botanic Garden, but the most striking consignment was donated by the veteran botanist Aylmer Bourke Lambert. This contained 77 different species of *Cereus* varying from 1 to 15 feet high, 87 plants of different species of *Opuntia* varying from 1 to 12 feet high, 2 large *Echinocactus*, 24 other species of *Cactus* and 12 other plants. These additions necessitated rearrangement of the plants in the glasshouses and increased pressure on space.

Two glasshouses in the Ferneries group had their heating arrangements changed from the flue type to a hot water system and a newly-built propagating house was provided with a similar system, thus making some progress towards reducing the amount of soot deposited on the houses and plants. The four acres of land which comprised the wedge stretching from the site of the present Main Gate to Kew Palace was now added to the botanic garden. John Smith presented a paper to the Linnean Society which drew attention for the first time to the phenomenon of apomixis which he had noticed in a holly-like plant *Sapium aquifolium*, now called *Alchornea ilicifolium*, three plants of which had been sent to Kew in 1829 by Allan Cunningham from the Moreton Bay area. This plant had no male flowers but produced seed from which Smith had, in several successive generations, raised new plants. Smith also published in the *Journal of Botany* an arrangement of the genera of ferns which was a substantial advance in the study of these plants. These achievements brought a small rise in salary and the retitling of his post as that of 'Curator'.

The building works undertaken in 1842 involved the destruction of the three historic plants introduced in 1788–9, the first in each case of its kind, the *Hydrangea hortensis*, the Tree Paeony and the fuchsia, which for over 50 years had grown in the same spot. The Orangery housed a miscellaneous collection, the larger trees and shrubs of which were suffering from lack of light. William IV's plan for windows in the ends matching those of the front was therefore revived and carried out. At the same time the arms of William IV were placed over each door and the elegant letter 'A' for Augusta over the two front doors with the date 1761 and the shield in the centre.

Sir William and Lord Derby, together with the Duke of Northumberland, co-operated in sending William Purdie to collect in Jamaica and New Grenada and James Burke to western North America, both leaving in the early summer of 1843. At the same time Mr John Parkinson, the British Consul in Mexico, presented a

[177]

The Orangery showing the arms of William IV which were added to the end gable and the medallions showing 'A' for Augusta which were placed on the front gables.

collection of *Echinocactus*, some of which were 36 inches in circumference. Unfortunately a number had decayed through being packed in a tin case. On 20 July seeds collected in Chile by Thomas Bridges were purchased from his agent H Cuming. Among them were the seeds of the Chilean honey-palm, *Jubaea spectabilis*, from which several plants were raised. One of these still survives in the Temperate House, a vast palm, the largest tree in the Gardens, reaching to the roof.

Little more than a month after the presentation of the *Echinocactae* an even more spectacular addition to the collections arrived. On 29 June 1843 the Duke of Bedford had written to Sir William telling him he was going to present his collection of orchids to the Queen and Prince Albert. The Queen asked that they should go to Kew and on 16 August they arrived, filling up half of the orchid house.

Discussions continued during 1843 on a proposed new house for palms. There was no room for it in the existing botanic garden area and Sir William therefore asked for seventeen acres of the Pleasure Grounds to be added to it. To his delight the Duke of Cambridge advocated surrendering 46 acres to enable both the botanic garden and the Pleasure Grounds to be improved, and the Commissioners of Woods and Forests agreed. As the proposal withdrew land from the royal control the consent of the Queen had to be obtained. This revived royal interest in Kew and she and Prince Albert visited Kew on 3 October 1843. Sir William conducted them over the botanic garden. Thereafter the Prince Consort made a number of visits, asking to be informed when any of the finer trees had to be cut down. The royal children were also brought to the garden several times without their parents.

The precise order of events with regard to the design of the Palm House which now occurred is not easy to follow. A close study of all the documents seems to show that Richard Turner, ironmaster, of Dublin, having heard of the proposal, approached Sir William of his own volition with a design of his own and that this was sent to the Board of Works together with an estimate, but the Board felt that it ought to have an architect's view and brought in Decimus Burton. After the Board had met with Burton present Turner was asked to make 'full drawings and plans of the range of centre and wing houses immediately' according to this estimate. Burton received these about mid-February and on 27 February showed a revised and digested version to Sir William and John Smith, neither of whom liked it, principally because 'there were so many' interior 'pillars' and 'they were so close together that there would not be room for the full expansion of the leaves of the larger palms'. When Turner saw them he was appalled, calling them 'a most absurd set of plans, the singular production of a civil engineer, whose aid was called in by Mr Burton'. He commented that 'there are too great a variety of roofs, nor will the doorways at ends, nor indeed, the principal approaches ... look well. But the grand objections ... are the mode of support. It seems ... wildly extravagant, its interior will be much encumbered ... with a series of these immense massive trussed arch supporters.' Burton was persuaded to try again and produced the design which was accepted.

The site fixed on for the new Palm House was on the lowest ground in Kew, which had orginally been a series of lagoons and swamps connected with the Thames. When John Smith pointed this out the objection was ignored as of little importance, but the continuing expense that has had to be borne over the years because of water which accumulates there from time to time amply vindicates the validity of his objection. The site was, of course, chosen because the Palm House would look out over the lake and would be reflected in it.

[179]

On 23 May the Commissioners accepted Richard Turner's tender for £18,500 for the central portion of the house, but rather put a damper on his enthusiasm by allowing only £5,000 to be spent before 31 March 1845, which was sufficient for little more than the foundations. He had hoped to make the ironwork in the winter and on this he had had a new idea. On 25 May he put forward the view that it would be preferable to use wrought iron rather than cast iron in the framework. An article published in the *Builder* in 1849 explains why this change had become feasible. It was the development that had made it possible to build large iron ships. 'Great improvement' had been made 'in the manufacture of wrought iron (deckbeam) scantlings.' The ribs for the Palm House were to be formed of '9-inch deck–beam iron ... in lengths of about 12 feet' which would be welded together to the length required, about 42 feet, and 'bent upon a templet to the necessary curve.' The ribs were to be '12 feet 6 inches apart and fitted with cast iron sockets let into granite blocks upon a concrete foundation.' The upper ribs of the centre portion fitted into 'strong cast-iron columns' which also received the upper end of the lower ribs and bearers for the internal gallery. The column heads were connected by a continuous curb of scantling similar to that used for the ribs. When the visitor stands on the other side of the lake looking across to the Palm House, and thinks that, with its reflection, it floats like a great ship on the waters, his fantasy is nearer to the truth than he realises, for the strong beams that hold it there, and have held it for a century and a half in that place, are the great beams that also carried the British Navy and the vast British cargo fleet on their journeys opening up the world in the hey-day of the British Empire. How fitting that connection is will already be apparent: it was to become even more apparent as the years passed.

An ingenious method was used by Turner to brace and strut the ribs which was regarded as novel at that time. The connecting bars between the ribs, which acted as purlins, were formed of a small round bar, one-eighth of an inch in diameter, which was welded in long lengths and, passing through the ribs, formed a continuous tension-rod around the house. Means were provided for straining the rod as tightly as possible, and it was enclosed in a tube of wrought-iron which exactly fitted between the ribs and thus acted as a distance piece in opposition to the tension-rod. The arrangement knitted the entire structure together very strongly and was most effective.

The contract for building the foundations was let to Messrs Grisel and Peto and they got off the mark in early September. Discussions continued on various matters such as the siting of the internal spiral staircases, the siting of the ornamental tower some distance away from the boilers under the Palm House to act as a vent for their hot emissions, the use of these to heat a tank of water in the tower, a smoke-consuming apparatus, and a tunnel from the coke-yard by the tower to the boiler-room. The foundations were finished but, as John Smith had predicted, water gave trouble almost immediately and was at one stage 2 feet deep in the furnace rooms and in the tunnel from end to end. The method of ventilation was settled. Provision was included for rolling-sashes on the roofs, with vertical sashes hung on centres at the level of the gallery and in the lantern. Air could also be admitted through panels in the stone pedestal of the building. Both ventilators and windows were to be provided with simple machinery, invented by Richard Turner, so that they could be opened and shut simultaneously along each row. Until John Smith raised the matter, no one had given any thought to the question of glazing. His account of the incident has its funny side.

In answer to Smith's question about glass Turner said, in his characteristic fashion, holding up his hands 'Glass! You won't see there is glass, it will be so clear!' John Smith observed, so he says, with some sarcasm, 'This will be very pretty, but how are the plants to be shaded in summer? For if not shaded by some material the plants will be liable to be scorched.' He drew Turner's attention to the plant houses in the garden being covered with canvas shades during bright sunshine in summer. Both of them could see that canvas was impracticable for a house of the size and design of the Palm House and John Smith suggested green glass. This was a new idea for Turner but glass of this colour was already in use in the garden. The matter was investigated scientifically and green glass was eventually used, although it has long since been abandoned as unnecessary.

Parallel with the designing and construction of the Palm House action was taken to decide what should be done with the remainder of the new land. W A Nesfield, a well-known landscape gardener of Eton, was aked to prepare a plan to include the establishment of an arboretum. In July 1945 he produced a report which recommended the laying out of the garden on the lines that still exist. The main skeleton around which the plan was built were three vistas radiating from the western door of the Palm House. The first, the Sion Vista, took the eye across the river to the grounds of Sion House, and was thus at right angles to the long axis of the Palm House. The second, the Pagoda Vista, looked from the same spot towards the Pagoda and the third radiated at a similar angle to the north-west. From the Pagoda another vista, the Cedar Vista, looked towards the river end of the Sion Vista, making a triangle with that vista and the Pagoda Vista.

Purdie continued his collecting in Jamaica and then moved on to Santa Marta in Colombia. His work was not without hazard. He encountered the savage Guaggira Indians on the Rio de la Hacha and fearful storms in the Sierra de Marocagua. Burke had been even more affected by the weather. He struck a very bad season, getting only as far as Jasper's House in Alberta and collecting virtually nothing.

A remarkable plant was received at Kew in 1844 of which a report was published in the *Illustrated London News* on 4 January 1845. The plant was one of a group of *Echinocactus* received from Mr Frederick Staines of San Luis Potosi in Mexico. It weighed 235 lbs, was 3 feet 4 inches high, and had a circumference of 5 feet 7 inches. Immediately on arrival and potting up in a tub at Kew it threw out more than a hundred flowers.

Parliament had requested annual reports from Kew, the first being issued in May 1845, revealing among other things that attendances by the public had increased from 9,174 in 1841 to 15,114 in 1844. The next year the attendance almost doubled to 28,139 and the services of a Metropolitan Police constable were hired in the summer months, one of Sir Robert Peel's new 'peelers'. This was the genesis of the Kew Constabulary, although it was some time before this security force became part of the Kew staff paid directly by Kew.

Progress on the Palm House was slow during 1845, the delay being due to the time taken to manufacture the ironwork and, although the Broad Walk designed by Decimus Burton was brought down to the Palm House Lake during the year it could not be carried round the Palm House until that was finished. Accessions to the collections continued to pour in and further alterations had to be made to the smaller glass houses to accommodate these. Mr Staines of San Luis Potosi surpassed his previous effort by sending over an *Echinocactus* weighing 713 lbs.

During 1845 some of the old walls and boundaries within the garden were removed, the collection of British native plants was doubled in size, the mound covering the ice-house was planted up with evergreen shrubs and the large Mound near the Palm House Lake was cleared of coarse shrubs and unsightly trees. The decayed Temple of Aeolus on this Mound, relic of Sir William Chambers and Princess Augusta, was cleared away and a replica erected by Decimus Burton to the original design but without the rotating interior.

Purdie must have been somewhat dismayed at this time as, in spite of immense difficulties arising from the terrain and the weather, he received complaints from Kew about the paucity of his collections. Among other things, he forwarded from Ocana a glass case with more than 100 plants of *Phytolephas macrocarpa*, the ivory-nut palm, the bottom of the case being covered with the seeds of the plant. His troubles were crowned when after a long journey through very wet fever-ridden country between Santa Marta and Ocaña he was virtually arrested by the authorities as a vagrant. 'I arrived in Bogota', he says 'with only $\frac{1}{2}$ rial ($4\frac{1}{2}$p English), in debt to my servants and almost all my clothes in rags.' It is difficult to avoid the impression, reading the correspondence, that Sir William, who had done no collecting himself in such countries, had very little idea of what conditions were like, or disposition to make allowances for them.

Burke had eventually got across the Rockies and into the Snake country but misfortune still dogged him. His baggage horse took fright and fell, smashing up much of his precious equipment. Vegetation was sparse here and not much better in Utah southward but he found more around the head of the Missouri. There was danger all the time from Indians and he had to be always on the alert, not the best of conditions in which to try to collect plants and his results were meagre.

In April 1846 the new gate on Kew Green, since its opening always called the Main Gate, was completed and came into use. It consists of a double gate in the centre for carriages, and one each side for pedestrians. The gates were made at York to Decimus Burton's design and are considered very elegant. They have the Royal Arms in the centre with the letter 'V' in the middle, the carriage gate being surmounted by a crown. The gates are 13 feet high and are executed in wrought iron in the style of the ornamental and polished ironwork of about the time of James I. A curved iron railing extends on both sides, terminated by stone piers bearing vases, the vases being those originally set up by William IV. The iron railings and stone plinth were taken from the fence that George IV erected to enclose a portion of Kew Green. These glorious gates have been, since their erection, one of the beauties and attractions of Kew.

For a time the large *Echinocactus* weighing 713 lbs was dwarfed by a very much larger one, a huge *Echinocactus visnaga*, which weighed over a ton. This monster had arrived on 10 July 1846 'in a very good state' but had 'two or three small bruises' which it was presumed would heal. Unfortunately, this expectation was not borne out and the plant rotted, leaving the field to the smaller one, but this still had much attraction for visitors who had not been lucky enough to see the larger one.

Decimus Burton had finalised Nesfield's plan which now covered almost the whole of present-day Kew, the King of Hanover having given up the portions over which he had had control, so that Sir William's empire extended almost down to Richmond. Burton sent the plan, together with his own recommendations, to the Commissioners of Woods and Forests, who received it on 1 June 1846. The letter and plan were then the blueprint for future Kew. Although the decisions were not made immediately, the recommendations were accepted and, except for a few minor points, carried out as they stood. The Royal Botanic Gardens as they are today still bear the shape that was given to them by this report, which is thus one of the most important documents in the history of the Gardens.

With the establishment of a royal kitchen garden at Frogmore, the royal kitchen

[183]

garden at Kew had become redundant and in June 1846 this area, with its forcing houses, was added to the botanic garden. The whole comprised 15 acres in the north-east corner of the Gardens. Among the buildings taken over with it was a sizable fruit store, which Sir William immediately seized on for use as a museum of economic botany. The first specimens were put on the shelves on 9 July 1846. They included examples of pine and *Banksia* cones, *Lecythia* and other 'curious capsular fruits', small specimens of wood, and pieces of Tapa cloth and similar curiosities which had been collected by John Smith and specimens supplied by Sir William, including fruits in bottles preserved in spirits from the days of his professorship at Glasgow.

Purdie continued to collect and send specimens in the earlier months of 1846 but on the death of David Lockhart he was appointed Curator of the Trinidad Botanic Garden and took up duty there at the end of September 1846 without returning to England. Burke, who had used Fort Hall as a base, returned to Vancouver for a time but was back at Fort Hall by June 1846. He made another attempt to collect on the headwaters of the Snake and Green Rivers but was again frustrated by hostile Indian activity. His next trip had to be cancelled because of the arrival of an emigration wagon train. Lord Derby and Sir William Hooker were both dissatisfied with the little they had received from Burke and had decided to terminate the arrangement with him.

Burke now received from Sir William a letter which had been written over a year earlier accusing him of neglecting his duties, which greatly incensed him, but he did not reply to it until he had taken part in an historic trip. Jesse Applegate and a party of young men cut and marked a road from Fort Hall to the Williamette Valley in Oregon preparatory to the passage through of a wagon train of emigrants comprising ninety to a hundred wagons. This was the first such train over a trail which was afterwards much used and came to be known as the 'Applegate cut-off'. Burke accompanied the trail-breaking party and describes it in a letter written on 17 October 1846 but gives little detail, doubtless because of his state of mind as, at the end of the letter, he resigns from Hooker's service. No one who knows his story can do anything but sympathise with him.

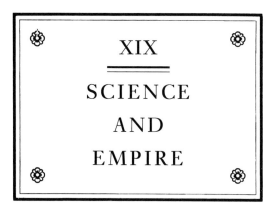

XIX

SCIENCE
AND
EMPIRE

'Growth is the only evidence of life.'

Cardinal Newman

The task of naturalist on board *HMS Herald* under the command of Captain Kellett, which was surveying in South American waters, was being carried out by the ship's assistant surgeon but he was accidentally shot and Berthold Seemann, a native of Hanover who was working at Kew, was sent out to replace him. Seemann had to wait some time at Panama before he could join the ship, which he was able to do on 17 January 1847. While waiting he collected and sent several consignments to Kew.

The commercial plant collector Thomas Bridges had stumbled across the giant water-lily *Victoria amazonica* while exploring the province of Moxos in Bolivia in 1845 and brought 25 seeds to Kew on 7 August 1846. Only two of these vegetated. They grew at first well enough to form leaves 'the size of a half-crown piece' but, having germinated so late in the summer, they ceased to flourish as the autumn drew on and died in the dull weather of November.

By the end of 1846 considerable progress had been made on the Palm House, the framework of the central portion being completed and much of the side wall, including the ventilators, being filled in with glass. The gallery had also been

The Palm House in the course of construction in the 1840s.

formed and a spiral staircase. The wings, too, had been commenced, the concrete foundations having been laid and some of the granite blocks fixed, together with several ribs.

The taking down of the walls in and around the botanic garden, the removal of hedges and other changes led to the breaking up and loss of many of the plants in the herbaceous and grass collections which grew in beds near the ice-house and a new set of beds, with the plants arranged by family, was established in 1847 in the old kitchen garden ground next to the Kew Road wall, where these collections have remained ever since.

Sir William had been told in 1844 to prepare a guidebook for the Gardens for sale to visitors and his effort in this direction was put on sale in 1847. It contained

Berthold Seemann, a German who trained as a student-gardener at Kew and afterwards became a
noted plant collector and distinguished botanist.

56 pages and was illustrated with 61 woodcuts. The rules under which visitors
were allowed in the Gardens in those days, while much shorter, are in some
respects stiffer than those of the present day. Smoking, eating and drinking for
example, are forbidden and visitors must be 'respectably attired.' Anyone
abstracting flowers or cuttings without authority was liable to 'disgraceful
expulsion'. The gardens were intended for 'agreeable recreation and instruction,
not for idle sports' and there must be no 'leaping over the beds or running'. Among
the plants mentioned in the book were two specimens of the agave *Fourcroya
gigantea* which had been in the royal gardens, first of Hampton Court and then of
Kew, probably from the earliest introduction of the species more than a century
before. Each produced, in the summer of 1844, a flowering stem which grew at

[187]

first at the rate of 2 feet in 24 hours. When they reached a height of 26 feet an opening had to be made in the roof of No 1 House, in which they were kept, through which the spikes passed, eventually reaching a height of 36 feet. Sir William's Guide appeared not a moment too early. Also on sale in 1847 was *Jeffs Handbook to Kew Gardens*, a private commercial venture which covered much the same ground as the official guide but in less detail.

During 1847 Sir William induced the Commissioners of Woods and Forests to obtain from the Treasury a rise in salary for himself from £300 per annum plus £200 in lieu of a house to £800 overall, for John Smith a rise from £130 to £150 per annum and for the gardeners a rise in the basic rate from twelve shillings to fourteen shillings per week, the senior men having had a rise the previous year.

The *Herald* completed its survey of Panama and moved on to Callao to spend some time surveying the River Guayaquil. Seemann took the opportunity to make an expedition, together with a companion named Bedford, which took him through the Peruvian deserts. On his return the survey was continued and on 5 November 1847 the vessel was at Buenaventura in the Bay of Choco, arriving back at Panama on 14 November.

In the autumn of 1847 Burke arrived back in England. The results of his activities had been very meagre and neither Kew nor Lord Derby got a reasonable return for their money. Nevertheless, his treatment by Sir William Hooker, in the view of the modern commentator, Susan Delano McKelvey, leaves much to be desired: the circumstances of the failure in her view suggest poor planning by those who sent him into the field as much as anything else, but he also had bad luck and exceptionally poor weather against him. He did get into botanically untouched regions at times and had his collections reached England in a reasonable state he might at least have contributed to the knowledge of plant distribution but his efforts were unfortunately wasted.

At the end of the year Sir William was asked by the Admiralty to prepare the botanical part of a manual which they were having produced for the guidance of naval officers on scientific matters. The section gave officers a few plain instructions on collecting, preserving and transporting plant specimens and asked them to look out for material suitable for display in the museum of economic botany. It pointed out that much of the world was still *terra incognita* to the naturalist and objects worth collecting could be found almost anywhere. A list of botanical books was included and, in later additions, seven pages of queries about various economic products.

Dr Joseph Hooker, Sir William's son, had been occupying himself in various ways since he returned from the *Erebus* and *Terror* expedition and had finished the

[188]

METROXYLON Sagu.   SAGUS elata.

An illustration from the *Historia Naturalis Palmarum* of von Martius published early in the nineteenth century showing two sago palms, *Metroxylon sagu* and *Sagus elata*, such as grow in the Palm House, in an artist's impression of their natural habitat.

Flora Antarctica resulting from that expedition. He now undertook a collecting expedition to the Himalayas, and arrived in Calcutta on 12 January 1848. After a few weeks travelling and collecting in the area he went on up to Darjeeling to await opportunity to begin the expedition proper.

A Royal Commission examining the nature and functions of the British Museum in 1848 raised for the first time a question that other similar bodies were to raise over the years. Members of the Commission noticed that while botanical specimens and a botanical and general library existed at the British Museum, and scientific work on plants was done there, the botanical collection of plants was at Kew, some distance away. It seemed to them desirable that these should be

[189]

brought together, but the questioning did not result in a recommendation.

During the spring of 1848 the Palm House was completed and the boilers tested and found adequate to maintain the temperatures required. The first plants put into the Palm House were the large specimens of the palm *Sabal umbraculifera*. The roots and soil in which these grew had been enclosed in brickwork in 1828 and on its removal the whole of the ball of earth consisted of a mass of roots, which were enclosed in strong wooden boxes. The largest plant weighed 17 tons and the other not quite so much. The assistance of engineers with tackle from Deptford Dockyard was utilised to raise the plants, which were then conveyed nearly half a mile to the Palm House on rollers. They were then drawn up the steps of the east centre door by a windlass. These were followed by the two large date palms (*Phoenix dactylifera*), one of *P. reclinata*, two of *Chamaerops martiana*, one large *Pandanus odoratissima*, a tall *Strelitzia augusta*, and two tall *Cocos* and *Caryota*. They were all placed in the centre of the house and, although some distance apart, gave a good impression. A number of young plants had been raised against the time the Palm House would be ready to take them but it was some time before the house began to take on a fully occupied appearance.

Water continued to be troublesome in the tunnel and furnace room and a deep well was sunk into which the water drained and as it did so was pumped to the steam engine in the chimney tower and from thence discharged into the pond. However, this did not completely solve the problem and in the summer of 1853 the floor of the furnace room was raised by 20 inches. There was trouble then with the draft which became very sluggish because the lifting of the furnaces had brought them almost on a level with the flues. Rebuilding of the flues to rectify this raised the heat in the boiler room to an almost unbearable level and ventilation had to be devised to overcome this. Eventually, however, a tolerable situation was reached.

The *Herald* was ordered in April 1848 to break off its survey and proceed to the Arctic to search for Sir John Franklin and continued searching until driven back by the winter, returning to Panama on 19 January 1849. In the meantime Dr Joseph Hooker had obtained permission to pass through Nepal and Sikkim and on 27 October 1848 made an abortive attempt which succeeded in reaching 16,000 feet so that the party was able to look down into Tibet but was forced to return by

Opposite: Interior of the Palm House showing iron gratings over the heating pipes which serve as paths, with a fan-leaved palm and the Giant Bamboo prominent in the picture. The latter plant grows from ground-level to the roof in one season, a distance of more than 60 feet.

A New Zealand palm, *Rhopalostyus sapida*, often grown as an ornament in sub-tropical gardens, in the Palm House.

Sarracenias and Darlingtonias, plants that trap and digest insects in their long pitchers.

Cacti and succulent plants from hot dry areas of the world growing outdoors at Kew in the summer, with the rock garden in the background.

snow in the passes.

Since Thomas Bridges had brought the first seed to Kew in 1846 other attempts had been made to grow the *Victoria amazonica*, but none had succeeded. In January 1849, however, six plants were established from seed sent by Dr Boughton from Demerara. By May one of them was filling a shallow tank 9 feet in diameter. A larger tank was rapidly constructed, 25 feet long by 11 feet wide and on 21 August the plant was moved into it. At the same time the Duke of Devonshire's gardener, Sir Joseph Paxton (afterwards a railway tycoon and designer of the Crystal Palace) was cultivating another of the plants and a race took place as to who would flower the plant first. By 11 November the Duke had won, his plant by then having come into full flower. The Kew plant produced a bud but too late in the season for it to develop. Nevertheless, a start had been made and the Giant Water Lily soon became one of the most famous sights of the Gardens. It is grown each year from a seed the size of a pea sown in January and by August has filled its large tank with leaves 6 feet across.

On 29 January 1849 the *Herald* left the Bay of Panama once again on surveying work which afforded Berthold Seemann further opportunity for collecting. The vessel then sailed for the Sandwich Islands, arriving at Honolulu on 7 April. Seemann had more than a month in which to collect before the vessel sailed again to recommence its search of the Arctic for Franklin, on which it was engaged from the end of June until mid-November, when it sailed for California. While the *Herald* was surveying the Californian coast Seemann took the opportunity to make a journey into the interior of Mexico.

Dr Joseph Hooker collected a great deal of material around Darjeeling and on his journey back from it but many of the living specimens perished in the heat of the plains before they reached their destination. On 3 May he set out on a second and longer Himalayan journey through eastern Sikkim. Successive climbs brought him to Manay which, at a height of 15,000 feet, with its great yak pastures, the highest in Sikkim, proved to be 'an ideal place for observations of all kinds . . .'. On 9 September he went on to the Donkiah Pass, nearly 18,500 feet high. From here in order to obtain a still wider view of Tibet, Joseph scrambled up the mountain-side another 1,000 feet. This height remained a record for some time. The trip was botanically very rewarding. He returned to Manay and then repeated the high climbs, spending four days in Tibet and returning at the end of October. The long journey back ended in a bizarre contretemps. His party was told to go via Tumboong over the Chola Pass but after ascending the pass on 7 November they were assaulted and imprisoned by the Dewan and his men. They were not released until Christmas Eve.

Sir Joseph Hooker in middle age.

On 9 October 1849 W T Aiton died at Kew. Unfortunately all his records and other papers were burnt, together with whatever early material survived from his father's times, a loss of archives that would have been of incalculable value to garden historians. At Michaelmas 1849 the final vestige of royal control over the Gardens disappeared as the King of Hanover relinquished the game preserve by the river of which he had retained use. The way was clear to carry out Nesfield's plan, as modified by Burton, in full. Progress had, indeed, already been made and the main vistas and the development around the Palm House almost completed. Much culling and replanting, however, remained to be done in the woodland before the national arboretum could be said to have come into existence. Smeaton's horse-driven water-pump no longer produced an adequate supply and

The Palm House in Kew Gardens in mid 19th century

A Victorian print of the Palm House and the tropical water-lily house next to it.

more modern engine-driven arrangements were introduced which have been improved from time to time as developments have required. A minor but interesting event which occurred in September 1849 was the repurchase for £7 of the Unicorn which had formerly decorated one of George IV's gate lodges on Kew Green. It now adorns a small private gate into the Gardens from the Kew Road. The Lion which decorated the other lodge may be found on the public Lion Gate at the south end of the Gardens.

Seemann rejoined the *Herald*, which returned to the Sandwich Islands, anchoring at Honolulu on 16 May 1850. After a further unsuccessful search for Franklin it came back to Honolulu on 16 October and then, after a refit, sailed for Hong Kong and England, its task finished. Seemann developed very rapidly into a

A jungle-like corner of luxuriant vegetation in the Palm House.

distinguished botanist, taking his PhD at Göttingen in 1852 and publishing both a narrative of the voyage of the *Herald* and separate volumes on the botany of the five-year voyage. He also founded and edited the scientific journal *Bonplandia*.

Joseph Hooker's experience rendered him useful to the army but a desire to return to Nepal was frustrated as it was considered unwise. In the meantime his father had got Walter Hood Fitch, the botanical illustrator, to work up his drawings of rhododendrons and had published them in *The Rhododendrons of Sikkim-Himalaya 1849-51*. The rhododendrons he introduced were of outstanding horticultural importance. In time they altered the look of the British countryside because from them were raised hardy hybrids with far larger and brighter flowers than anything hitherto seen. These were planted extensively on country estates, producing much more colour in the summer and more attractive evergreen foliage in the winter than had been available in the past. As he could not go to Nepal, Joseph undertook a journey to the Khasia Hills, then returned to Calcutta and was in England by 25 March 1851.

Berthold Seemann and Joseph Hooker were the last two major Kew plant collectors. Relations with Empire countries and their botanic gardens which were being established and other institutions and individuals had begun to produce an ever-increasing flow of specimens. There was also a lively interchange between Kew and the various botanic gardens on the Continent. It was, in the main, usually necessary in the future only to ensure that, if possible, expeditions into botanically unexplored parts of the world included someone who would collect for Kew.

Queen Victoria's interest in Kew had always been high: in 1851 she decided that she liked the Queen's Cottage grounds so much that she would have the area fenced off for her own use. It is still fenced off and kept in the semi-wild state which she enjoyed but is provided with a walk so that visitors may go through it and experience the pleasure that she valued.

Although the layout of the gardens had reached its modern form and the work of fostering the plant resources of the Empire was making progress, the scientific work of Kew had, in 1851, hardly yet begun. Outside botanists such as George Bentham used the living collections but only Sir William and his son Joseph and John Smith were doing scientific work at Kew, and the Hookers used Sir William's private collections and library at West Park: they had, as yet, no accommodation for such work in the Gardens. The accumulation of dried specimens was presenting a problem. By good fortune, two occurrences in 1851 combined to provide a solution: a house on Kew Green was made available by the Queen as an official residence for the Director of the Royal Botanic Gardens and another, Hunter House, became available to house a herbarium and library. In 1852 both

A view of the Herbarium during 1943, when work was much reduced by the exigencies of the war.

were brought into the service of Kew.

Sir Joseph Banks, had he been alive, would have highly approved of the way things were going. He had always had the vision of Kew spearheading the development of Empire resources: he had also cherished the notion that Hunter House might be used as a Herbarium and Library. Both these ideas were coming to fruition. There were many uses to which the new plants could be put, the feeding and clothing of men and animals, in medicine, in construction work, in reclamation of land, for ornamental purposes and a host of other activities beneficial to humanity. Someone had to look at the thousands of new plants becoming available, sort out their relationships, and give them names by which they could be distinguished from one another by those who used them, otherwise

Scientists at work in the Herbarium in the bays between the stacks of cabinets which contain the collections of dried specimens. The worker in the foreground is comparing the specimen in her hand with some of the specimens from the cabinets to determine its botanical status.

[199]

the situation would be chaotic. Kew, where a substantial proportion of the plants was being grown and where they could be examined as living specimens, was the obvious place to carry on the work of taxonomy, or systematic botany, as the work of plant classification is called, though in practice taxonomists use the living plant as a reference point far less than the layman might expect. The move was made and the base established and so, in 1852, three hundred years almost to the day after William Turner, the first Englishman to tackle this branch of botanical science, left his garden at Kew where he grew exotic plants to assist his studies to become Dean of Wells, the wheel came full circle and these studies returned to Kew, where they have been pursued ever since.

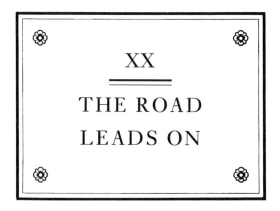

XX

THE ROAD

LEADS ON

'Progress, therefore, is not an accident, but a necessity
... It is part of nature.'

Herbert Spencer

Early in 1852 Miss Eliza Bromfield offered to Kew the herbarium and library of her late brother, Dr William Arnold Bromfield. This was at first kept in packing cases in a garden shed at West Park but was moved along with Sir William's into Hunter House when that became available. The 600 books included in this gift were the foundation of the present-day Kew Library, one of the finest botanical libraries in the world. The Bromfield gift was followed in 1854 by another from George Bentham, who offered his own herbarium and library of 1,000 volumes to Kew provided he was allowed to work with it there. The offer was accepted. The Kew Herbarium and Library became almost immediately a magnet for taxonomists and within five years of its establishment it was attracting upwards of fifty scientists a year to work there, many from overseas.

In 1856 Sir William adumbrated what became the ground-plan of future work in the Herbarium. At that time research of one kind or another was being done there on floras of New Zealand, Tasmania, Ceylon, India, South Africa, Madeira and the West Indies. He suggested to the government that a scheme should be adopted for the preparation of a series of Floras or descriptions in the English language of the indigenous plants of British colonies and possessions. Sanction was given for the compilation of such a scheme and Sir William began to work on more detailed proposals.

Since the railway had been brought to Richmond in the late 1840s numbers of visitors to the Gardens had risen sharply, almost four times the number that visited in 1846 coming into the Gardens in 1850, when the total reached 179,627. The next year, 1851, was the year of the Great Exhibition and numbers leapt to 327,900. The following year was lower, but this was a temporary fall, the 1851 figure being surpassed in 1853. From then on numbers rose each year, the Gardens becoming very popular with London's East End poor, for whom it was a cheap day out in the open air, a great contrast to the fetid streets of Dickens' London in which they lived. The increased numbers and the need for better control of visitors led in 1857 to the gatekeepers, park constables and museum attendants being put into uniform.

The Museum of Economic Botany was a great attraction. The vegetable products of the Empire were then entirely new and there were so many of them that one wondered at which to stare. In 1855 Sir William produced a Guide to the Museum for sale to visitors. The old fruit store which was being used as the museum was, however, inadequate to house all that was being acquired and money was provided for the erection of a new purpose-built Museum facing the Palm House across the lake. It came into use at the beginning of 1857.

Sir William's relations with the Cambridge family, now the sole representatives of the royal family residing at Kew, were always very cordial. The old Duke Adolphus, George III's youngest son, died in 1850 but the family still lived on in Cambridge Cottage, Lord Bute's old house on the Green, which had been enlarged, and Princess Mary of Cambridge in particular was fond of gardening and the Gardens. She concerned herself closely with summer bedding plans and other matters which she used to discuss with Sir William, for whom she had the affectionate nickname of 'Old Hookey'. Cambridge Cottage saw many famous people at dinner parties and as visitors at other times. The young Prince of Wales, the future Edward VII, when rowing on the Thames, would moor his boat and come to see his aunt and cousin. It was, indeed, at Cambridge Cottage that he attended his first dinner party.

The international development of the scientific work and the great expansion of the Gardens in area, buildings, plants and visitors induced the Treasury to sanction the appointment of Sir William's son Joseph as Assistant Director from June 1855. Joseph's stature as a scientist had now risen into the very highest class and he took on special responsibility for the Herbarium.

[202]

An artist's impression of the original Museum of Economic Botany established in the 1850s.

The Commissioners of Works and Buildings, who had taken over responsibility for Kew from the Commissioners of Woods and Forest, had their own ideas as to the uses to which the Gardens might be put. In 1855 a tree nursery was established at Kew to supply the parks of London, which were at that time in process of formation. Sir Benjamin Hall, First Commissioner of Works, after whom Big Ben was named, considered that the Gardens were not colourful enough. The new and attractive flowering plants brought in by plant collectors had stimulated the new fashion of 'carpet bedding' and in 1856 Sir William, under orders, brought into being in the Gardens fifty beds, 'each filled with peculiarly coloured flowers harmoniously arranged'.

Changes following the Indian Mutiny in 1857 led the Honourable East India Company to transfer to Kew in 1858 the collection of plants made by their officers, which had been accumulating for thirty years in the cellars of India House. They filled eleven large wagons and from them a selection was made at Kew, and sorted into the Herbarium collections, for use in the preparation of a Flora of British India. The consignment contained much valuable material which had been collected by well-known key figures in the investigation of the flora of India.

Although there had been no formal course, young gardeners had come to Kew for many years for training and had usually stayed two years, going through all parts of the Gardens. Many of them went overseas to serve in Empire countries and it was on them that the economic development of the Empire was built, since much of that development depended upon the exploitation of the indigenous plant populations, and the distribution of these around the world to test their suitability and economic value in other countries. Kew-trained men played the key role in this work because of their training in the cultivation of a large number of exotic plants and Kew itself, with Sir William and his successors at the head, acted as a clearing-house for information as well as providing the trained men, and gave a guiding hand when needed. The prime motive was, of course, the encouragement of trade to ensure an adequate return for investment, but the chief actors in the forefront of this scene, the pioneers who set it going, made little profit from it and often lost their lives or had them shortened by the awful diseases of warmer climates. The pages of the records are full of the names of young men who went out to Empire countries and, in a few months, were dead of fever, to be replaced in succession by others. On their work the present economic development of many of those countries was built and without them they would have been the poorer. It is fashionable now to denigrate the role of the British Empire in world history, but when the unbiased story comes to be written in future centuries, the role of these young men will be recognised. Their history cannot be told in detail here, but their work is the background against which this tale of the state botanic garden is set for the first 100 years of its existence, after it burst out of the cocoon of the old private garden. At the point this narrative has reached, in 1859, the young gardeners were for the first time given formal lectures.

Some 16,000 yards of gravel had already been used from the Gardens for the repair of public roads: now another 10,000 yards was used to provide a terrace on which to build a new glasshouse. The increasing size of the large number of trees and shrubs in various glasshouses which were not frost-hardy made it imperative that another large house should be provided, if the plants were not to be destroyed, which was unthinkable, because they included some of the most prized and

[204]

striking plants in the Gardens. In 1860 the erection of such a house, to a design by Decimus Burton, was commenced. Although the completed design provided accommodation as spacious as the Palm House, it was divided into five parts, a high central portion with octagons at each end and beyond those another rectangular house at each end. The hole left by the extraction of the gravel was turned into a lake, a connection being made in 1861 to the Thames, so that the tidal waters filled it. The new house, which was sited between the lake and Kew Road, was called the Temperate House.

Kew took part in 1860 in one of the most important horticultural operations that has ever taken place. An expedition to South America by Clements Markham, with the help of the sick Richard Spruce, a botanist and plant collector, managed to obtain seeds and young plants of the *Cinchona* tree of South America, the efficacy of the bark of which, known as 'Jesuit's Bark', which contains quinine, against fever, particularly malaria, had been known for hundreds of years. Plants and seeds reached India in 1860. It was found that the Red *Cinchona* which Spruce had collected from the slopes of the giant Chimborazo, one of the highest mountains of the Andes, thrived the best and within five years a million trees had been distributed. This action, in which Kew assisted, the Treasury having financed a special glasshouse at the Gardens for the raising of the seeds and the rearing of the young plants, saved an incalculable amount of human suffering, because it soon became possible to buy quinine in India and elsewhere very cheaply and it was not until the Second World War that any more useful specific against malaria was discovered.

Richard Spruce was only one of the plant collectors who contributed to the Kew collections in the 1850s. There were seven others from whose activities Kew profited in this period: M Bourgeau, who accompanied Captain Palliser's expedition into the unknown territories of British North America on the eastern side of the Rocky Mountains; Dr John Kirk, who was with Livingstone in the interior of tropical East Africa on his journey to the Zambesi in 1858; William Milne, who was on Seemann's old vessel the *Herald* on its expedition to Fiji between 1852 and 1856; Dr David Lyall and John Buttle, both on the British Columbia Boundary Commission, 1858–61; Charles Wilford, who collected plants in Hong Kong, Formosa, Korea and Japan in 1857–9; and Charles Barter, who was on Dr Baikie's second Niger expedition 1857–9.

The expansion of the Museum had necessitated the appointment of a Keeper in 1847 to take charge, the post having first been occupied by John Smith's son Alexander Smith who now, in 1860, had to give up the post on account of ill health, Mr J R Jackson taking his place. For similar reasons it was now necessary to appoint someone with special responsibility for the Library and collection of botanical illustrations, which had been greatly augmented by gifts, and Daniel Oliver, FLS was appointed in 1860 with the title of Librarian to undertake this task.

Although the central portion of the Temperate House had been commenced, the octagons at each end of it came into use first, being filled with the contents of Princess Augusta's 'great stove' built in 1761, the oldest glasshouse in the Gardens, which was now pulled down. The large *Wisteria* plant which had been growing over it for many years was retained, and provided with an iron frame, over which, 120 years later, it may still be seen growing. When the central portion was ready towards the end of 1861 the contents of the glasshouse by the Main Gate (No 1) were transferred there, being replaced by members of the Arum Lily family and other tropical large-leaved plants, particularly climbers. The large plants growing in the Orangery were also moved to the Temperate House, leaving that building available to be used as a Timber Museum.

The Temple of Victory on the Mound near the Temperate House had fallen into decay and was removed to make way for a new attraction, a large flagpole presented by Mr Edward Stamp of British Columbia, which had been made from a Douglas fir said to be 250 years old and 220 feet in length, which had been cut down to 159 feet. This was, in fact, the second spar presented to Kew by Mr Stamp, the first, 128 feet long, having been broken in course of erection. As each pole has aged it has been replaced by a new one, each new pole being larger than the one before it. The current pole is 225 feet in height, having been cut from a tree 275 feet tall. The Kew flagpole is a well-known and familiar landmark.

Aid continued to be rendered by Kew to Empire countries as they required it. In 1847 William Wren had been sent to Ascension Island, which was almost a desert, with a large quantity of trees and shrubs, which had become established there, together with Bermuda grass. In 1863, at the request of the Admiralty, further large consignments were despatched. Similar consignments were sent, at the request of the Governor, to St Helena.

The scheme for the preparation of Colonial Floras that Sir William Hooker had tentatively advanced in 1856 he now formalised, seven years later, in a memorandum to the Colonial Office which was printed as a Government paper. The work proceeded on the basis proposed. Floras of Hong Kong, New Zealand, the West Indies, Ceylon and South Africa were completed between 1861 and 1865; a Flora of Australia was begun in 1863 and completed by 1878; a Flora of Tropical Africa between 1868 and 1877; of Mauritius and the Seychelles in 1877; and a Flora of British India between 1875 and 1883.

A quiet water-lily pool in the Temperate House.

An important work undertaken at Kew at this time, of which the first volume was published in 1863, was the *Genera Plantarum* of George Bentham and Joseph Hooker, a standard background classification of the genera based on ideas of 'natural' evolutionary arrangement. It is on this system, which is used by a substantial part of the world of botanical science, that the dried specimens in the Herbarium at Kew, which total several millions, are arranged.

The posts of Keeper of the Herbarium and that of Librarian were merged in 1864 under the title of 'Keeper of the Library and Herbarium'. In the same year John Smith, whose sight was failing, retired from the post of Curator, an event that drew from Sir William Hooker the comment that it was the 'most important change' in the botanic garden which had been made since he became Director in 1841. Smith was to some extent embittered by what he felt was a failure to recognise his knowledge and abilities and it is, indeed, difficult to escape the

[207]

conclusion that he never got the recognition or pay that he deserved.

In his earlier days Smith's patient work on cultivating ferns and sorting them out laid the foundation not only of their culture and botanical treatment, but also demonstrated their attractions so effectively that it played a large part in the stimulation of the Victorian craze for ferns. His work with David Lockhart on the cultivation of epiphytic orchids was also a notable advance in the culture of plants that had defeated his predecessors. Kew owes much to John Smith, who kept a taut ship in the bad times of 1820–41. Had he failed in his task in those times, the Committee of Enquiry in 1838 might have seen a Kew of which they despaired, and written it off as beyond recovery. That they did not, is entirely due to John Smith. His name stands very high among those who have served Kew, and he deserves to be honoured accordingly.

John Smith's replacement was, by a coincidence, also named John Smith. He took up duty on 16 May 1864, having served as gardener to the Duke of Northumberland at Sion House across the Thames. Almost the first action he was required to take was to clear the original arboretum near the Orangery of trees past their best and replant with more ornamental varieties. Action was also initiated for a comprehensive review and renewal of the new vastly bigger arboretum which had been established in the Pleasure Grounds. Here some three thousand species and varieties had been planted in the last twelve years. The poor soil of Kew, some dry summers, and disease from the roots of old trees and thickets still in the ground, had rendered results very unequal. Unthrifty specimens that had proved too tender or otherwise unsuitable had to be removed and new young trees given the protection of clumps of shrubs.

Among other moves on the economic front, plants of ipecacuanha were obtained from South America in 1864 for testing in Ceylon as to the suitability of the plant for commercial cultivation in that island. Cork oaks (*Quercus suber*) had been raised at Kew and established in South Australia in 1864, prompting requests for plants of this useful tree from Victoria, New South Wales and Queensland. On 12 August 1865, however, Sir William Hooker died. His son Joseph, the obvious successor, was appointed director in his place. Of his father he wrote that 'the late Director of Kew has won the esteem and gratitude of his countrymen, and left a name that will ever occupy one of the most prominent positions in the history of botanical science.' Much more was written but this sentence is all that is really needed as an epitaph.

A scene near the mansion at Wakehurst Place, Kew's satellite garden in Sussex.

Contrasting colours among the trees and shrubs around the upper lake near the mansion at Wakehurst Place, Kew's satellite garden in Sussex.

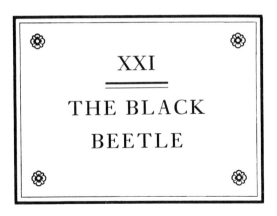

XXI

THE BLACK BEETLE

'... how seldom see we sons succeed
Their fathers' praise, in prowess and great deed.'

Bishop Joseph Hall

The change of Director enabled the post of Assistant Director to be abolished, on the ground that the duties could be split between the Curator and the Keeper of the Herbarium and Library. In effect this merely transferred the bulk of the duties of the abolished post to the Keeper, who from then on became the effective Assistant Director. Two substantial accretions to the Herbarium collections came to Kew in 1865: Dr John Lindley's orchid collection, numbering 3,000 specimens, and the collection of the explorer William John Burchell, who had travelled extensively in South Africa and South America.

Frost and snow in January 1867 inflicted unprecedented damage on the plants in the Gardens. Many of the oldest trees together with most of the tender conifers and upwards of half the shrubs were destroyed. Among other things all the specimens of *Cupressus macrocarpa*, including the oldest in Europe, which were nearly 50 feet high, were killed. The hybrid rhododendrons and the Sikkim species were devastated and much of the newly-acquired material from China, Japan, North India and California perished.

[209]

The herbarium, library, botanical illustrations and collection of portraits which had belonged to Sir William were bought by the Treasury in 1867 for £7,000, which was far below their value. Apart from the dried plant specimens accumulated over sixty years, many of the books were of considerable worth, being large hand-coloured illustrated editions bought at the time of issue. As he acquired them over the years, Sir William was laying up a storehouse of inestimable use at the present day.

Between 1866 and 1868 new arrangements for the supply of water to the Gardens were brought into being. The river water hitherto used left a deposit on the leaves of the plants which interfered with their growth. An engine house was built in the Arboretum Nursery and the tidal water which enters the lake from the Thames, after being allowed to settle, was passed through a filter bed in the nursery and pumped up to a reservoir in Richmond Park, coming down from there to an eight-inch main under the road to be distributed at high pressure through the Gardens. In the 1960s the supply from the reservoir, which by then was taken directly from the Thames and not through the Gardens lake, was incorporated by the Metropolitan Water Board into the public system.

A lodge was constructed and a gate opening made in the Kew Road wall near the Temperate House in 1867–8 to allow easy access from a projected railway station. The station site was, however, changed and the gate opening never used but the opening, at the instance of the nearby residents, who appreciated the glimpse of the Gardens afforded by the opening, filled in with railings instead of restoring the wall.

The Palm House heating was still giving trouble because of water in the stokehole. Several possible solutions were considered but the only one that was certain of success and reasonably cheap was the erection of flues passing up through the building itself. The work was carried out in 1866. The tops of the flues projected through the Palm House roof, but there was no way of avoiding this disfigurement.

Eight old glasshouses were demolished in 1868 to make way for new houses on the site now known as the T-range, near the Rock Garden (which, in fact, had not yet been made). One of the new houses was provided with a large tank for the *Victoria amazonica*, the house originally designed for this plant near the Palm House having proved too small. This, House No 15, is used for smaller tropical water-lilies. At the same time as this work was being carried out, a new gate was opened in the Kew Road wall at the end of the Herbaceous Ground, on the site of stables that had been demolished in 1867. It was erected at the expense of J G D Engleheart, the adjoining ground landlord, and called the Cumberland

Gate in memory of the King of Hanover.

The changes in heating in the Palm House and T-range were part of a general modernisation of the glasshouse heating arrangements. More efficient hot water heating systems had become available. During the years 1868–72 the work of replacing shrubs and trees in the Arboretum was continued, many of the older trees having been blown down or reached the end of their life. Various walks were made and collections planted, slowly bringing the arboretum arrangement into the form in which it may be seen today.

In 1872 a new entrance was made, with a drawbridge over the ha-ha, on the river side of the gardens, to serve visitors who came by the Isleworth Ferry or walked up the towpath from Richmond. During 1872 a new basis for the control of visitors to the Gardens came into being, as Kew was included within the scope of the Parks Regulation Act passed in that year.

The Director's annual reports indicate the extent of the economic and other assistance being rendered by Kew to Empire countries. That for 1872 is an average sample. This report mentions tobacco, efforts to establish which had been made in a number of countries, the introduction of teak into Jamaica, *Cinchona*, tea, Liberian coffee and chocolate into Ceylon, and *Cinchona* in India. The same report includes the names of Kew-trained men who went to overseas posts in that year, mentioning as destinations, Natal, Constantinople, Calcutta and Mauritius. The Gardens was now approaching its peak as a prime factor in the development of the Empire.

Against this story of success must be set the Director's troubles at home. Acton S Ayrton, the First Commissioner under Gladstone in the early 1870s, had nothing but contempt for scientists and did everything he could to thwart the Director and to exercise arbitrary authority over him. In 1872 the wrangle blew up into a *cause célèbre*, which even reached the august ears of Gladstone himself. Ayrton is remembered mainly for one remark. Defending himself against attack 'he exerted', according to the *Spectator*, 'his whole capacity in developing this thesis, that when, as Justice Maule said 'God Almighty was addressing a black beetle', he could not be expected to choose his words.' Presumably the Director of Kew was the 'black beetle' and Ayrton God, but it seems an arrogant assumption, even for a Victorian politician!

The scheme for the education of young gardeners received a boost during 1873, Sir Joseph Hooker, who was made a Swedish Knight of the Polar Star during the year, persuaded the Treasury to accept a case for extra tuition and £100 per annum was made available, which was enough to pay for lectures in four different subjects. This was the start of the formal student-gardeners' scheme. This year

The first Jodrell Laboratory, built in 1876.

was a notable one for Sir Joseph, apart from his Swedish knighthood. He had already, in 1868, served as President of the British Association for the Advancement of Science. Now, in 1873, he was elected President of the Royal Society. In this year the Pagoda came into use for a novel purpose, the Meteorological Office finding it suitable, as a high isolated building, for temperature experiments.

So many specimens had accumulated that Hunter House had become full up and it was necessary to make further provision. Opposition both from the Cambridge family, who did not wish to see the old house, with its royal associations, changed, and the First Commissioner of Works, Lord Lennox, who wanted a new building altogether, was eventually overcome. These objections were put aside when the receipt was found for the sale which has previously been mentioned in which George IV is shown to have been paid £18,250 for the property when he sold it to the state in 1823. The large reception rooms at the back

Jodrell Laboratory plant anatomists cutting sections of timber for microscopic examination.

were pulled down and a hall erected for the reception of the Herbarium and two new library rooms constructed in front of the old building. The work was finished by 1877.

The year 1875 saw the revival of the Assistant Directorship, primarily to handle 'the conduct of scientific business with public departments', whatever that broad phrase meant but really to assist with the heavy load of day-to-day business. The post was filled in June by W T Thiselton-Dyer, Sir Joseph's son-in-law. In the Fourth Report of the Committee on Scientific Instruction and the Advancement of Science it had been recommended that the opportunity to investigate plant physiological problems should be established at Kew. T J Phillips Jodrell, a friend of Sir Joseph, donated £1,500 to this end, of which £1,000 was spent on a building in 1876 and the rest on equipment. The new laboratory was built away from the Herbarium as it was thought it might constitute a fire risk to the irreplaceable specimens contained in the collections in that building. No staff were provided for

Dr Dukinfield Henry Scott, Honorary Keeper of the Jodrell Laboratory, 1892–1906.

the new laboratory, the intention being that it should be made available to any research worker competent to use its facilities. It was a provision made none too early. In continental laboratories researches were being pursued in the structure and physiology of plants that had as yet no counterpart here. Young men who had studied abroad were frustrated when they returned. These studies were complementary to the taxonomy that was making such strides in the Herbarium. It was not long, therefore, before men who were later to become very distinguished were using the facilities. Their studies were closely connected with similar work at London University. The high standard of the work pursued at Kew may be judged by the fact that six of those who worked at the laboratory in its first thirty years were elected Fellows of the Royal Society.

There occurred in the summer of 1876 what was probably the most important single event in the efforts of Kew to foster the economic life of the Empire. For a number of years the commercial possibilities of several rubber-producing plants had been under investigation and some had been grown at Kew and sent to India and Ceylon for further trial. Opinion had gradually crystallised into the view that *Hevea brasiliensis*, source of Para rubber, was the best because this species not only produced the precious sap freely but healed the wounds caused by tapping without difficulty. Some plants of this species were sent to India in the mid-seventies but it had not yet been established there. Seed lost its viability very quickly. It was desirable, therefore, that any move made should proceed without a hitch as quickly as possible.

The India Office commissioned Henry A Wickham, resident on the Amazon, to obtain as many seeds as he could and himself bring them post-haste to Kew. On 14 June 1876 a hansom cab rolled up to the door of the Director's house at 55, Kew Green. Wickham got out and, knocking at the door, was welcomed in with his package which, to the Director's delight, turned out be 70,000 seeds of *Hevea brasiliensis*, gathered on the River Tapajos. Under their joint supervision, the seed was sown in one of the houses in the T-range. For the next few days they watched with bated breath. Then, on the fourth day, to their great satisfaction, seedlings began to appear. About 1,900 plants were raised in all, which were sent on 12 August 1876 in 38 Wardian cases, specially made to accommodate the rapid growth of the seedlings, to Ceylon. From that consignment of plants arose the great rubber industry of the Far East. This was an effort by Kew as momentous in its consequences as the introduction of *Cinchona* into India.

Further flooding of the Palm House stokehole took place in the early months of 1877. New boilers were required and, in an effort to prevent further trouble from water, the floor was puddled with 15 inches of clay before 9 inches of concrete and 3 inches of paving were laid on it. Later in the year Sir Joseph, disturbed by the difficulty of controlling the crowds that gathered on Kew Green during public holidays, successfully opposed the licensing of a new public house on the corner of Kew Road opposite Cumberland Gate on the grounds that the congregation of people there on a busy road opposite such a gate was liable to lead to difficulty and perhaps injury. In this year also the height of the Kew Road wall, much to the disgust of the residents of the new houses which were replacing the market gardens on the other side of the road, was raised by three feet to give protection where the existing wall was only five feet high and screen the public conveniences and workplaces immediately inside the wall from the view of the upper storeys of the houses. Sir Joseph also opposed agitation to open the Gardens to the public before one o'clock, insisting that only bona fide students coming to the Gardens for serious study could be admitted before that hour.

Early in the morning of 3 August 1879 a hailstorm of tropical intensity broke over Kew. The hailstones averaged five inches in circumference and fell with such velocity that they buried themselves in the ground. The number of panes of glass broken in this extraordinary visitation amounted to 38,649 and the fragments weighed eighteen tons. A supplemenatry vote was needed from the Treasury to rectify the damage, pay for the tents and tarpaulins to protect the plants meanwhile, and defray the cost of reinstatement. Losses of plants were surprisingly few.

This year saw the building of a tank for hardy aquatic plants 80 feet long, 20 feet broad and 20 inches high above the ground. It was sited near the original Museum of Economic Botany, George III's old fruit store, the name of which had been changed to Museum II, the new Museum on the Palm House lake being Museum I and the Orangery Museum III. During the years 1878 to 1880 the India Office disbanded its India Museum at South Kensington and gave very large quantities of material to Kew. The Office also provided money to deal with it. Two temporary sheds built for workmen during the clearing up after the hailstorm of 1879 were used to sort the specimens. Some had to be destroyed because the labels had been lost in storage and a great deal of duplicate material was distributed to other institutions, but there was still left a very large accretion to the Kew Museums. Some measure of the size of the task may be gained from the fact that there were 2,000 rice samples alone, weighing together about three tons. There were also 36 tons of wood samples, but most of them had to be destroyed as useless because they could not be identified. Among the material received was one collection which immediately became a prized possession of the Library. This comprised 3,359 drawings of Indian plants which included a large number prepared for William Roxburgh at the Calcutta Botanic Garden during the period 1793–1813.

The money made available by the India Office included £2,000 to provide accommodation for the material at Kew. With it was built an extension to Museum I, a wing 50 feet long and 28 feet wide thrown out at the back like the leg of a T. An extension 30 feet long by 25 feet wide was also added to Museum II, turning it into the long low building which it appears now. The India Office also transferred to Kew from the India Museum what was called the Iron House or Iron Room, a large metal clad shed that was divided into two by a brick partition. This building will be remembered by generations of ex-Kew student-gardeners because from 1880 onwards it was used as lecture-rooms for their instruction, being sited next to the Jodrell Laboratory. It did not go out of use until it was pulled down in the early 1960s when the Jodrell Laboratory was enlarged and rebuilt to contain a modern

[216]

An artist's impression of the new Jodrell Laboratory and Lecture Theatre built in the early 1960s.

lecture-room covering the site on which the Iron Room formerly stood.

In 1880 another exhibition building was erected at Kew which has proved to be one of its permanent attractions. It is situated by the Kew Road wall opposite the Temperate House and houses a collection of oil-paintings of plants in their natural habitat made by Miss Marianne North during a period of thirteen years' travel. There are 627 pictures in all. They include scenes from Teneriffe, Brazil, Jamaica, United States, India, Sri Lanka, Singapore, Borneo, Java, Japan, Australia and New Zealand. The building was erected at Miss North's own expense and was designed by James Fergusson, FRS. It consists of a gallery measuring 50 feet long by 25 feet in breadth, and has a small studio and caretaker's house attached to it. Miss North later added another room and an entrance porch. The building is of red brick, with Bath stone dressings, and is in a plain classical style, with a low-pitched roof covered with zinc and terminating in pediments at either end. Lighting is by windows between pilasters in the upper part of the walls below the ceiling, and immediately above a narrow gallery that runs all round the room. The lighting scheme is generally considered effective and the building pleasing, though now old-fashioned, but most visitors find the pictures so crowded that they have patience to examine only a few and the general effect is rather of a kaleidoscopic pattern than of individual pictures. The Gallery, called the North Gallery, was

The new Jodrell Laboratory and Lecture Theatre built in the early 1960s.

opened to the public on 8 June 1882.

There had been a great increase in the popularity of rock-gardening in the period 1860-80. Kew had a small garden of this kind on the mound covering the ice-house, but near the end of 1881 some interested individuals memorialised the Office of Works urging the creation of a larger one, both for the benefit of botany and for the general public. As usual, money was the difficulty, but a bequest forced the issue. George Curling Joad, of Oakfield, Wimbledon, left his collection of herbaceous plants to Kew on condition that they were immediately removed there. The legacy was so opportune and so good that the Treasury were persuaded to provide the money to make a rock garden on a scale consonant with the size of the collection.

The site chosen for the new garden was between the wall bounding the Herbaceous Ground on the west and the T-range of glasshouses. The garden constructed attempted to reproduce the rocky course of a stream such as may be found in some of the side valleys of the Pyrenees. In these valleys the streams dry

The interior of the North Gallery showing how Miss North's paintings are arranged.

up after winter, and are bounded by rock-piled banks in the crevices of which summer vegetation grows freely. Above the rocks an evergreen shrubby growth springs up wherever the soil is of sufficient depth. The path at the bottom of the rock garden represented the dry bed of the stream, and was 8 feet wide and 514 long. Numerous stand-pipes were sited among the rocks to provide a water-supply, and suitable drainage also provided. The stone came from various sources, the Rev H Ellacombe providing weathered Bath oolite and Col A M Jones weathered limestone from Cheddar cliffs. The 'Stonehouse' in the southern part of the Gardens, made from stone from Queen Caroline's buildings, was also drawn upon but this was more difficult to use because much of it had been squared for building, but the gardeners did their best to make it look like uptilted stratified rocks. Joad's collection amounted to 2,630 plants which, planted out, soon produced a fine effect.

Another garden was made at this time which was a reflection of current fashion. William Robinson was advocating the 'wild garden' in reaction to the formal bedding that had been in vogue for so long and in 1881 the Mound surmounted by the Temple of Aeolus, which had been used by visitors as a playground for their children, was converted into such a garden, being planted up with bulbs, spring flowers and later, ferns and other suitable plants. The Azalea Garden, one of the most secluded and beautiful retreats in Kew, was also created about this time not far from the Rhododendron Dell (the former Laurel Vale).

The demand for trees for the public parks of London having dwindled, the special nursery for the production of these was discontinued in 1881. Sir Benjamin Hall, who had established this nursery, had also ordered surplus bedding plants produced in it to be given away to the London poor. Another activity was put on a more formal basis in 1882, the supply of material for educational purposes being facilitated by the provision of a small heated sunk-pit solely devoted to the cultivation and maintenance of plants for this purpose: these mainly went to university science classes at South Kensington.

In 1882 numbers of visitors to the Gardens suddenly jumped by some 50 per cent and, at 1,244,167 for the year, the million was passed for the first time. Figures are not very reliable because there were then no turnstiles and the gatekeepers merely kept a tally, but there was no doubt that the popularity of the Gardens was increasing rapidly, bringing with it new difficulties arising from the large numbers of people. The annual bonfire on the Green had been prohibited from 1874 and football also had to be banned in 1881, but a place had been found for cricket (this would have pleased Prince Frederick of Wales), a ground being authorised in 1876.

Although for a time there had been a small group of ex-Crimea pensioners used as Park Constables, these 'old soldiers' had not been wholly satisfactory and the Metropolitan Police supplied the backbone of control. Additional patrols by members of the Gardens staff on Sundays and holidays were regularised in 1882 by the provision of an official armlet with a badge. In 1883 it was decided to reduce the Metropolitan Police establishment by a sergeant and five constables and employ the equivalent directly as part of the Gardens staff in addition to the gatekeepers. This was the foundation of the Kew Constabulary as it is at the present day. The constables, like the gatekeepers, were required to do a certain amount of manual labour as part of their duties.

In 1882 the Jodrell Laboratory was the scene of work which had wide and lucrative industrial consequences. C F Cross and E J Bevan carried out basic research there on the chemistry of lignification which laid the foundation, years later, of the 'rayon' or artificial silk industry, a noteworthy landmark in the history of that small Laboratory and one of the most important events, because of its

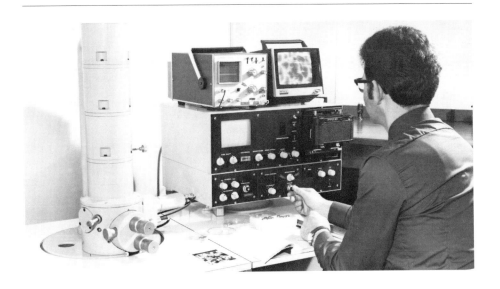

A Jodrell Laboratory scientist at work.

commercial implications, in the history of the Royal Gardens, ranking alongside the work on *Cinchona*, rubber and other plant products which had similar economic and financial consequences.

Bentham and Hooker's *Genera Plantarum* was completed and published in three volumes in 1883. This work defined the characters of all known genera of flowering plants and is widely accepted as standard: it embraced 202 orders, and 7,585 genera, including 95,620 species. In providing a framework for the study of taxonomic botany, not the only possible one and not necessarily the final word, but a workable tool, these two eminent botanists had done an inestimable service to their colleagues. It is one of the basic works upon which the fame of Kew as a botanical institution rests.

Sir Joseph Hooker retired from the Directorship of Kew at the end of November 1885 with many years of active scientific life still ahead of him as he did not die until 1911. He is one of the Victorian giants, and stands alongside his close friend Charles Darwin, as he did literally at the famous meeting of the British Association at Oxford on 30 June 1860, when Bishop Wilberforce ('Soapy Sam') set out to demolish Darwin's Theory of Evolution by ridicule, and was himself routed and had to slink away discomfited.

[221]

XXII

CLOUD OVER
THE SUN

'Pride goeth before destruction, and
an haughty spirit before a fall.'

Proverbs

There was considerable public criticism of the poor standards of cultivation in the Gardens in the early 1880s. So far as the glasshouses were concerned, suspicion fell upon the green glass used in them. The glass now supplied was noticeably darker than W T Aiton's 'Stourbridge Green' and a new test showed that its composition had, in fact, changed, so that it was keeping out much more light than it should have done. In any case the shading effect for which it had originally been adopted was no longer needed because of the haze arising from urban London which had now spread out beyond Kew. It was accordingly replaced in 1886 throughout the Gardens, although the last of it, in the Ferneries and Palm House, did not go until 1895. This move, coupled with the replacement in 1886 of John Smith II, whose performance had deteriorated, by George Nicholson, soon had an effect.

George Nicholson was an outstanding horticulturist who already had a national reputation because of his *Dictionary of Gardening*, published 1884–7, his own speciality being hardy trees and shrubs. Many plantings had failed in the past because of the poorness of the soil and over the next few years hundreds of poor trees were felled in the Arboretum. Vast quantities of loam from elsewhere, together with similar quantities of manure, were incorporated in the surface layers to bring up fertility. These measures improved matters and, in a short time, cultivation at Kew was again being held up as an example to others.

In 1885 the distribution of seeds was put on a regular basis by the preparation of a printed list for circulation to governments, botanic gardens and like institutions. In an establishment growing so many plants as Kew, with species of the same family planted adjacent to one another, the possibility of unplanned hybridisation was always present. Not until the 1960s was any attempt made to produce a totally reliable seed list. Although the Rock Garden contained many upland and mountain plants there were many others which would not tolerate the English climate and needed to be kept under controlled conditions to flourish. For them an Alpine House was built in 1887 next to the Herbaceous and Alpine Yard behind Museum II. This very popular house was enlarged in 1892 and replaced by a much larger house in the Melon Yard in the late 1970s. The rules had hitherto forbidden eating in the Gardens but in 1887 a Refreshment Pavilion was built in the southern part of the Gardens.

Annual reports to Parliament on the work of Kew were discontinued in 1882 but the information they contained continued to be published when the *Kew Bulletin* began to appear in 1887. The will of George Bentham, who died in 1884, left a substantial sum in trust to be administered by Kew to foster botanical work, particularly its publication, and to purchase books for Kew. This Trust, formally established in 1887 under the name of the 'Bentham Trust', was augmented in 1916 by a settlement made by Mr A E Moxon and his sister Miss Margaret Louisa Moxon, a painter of Swiss alpine plants whose drawings, numbering about a thousand, were presented to Kew by her brother in 1920. At the request of the donors the bequest was named the 'James Edward and Louisa Sarah Moxon Memorial Fund'. Its administration was undertaken by the Bentham Trustees and their name altered to the 'Bentham-Moxon Trustees'. Many other funds, totalling upwards of twenty-five in all, were placed in the hands of the Bentham-Moxon Trustees during the Directorship of Sir George Taylor from 1956 to 1972.

The gate opposite the Temperate House, which was intended to serve visitors coming to Kew via a railway station which, however, was never built, was moved in 1889 to a position opposite the end of Lichfield Road, which leads directly from the station which was eventually built to the Gardens. It was named, in honour of the Queen and her recent Jubilee, the Victoria Gate. In 1892 an additional botanical attraction was added to the Gardens, a bamboo garden being established

[223]

in a dip opening off the Rhododendron Dell. In the same year a glasshouse was provided in the Ferneries to house the filmy ferns but the house had to be closed to the public because it was found that the continual opening and shutting of the doors affected the plants. In the 1960s a much larger house in which they could be seen through a glass screen and which thus avoided this difficulty was built behind the Orangery. In 1892 also the old *Araucaria araucana*, one of Menzies' Monkey-Puzzles, long known as 'Sir Joseph Banks' Pine' was destroyed as a ruin and an eyesore no longer worth preserving. The Jodrell Laboratory also took a step forward in 1892. The concession was made that Dukinfield Henry Scott, who was working on plants of the Coal Measures, might serve as Honorary Keeper of the Laboratory. He had to pay for assistants out of his own pocket. One of them, L A Boodle, specialised in plant anatomy.

Taxonomic botanists consulted Steudel's *Nomenclator*, which listed all published names of plants, to avoid choosing a name for a new plant which had already been used. Charles Darwin was aware of the usefulness of this work and also of the fact that, with information added to it, it could be of even more value. He therefore made funds available at Kew to prepare a new work enumerating the names and bibliography of all known plants, based on Bentham and Hooker's *Genera Plantarum*. B Daydon Jackson of the Linnean Society undertook the work, publishing the first volume in 1893. This covered the period from 1753, when Linnaeus established the binomial system of naming, until 1885. By the time publication, which took two years, was completed, a supplement covering the period 1885–90 had also been prepared. Five-yearly supplements have been published ever since. The *Index Kewensis*, as this work is called, has a fair claim to be regarded as Kew's greatest contribution to botanical science.

For a number of years student-gardeners had met in the evening for discussion purposes, each one giving a talk in turn, a very useful introduction to speaking in public. This meeting led to the formation of the Mutual Improvement Society, an evocative Victorian name for an association that still exists. In 1893 a wider body, the Kew Guild, was formed mainly to keep ex-Kew students and employees in touch with one another. It publishes a Journal which has continued until the present day.

Unprecedented cold marked the early months of 1895, the temperature between 7 and 12 February hovering between 1°F and 5°F. Again many plants were killed and others badly damaged. One unexpected inhabitant of the hothouses survived, however, which for a time gave rise to a puzzling noise, the origin of which was not obvious. On quiet evenings 'shrill whistling notes' were heard which 'resembled the piping of a nestling bird'. A close watch eventually

The Stag Horn Fern (*Platycerium grande*).

revealed the originator, concealing himself between the pots and orchid baskets. He turned out to be *Hylodes martinicencis*, a small West Indian frog called familiarly 'coqui' in Porto Rico, which had begun to colonise his new habitat.

During 1895 the Old Queen began to relinquish her hold on the parts of Kew still used by the royal family. She released to the Gardens the 4½ acres of the Palace Meadow attached to Kew Palace, the existence of which had been the reason for the Broad Walk from the Main Gate taking a sharp turn left at the Orangery. The fence was removed and the ground incorporated into the Gardens. In the same year the wire fence which still separated the botanic garden from the Pleasure Grounds (the Arboretum) was also removed. This fence had for a long time prevented easy communication between the two parts of the Gardens and had on occasion given rise to criticism from the public. The stable block and residence which stood adjacent to the Palace near the end of the Broad Walk were also demolished after storm damage to the roof in 1905.

Interest in plants at Kew was such that it was considered that lists of species actually growing in the Gardens would be of considerable use to professional visitors or those building up a collection. Accordingly, in 1895 the first *Hand Lists* were issued. The first covered part of the *Trees and Shrubs* collection in the Arboretum. It was immediately followed by similar lists of *Ferns and Allies*, *Herbaceous Plants* and, in 1896, *Orchids* and the second part of *Trees and Shrubs*. The plants named in these lists could be seen growing labelled with their correct names in the Gardens and could thus be used as a check by others on the names of plants which they possessed.

Only the central portion of the Temperate House and the octagons had been built in the 1860s but sanction was now obtained to complete the House in accordance with Decimus Burton's original plan. Building of the south wing accordingly commenced in 1895 and was finished in 1897. The north wing was started in that year and completed in 1899. Closed for some years recently for restoration and internal replanning it is now restored to its full splendour.

Carnivorous plants are always intriguing to visitors to Kew and none more so than the *Nepenthes*, the pitcher plants, of which there are a number of species. To show these off rather better and provide improved conditions for their cultivation a new glasshouse was built in 1897 in the T-range. This had no external doors, but opened at each end into the adjacent stove house. The heating pipes were sited low down so that if the humidity needed to be raised they could be covered with water. The plants themselves are grown in hanging baskets so that the pitchers, which hang down from the plants, can be displayed to the best advantage.

The accumulation of mud in the lake was causing trouble with the water-supply

[226]

and in 1891–4 it had to be dredged clear, an operation that still has to be repeated at intervals. In 1897 a pumping engine of greater capacity was installed, a larger main provided and a new pipe system laid throughout the Gardens. Warm water from the engine-house drained into a pond outside the Arboretum nursery, in which for a time tender water-lilies could be grown, but a later change to a different system cut off the supply of warm water and the pond had to revert to the hardier sorts.

The areas of water within the Gardens had new denizens at this period. A pelican was given to the Gardens in 1890, and another in 1896. The latter died after a few months but the former flourished until, one day in 1897, it developed wanderlust. Taking off from the Gardens, it was for a time at Southall, but disappeared again, only to be shot by a gamekeeper in Sussex. More pelicans were given to the Gardens and in their turn became an additional attraction, particularly for the children. In 1899 three penguins were installed and also became favourites, but these species are not represented now, the largest birds being the black swans, the black-necked swans and the Canada geese which have long been denizens of the lake, together with a number of smaller species of wildfowl, some of which, like the Paradise Shelduck added in the 1960s, are relatively uncommon.

In 1898 the First Commissioner instructed the Director to open the Gardens to visitors in the summer months at 10 am for an experimental period. It was found that interference with the work of the Gardens staff was minimal and the arrangement became permanent. The new opening hours did not apply to the glasshouses where watering and other chores would undoubtedly have been impeded.

The Queen's Cottage grounds were still used occasionally on behalf of the Queen but she relinquished these also in 1897 and, after tidying up and adjusting paths, they were opened to the public in 1898. The Queen made the express stipulation that these grounds should always be preserved in their semi-wild state because of the great pleasure that she took in the bluebells which grow there in masses. This condition has been strictly observed. The grounds are a sanctuary for wild birds, which are little disturbed by visitors walking through.

The house built for William Aiton in the north-east corner of the Gardens, the outside of which can be seen by visitors as it fronts on the corner of Kew Green but which cannot be seen by them from inside the Gardens because it is within the nursery called the Melon Yard, had been let after W T Aiton's death in 1849, but in the 1890s reverted to the Office of Works. In the 1880s it had been named *Descanso House* by a South American merchant who rented it during the period 1888–92 and this name, which means in Portuguese 'resting place', has since stuck to it, although it has no connection with the Gardens or the royal family. It contained, when taken over, five large bronze *relievos* showing scenes from French history of the late seventeenth century, which were removed by the Office of Works.

At the beginning of 1896, two girl gardeners were taken on the strength at Kew. It seems possible that this development was brought about by pressure on the Director. Before they were engaged he insisted that they should wear brown knickerbocker suits, such as were worn by boys, thick woollen stockings and ordinary brown cloth peaked caps. When walking to and from work they wore long mackintoshes, which must have been uncomfortable in the summer. 'There was nothing unseemly in the attire', says William Dallimore, Keeper of the Museums, 'but it created a sensation in the old-fashioned village of Kew.' The Director's reason for the special clothing was to make the girls as unattractive as possible to the young male gardeners, and it was understood that he had said that he was not going to encourage any 'sweethearting'. The most awkward item of dress for the girls appeared to be the cap. 'They wore their hair long and seemed to find it difficult to arrange so that they could wear the cap becomingly.'

The *Daily Telegraph* thought that 'Mrs Grundy will, no doubt, raise her hands in horror at the idea; but, after all lady-gardeners in trousers are much better equipped for the work than was the first gardeneress, Eve, when she showed Adam how to gather fruit, and afterwards eat it.' Another publication broke into verse (it should perhaps be pointed out, for better understanding, that 'knickers' as used in the poem below refers to the 'brown knickerbocker suits' and is not used in the modern sense of an undergarment!):

'*Plants Platonic.* A religious journal, advocating the costume favoured by the 'new' woman, says: 'When sex ceases to be emphasised in dress, the baser passions will have less stimulus'.

> Distinction in dress for the sexes
>   The pathway of virtue is blocking,
> A gown simply teases and vexes
>   The soul that is swayed by a stocking:
> Are 'they' shapely, or lean, or contorted?
>   But the girls to such secrets are stickers,
> Thus the plans of reformers are thwarted
>   By a foolish objection to knickers.

The first girl gardeners at Kew were taken on at the beginning of 1896. Permission to recruit them was given only on condition that they dressed as boys. Their appointment on this basis caused somewhat of a sensation and a certain amount of derision in the Press, which spread even to religious journals.

The white linen dicky which covers
　　The breast of the damozel pretty,
Can't chasten the thought of her lovers
　　If the coats of the charmer be petti;
The hot flame of passion still burning,
　　Alternately blazes or flickers,
Till she crushes the amorous yearnings
　　By putting her limbs into knickers.

Long skirts are undoubtedly rather
　　Seductive to masculine feelings;
How oft near a staircase we gather,
　　Expectant of dainty revealings,
Or gaze with expression sardonic
　　At the gambols of saucy high-kickers –
Yes, our love would be pure and platonic,
　　If the ballet were put into knickers!'

Trained at Swanley Horticultural College, the girls were quite as good as the men, and the sensation soon died down.

Daniel Oliver's long reign of 26 years as Keeper of the Herbarium and Library had ended in 1890, his place being taken by John George Baker who, in turn, gave way to William Botting Hemsley in 1899. Hemsley handed over to Otto Stapf in 1908, who held the post until 1922. The calibre of these Keepers may be judged by the fact that all four of them became Fellows of the Royal Society. By 1902 the Herbarium had again become congested with the continuing influx of specimens and the building of another wing was commenced, projecting from Hunter House towards Kew Palace. It was completed in 1904. *The Kew Bulletin* had, however, suffered a setback. Publication was suspended in 1901, probably as an economy measure arising out of the expenditure on the Boer War.

George Nicholson's health had deteriorated and in 1901 he had to retire from the post of Curator. His place was taken by William Watson, equally eminent in his profession, and author of a number of books of which his massive six-volume revision of Robert Thompson's *The Gardener's Assistant* is the chief.

Some aspects of the work of Kew directly impinged on that of the new Board of Agriculture, which had been created in 1889 and it seemed an obvious step when, in 1903, an Order-in-Council transferred Kew from the control of the Office of Works to the Board except for matter relating to buildings and some smaller items such as the care of the trees on the river bank and the use of Kew Green. Kew remained under the same control when the Board became a Ministry in 1919.

In the early 1900s H T Brown and F Escombe worked in the Jodrell Laboratory on the diffusion of gases through membranes perforated with fine holes to represent stomata. Their conclusions were a notable advance and led to a much greater understanding of the way in which gases are exchanged between plants and their surroundings.

Kew was not immune from the dissatisfaction of 'working' men with their lot which was causing the rise of the Labour party. Wages of gardeners, which were twelve shillings per week in 1841, had risen only to twenty-one shillings per week in 1895, and the first girls were paid as little as ten shillings per week. Frequent complaints were brought to the Director that the men could not live on their wages and in 1905 there was the threat of a strike. The matter was not settled until the aid of Labour MPs was invoked.

Sir William Thiselton-Dyer retired on 15 December 1905. He had done quite a lot to improve the condition of the men but his rule was rather autocratic, which from time to time gave rise to difficult situations, not only in connection with his own staff but in relation to those above him. His strongest side was his care for the economic affairs of the Empire, in which he worked hard and long to carry on and improve on the achievement and success of those who preceded him.

Princess Mary of Cambridge had married the Duke of Teck in Kew Church in 1866. Her daughter, later Queen Mary, wife of King George V, was often brought by her mother from White Lodge in Richmond Park where they lived to Cambridge Cottage, and got to know the Gardens very well, catching the enthusiasm of her mother for it. The Duke of Cambridge himself, son of the old Duke who had first taken Cambridge Cottage, was often at Kew in his declining years, and used to ride in the Gardens before opening hours. When he died in 1904 and the cottage was given up, Queen Mary continued her visits to the Gardens and was a well-known figure there until just before her death.

After the Duke's death, when the Cottage reverted to the Office of Works, two of the old houses forming the western part were pulled down and the remainder adapted partly for offices and partly for a Museum of British-grown Timbers, being renamed Museum IV. All this was done in the time of Sir David Prain, who had succeeded Sir William Thiselton-Dyer as Director.

Prain's previous experience had been wholly in India and he was well aware, therefore, of Empire problems. His first task at Kew, however, was to calm the troubles of the labour force and he did manage to bring about a state of uneasy peace, though for many years, until long after his time, there were stormy meetings

The Chokushi-mon, the slightly scaled-down version of the original gateway in Japan presented by the Japanese government in 1911.

expressing discontent at which the staff pressed for better pay and conditions of service. In 1907 he succeeded in having the post of Assistant Director restored, a post to which Arthur William Hill, a Cambridge Lecturer in Botany was appointed. When Sir David Prain retired in 1922 Hill succeeded him as Director.

In the early years of Sir David Prain's rule the Gardens proceeded in a reasonably calm way with no great changes, while the Herbarium continued its work on the Colonial Floras. *The Kew Bulletin* was restarted in 1906 and back numbers which had not been issued during the ban were also published. D H Scott gave up his Honorary Keepership of the Jodrell Laboratory in 1906. The Treasury still would not agree to a paid replacement as Keeper, but a post as Assistant Keeper was authorised, to be paid at the rate of £90 per annum. L A Boodle, the plant anatomist, who had been working in the Laboratory for a long time as Scott's assistant, was appointed to fill it. A shy and retiring man, his specialist knowledge was of great use in answering the many questions put to the Gardens which involved a knowledge of this branch of plant science.

At the close of the Japan-British Exhibition in London in 1911 the Kyoto Exhibitors' Association presented to the Gardens a reproduction four-fifths the actual size of the Chokushi-mon, the 'Gate of the Imperial Messenger', an entrance to the Great Buddhist Temple of Nishe Hongwanje at Kyoto. The reproduction, like the original, is made of Hinoki wood (*Cupressus obtusa*). It was erected on Mossy Hill, near the Pagoda, where Sir William Chambers' Mosque formerly stood, and specimens of *Cupressus obtusa* were planted nearby. The appearance of the hill was greatly improved by Sir George Taylor when, in the 1960s, he had Japanese maples and azaleas planted on the mound.

The next year, 1912, plants in the orchid houses were the target for suffragettes, who did much damage. It was the first time, so far as is recorded, that such a thing had happened since the early years of George III, although there has always been some minor damage and theft by visitors. But worse was to come. The Refreshment Pavilion was set on fire one night by the agitators and burnt down. One of the suffragettes accused of doing this, Lily Lenton, was still alive in 1967 and appeared on television in that year, telling of her experiences of the movement. The Pavilion was rebuilt in 1914.

The flagpole, in spite of having been provided with a new pitchpine lower portion in 1896, had now decayed beyond redemption, and had to be taken down in 1913, so that Kew was without it at the start of the 1914–18 war, a time when perhaps it would have been appropriate to fly the Union Jack as high as possible in support of the patriotic fervour which stirred the nation. A replacement from Vancouver Island was given by the Government of British Columbia, but it did not reach England until the end of 1915, when erection was not feasible because of the war. The effect of that deadly conflict had, indeed, overtaken everything and Kew affairs, like almost everything else, gave way to the demands of the war effort, setting other things aside.

XXIII

THIS

NETTLE

DANGER

'How is the Empire?'

Last words of King George V

Sir William Chambers' finest small temple, the Temple of the Sun, which stood in the centre of the original botanic garden, was irretrievably smashed by a falling Cedar of Lebanon on 28 March 1916. To commemorate it, Queen Mary planted in the same place seven years later a young Maidenhair tree, *Ginkgo biloba*, close to the famous old specimen of the same species planted in Prince Frederick's time. This fine old tree is a male but in February 1911 female shoots sent from Montpellier were grafted on it. Four fruits ripened on these in 1919, but the shoots have since disappeared.

In 1916 an entrance charge of 1d was imposed as a contribution to the war effort. There was opposition to the charge because the Gardens were a popular resort for poor people from the East End. Following this view, the first Labour government took the charge off again in 1924, only for it to be imposed again in 1926 by the incoming Conservatives. The second Labour government removed it once more in 1929, but on their fall in 1931 it was reimposed. It remained at 1d until 1951, when it was raised to 3d. Successive Ministers of Agriculture, anxious to avoid trouble, left it alone for twenty years. With the advent of decimalisation the nearest equivalent of three old pence was one new pence but this, in fact, equalled only 2.4 old pence, so that the charge actually went down. In 1980 it was raised to 10p.

The replacement flagpole from British Columbia, which had been lying in the Berberis Dell in the Gardens since the end of 1915, was raised in position on 18 October 1919. The new spar was 214 feet high. At the same time changes were taking place in the Jodrell Laboratory. From 1914 onwards staff at the Laboratory provided the scientific back-up for the responsibilities of the Ministry of Agriculture in the statutory control of plant diseases. The Laboratory building was too small to house the additional workers. Room was found for them in part of a house now called Gumley Cottage on Kew Green but in 1919 they were moved to premises at Harpenden which became the Plant Pathology Laboratory of the Ministry of Agriculture. The Imperial Mycological Institute, which later became the Commonwealth Mycological Institute, also had its origin in the Jodrell Laboratory but, although it remained at Kew, ceased to have any connection with the Gardens.

The great drought in the south of England in 1921, when rainfall at Kew was only 13 inches instead of the normal twenty-five, caused unexpected losses of plants inside the glasshouses. The cause was eventually traced to the water, which at that time was drawn from the Thames via the Gardens lake and then pumped up to a reservoir in Richmond Park before it came down again to Kew. With the Thames very low, almost all the water that came into the Kew lake was sea water. While it was in the lake the hot sun caused evaporation, turning the lake into a miniature Dead Sea. To avoid this in the future internal tanks were provided in the glasshouses to store all rainfall which fell on them. Later, arrangements were devised which drew water from the Thames into the Richmond Park reservoir from above the level of salt water contamination.

Sir David Prain retired from the Directorship in February 1922 and was succeeded by the Assistant Director, Sir Arthur Hill. William Watson, who had been Curator during the whole of Prain's term of office, also retired in 1922, being succeeded by W J Bean, who continued the tradition of authorship. He had for a long time specialised in trees and shrubs, his labours bearing fruit in the exhaustive work entitled *Trees and Shrubs Hardy in the British Isles*, which immediately became the standard work on the subject.

Kew had suffered for a long time from urban pollution and the discharges into the air from the gasworks across the river, which had made conifers in particular very difficult to grow successfully. In 1924, in conjunction with the Forestry Commission, a national pinetum was formed on 50 acres of Forestry Commission

[235]

land at Bedgebury in Kent. Expenses of the Bedgebury Pinetum are shared equally between Kew and the Forestry Commission, Kew taking responsibility, under a joint directing committee, for the scientific side of the collection. The Bedgebury collection remained Kew's primary conifer interest until Wakehurst Place was acquired as a satellite garden in 1963 and the Clean Air Acts improved the Kew atmosphere, so that conifers would again grow reasonably well there.

The need for Kew to be involved in Empire affairs progressively lessened until the formation of the Empire Marketing Board in the 1920s when a grant from the Board to Kew financed the employment of an economic botanist, H C Sampson who, with other members of the Kew staff visited most of the Dominions and Colonies to advise in various ways and to collect plants during the years 1927–33, when the Board's activities were discontinued. A small glasshouse was erected in the Melon Yard in 1927 with EMB funds for use as a quarantine station for useful clones of bananas, and later cocoa and other plants, in transit from one Empire country to another. This service is still provided.

The high tide of 7 January 1928 which drowned some unfortunate people in basements at Lambeth flooded Kew Green and many houses near the river. Although the water came up Ferry Lane none fortunately got into the Herbarium. It found its way into the Gardens proper only at the south end of the Queen's Cottage grounds. Two pieces of statuary were installed in the Gardens in the late 1920s. The President and Council of the Royal Academy presented Hamo Thornycroft's 'A Sower' to Kew. It stands on a pedestal designed by Sir Edwin Lutyens at the angle of the Broad Walk near the Orangery. 'Out in the Fields', made by Arthur G Atkinson, the figure of a man with a spade, stood at first in the centre of the Iris Garden but in the 1960s was resited near the Jodrell Laboratory. This statue was the gift of Mr A T Hare, of St Margaret's, Twickenham. A third presentation to Kew at this time was a sundial designed to tell the time with great accuracy, designed by Professor Boys and presented by Mr George Hubbard. It was formerly in Cambridge Cottage garden but has been moved near the Orangery.

The assumption by many Empire territories of responsibility for their own economic destinies reduced the openings for trained Kew students overseas but the increasing interest of home local authorities in the improvement of their parks, sports grounds, cemeteries and other open spaces under their control created many new opportunities and the demand grew year by year for Kew-trained men to fill these posts.

The Chelsea Show of 1929 included an exhibition by Mrs Sherman Hoyt of Californian cacti and succulents, staged against a painted background of the

South African *Lithops*, plants that look like stones but which may be detected by the cleft that each shows.

Mohave desert, and that lady afterwards paid for a permanent glasshouse at Kew to which the display was transferred. The house, named the Sherman Hoyt house, was opened to the public in 1932. Another glasshouse was built alongside it in 1935, again with money from a private donor, to display South African succulent plants, including the small *Lithops*, which simulate stones so well that they are hard to distinguish from them until they produce their bright little flowers.

The pelicans and penguins which had formerly been well-known residents of the Gardens had been replaced by cranes and storks. The favourite among these was 'Joey', more well-known than the first Joey, a favourite haunt of his being round the Refreshment Pavilion. On 31 January 1935, however, he was found drowned in the lake, apparently having fallen through the ice and been unable to free himself. So widely known was he that his death was proclaimed on the placards of one London newspaper which announced 'Joey of Kew dead.' Next year saw a new Joey stalking the Kew lawns.

[237]

The Jodrell Laboratory was enlarged in 1934 by the addition of a studio for the Gardens artist and a photographic dark-room as well as increased facilities for science. The mantle of L A Boodle, who had retired in 1930, had been inherited by Dr C R Metcalfe who embarked on the work with Dr L Chalk of Oxford which made him, in the next forty years, a world authority on his subject, the *Anatomy of the Dicotyledons*, which was followed in due course by the *Anatomy of the Monocotyledons*, to which he also made a substantial contribution. These are works comparable in their field with the *Index Kewensis*, and the standard works produced by the horticulturists of Kew.

The seedling Chilean honey palm, *Jubaea spectabilis*, which had been raised from seed collected by Thomas Bridges in 1843, had by the 1930s become a superb tree, but was pressing on the roof of the Temperate House. It was decided to move it to a more central position in the house, where the top would have room to continue growing. Though the distance to be traversed was only from 15 to 20 feet, the weight of the palm with its ball of soil and shuttering to hold this in position was in the region of 54 tons. The transfer was effected successfully and the tree continued to flourish.

Crops of *Atropa belladonna* and *Colchicum* were grown at Kew as part of the 1939–45 war effort and both the Museums and the Jodrell Laboratory set aside their ordinary work to undertake special investigations. Dr Ronald Melville of the Museums put forward the suggestion early in 1941 that rosehips are rich in the anti-scorbutic Vitamin C and could be used as a source of this vitamin. The suggestion found favour and rose hip syrup was soon on the market as a supplement for the feeding of young children. The year 1941 ended in tragedy. The Director, Sir Arthur Hill, was riding early in the morning of 3 November in the Old Deer Park when his horse apparently stumbled and threw him, breaking his neck. Sir Geoffrey Evans, who had taken H C Sampson's place as Economic Botanist at Kew, assumed the mantle of Acting Director for the time being.

An interesting find was made in the Gardens in 1941. One of the lady gardeners thinning onions in the wartime allotment on the Palace Lawn found an Elizabethan gold signet ring set with an amethyst on which was engraved the profile of a woman. The ring was not classed as treasure trove, and was bought by the Victoria and Albert Museum from the lucky finder for £20.

On 1 September 1943 Professor E J Salisbury of University College, London, took up duty as the new Director. A botanist of immense reputation, his first effort in the Gardens was to make a chalk garden on the slopes of the ice-house mound, an attempt to create an ecological community, the first of its kind in the Gardens, but a new menace now presented itself. Early in the war there had been minor

[238]

A small plant of *Angiopteris evecta*, the Turnip Fern, which grows to large dimensions, having fronds 15 feet long when fully grown.

damage from bombs but in mid-June, 1944 V1 and V2 rockets began to fall, but there were no direct hits on the Gardens, which again suffered only broken glass. Working in the glasshouses during this period was, of course, very dangerous, as attacks came with very little warning from the V1s and no warning at all from the V2s. A klaxon system was adopted to announce imminent danger as soon as it was known.

With the ending of the war in May 1945 there was great need to organise training for the returning men. Kew played its part and on 1 October 1946 the first of the one-year courses under a Vocational Training Scheme organised by the Ministry of Agriculture began. Both theoretical and practical training was given. The course ran for several years but the Gardens eventually reverted to the normal student-gardener arrangements.

In May 1948 Dr N L Bor, brother of Max Adrian the actor, formerly of the Indian Forest Service, took up duty as Assistant Director, replacing J S L Gilmour, who had accepted the post of Director of the Royal Horticultural Society Gardens at Wisley.

A visit by the Director to Australia in 1949 resulted in a notable addition to the Gardens' glasshouses in the period 1950–52. Funds were made available by the Australian government for the building of a house in the Gardens for the purpose of exhibiting the flora of Australia. The site chosen for it was to the west of the Temperate House. The method of construction, new to Kew at that time, was the use of aluminium sections instead of the customary wood or iron. The Australian flora has marked characteristics of its own and the atmosphere and general feel of this house is quite unlike any other in Kew. Being somewhat tucked away, however, in the less frequented part of the Gardens, it receives relatively few visitors and many miss it who would otherwise have enjoyed it were it in a more prominent place.

A sign that the aftermath of the war was disappearing was the restoration in 1951 of the Clog and Apron Race, an event peculiar to Kew but not seen by the general public because it is an internal event always run after hours. The race starts from the Palm House end of the Broad Walk and finishes at the Orangery. The competitors, such student-gardeners as choose to run, wear the wooden clogs and gardener's apron that is their working garb in the hothouses. The noise of the clogs on the asphalt of the Broad Walk when the twenty or so young men and girls put themselves into motion is indescribable, reminiscent of a cavalry charge, but the race is exhausting and when the winners reach the Orangery the prizes are always large quantities of liquid refreshment, which is drunk immediately.

A more orthodox student event, called the Round-the-Gardens Race, is a race along the paths round the perimeter of the Gardens, a distance of $2\frac{1}{2}$ miles. This is a team race between the departments of the Gardens, and is also run after hours, unlike the Kew to Wisley (or the reverse) Relay Race, in which teams from the two institutions, and sometimes others, race along the public roads between Kew and Wisley Gardens, a distance of 17 miles. There are four runners in each team, each covering about four miles, but it has been known for a runner to miss his way and have to run two stages.

For some years the large number of old beech trees in the southern part of the Arboretum had been causing problems. Planted in the early days of the Gardens, they were, one by one, having reached their allotted span, falling into internal decay. A number had been removed already. No less than nineteen had to be removed in 1951, and others followed each year thereafter.

There are often protests by local residents and visitors about the removal of apparently healthy trees in the Gardens, but chances cannot be taken in Kew where many thousands of people congregate on holidays and other days. The need for such vigilance was illustrated in this very year, though it was not a beech which was concerned. On Sunday 9 December 1951, the top of a dead Turkey oak situated in the woods near the Rhododendron Dell snapped off in a gust and crashed down, killing a six-year-old boy who was playing with a group nearby. It was subsequently found that squirrels had eaten away a large cavity some fifteen feet from the ground and that it was at this point the fracture had taken place. This was the second occasion when such an accident had occurred in the Gardens, a branch of a large elm just inside the Cumberland Gate having fallen in 1913 and killed a man sitting on the seat beneath the tree.

The Palm House, now over 100 years old, had to be closed to the public in November 1952. There had been some movement of the main structural girders and glazing bars due to corrosion, and it was thought to be unsafe. Consideration of what could be done led to the suggestion that the house should be radically reconstructed using the arches which had been erected along the Mall for the Coronation in 1953. Most of those who knew of this and had a sense of history were not only appalled by the suggestion, but by the hideous appearance of the building it was proposed to construct from them, which replaced Burton's gentle curves with a sharp-pointed, angular, almost totally unbeautiful affair. Fortunately, the proposal was abandoned and the original building cleaned, repaired and repainted piece by piece until restored to its original safety and pleasing appearance. A reminder of the Coronation of Queen Elizabeth II was, however, placed near the Palm House. The Queen's Beasts which had decorated Westminster Abbey annexe during the ceremony were found so pleasing that stone replicas were made of the orginal wooden effigies and given to Kew by an anonymous donor. They stand in a row along the front of the terrace, a row of extraordinary heraldic beasts the like of which had not been seen on Kew ground since the days of Richmond Palace.

It was not only the Palm House that was showing signs of age. During 1952 several pieces of ornamental iron work fell from the Temperate House roof and it was decided to remove all of it as well as most of the stone urns which decorated the stone columns. No further action was, however, taken at this time, although it was obvious that it would not be too long before more fundamental work would have to be done on this house also.

Another Centenary fell to be commemorated in 1953, that of the founding of the Herbarium and Library. A printed brochure was prepared for the benefit of those, some seven hundred, who were invited to visit the exhibition mounted on 7 to 9 May, which attempted to show what had been done in the hundred years since taxonomic work began at Kew. It demonstrated how well Kew had stuck to the brief, for which authority had been obtained by Sir William Hooker, to concentrate on Colonial Floras, instancing the great African efforts, the *Flora of Tropical Africa*, the *Flora of West Tropical Africa* and the *Flora Capensis*. There was also the *Flora of British India*, the *Flora of the Malay Peninsula*, the *Flora Australiensis*, the *Flora of Tasmania*, the *New Zealand Flora*, the *Flora Antarctica* and the *Flora of the British West Indian Islands*, as well as a substantial number of floras of smaller regions. It illustrated also the monographs and miscellaneous works, including the vast number of smaller papers in a wide range of scientific periodicals, which had been produced, together with the effort put into the comprehensive basic enterprises carried out in the Herbarium, the *Genera Plantarum*, the *Index Kewensis* and the *Index Londinensis*. Work on the two long-running periodicals devoted to botanical illustration, the *Icones Plantarum*, started by Sir William Hooker, and Curtis's *Botanical Magazine*, which were edited and fostered from Kew, was also included. It was an imposing array of plant performance and erudition, and the Director was able to show that the work was being continued on the same lines with even greater attention, the staff of eighteen before the war having nearly doubled by 1953. Some may have thought it ironic that, as the Empire declined, effort at Kew on its floras greatly increased, but the exhibition did not deal with that point.

Sir Geoffrey Evans retired from the post of Economic Botanist on 31 December 1953 and T A Russell, formerly of the Colonial Agricultural Service, succeeded him in the post. Again, with Empire work having dwindled so far, no one seems to have asked whether the post, created for the Empire Marketing Board work in the

1920s, was still really needed. The Director himself retired in 1955. In his thirteen years, most of which were affected by the war and its aftermath, money and opportunity to make changes had been scarce, and his services had often been required by the Ministry for purposes other than those of Kew. Apart from the Chalk Garden, and a Clematis Wall near the Berberis Dell, he had done little to change the Gardens except for the very welcome addition of the Australian House. For the rest, he had continued to keep the machine going on the lines that had been followed in the past. For nearly seventy years now, this had been the policy of successive Directors. For the first thirty years of that time, up to the outbreak of the First World War, this had served well enough, although changes were already evident in the Empire work, but after that, in spite of the temporary nostalgic flare-up of the Empire Marketing Board, the candle of need for work by Kew on Empire matters had guttered lower and lower until, by the mid-1950s, it was virtually out. The taxonomic work went on under an ever-increasing impetus of its own, but the original base and reason for it had changed. Without an Empire, what need of Empire Floras compiled centrally by Kew, when the countries they covered had many of them become independent of Britain, and not infrequently hostile to her? It was becoming clear in the mid-1950s that Kew could no longer trundle along like a shabby superannuated Victorian hansom cab, running on its wooden wheels to its original destination. A new Director was needed, with a new vision. The hour produced the man.

XXIV

OLD INTO

NEW

'A state without the means of some change
is without the means of its conservation.'

Edmund Burke

Sir George Taylor took office as Director on 19 October 1956, coming from the
post of Keeper of the Department of Botany in the British Museum (Natural
History), in which he had made his career since 1928. His garden at
Rickmansworth, in which he grew many rare and difficult plants, was well known
to connoisseurs, and he had served long and ably on the Royal Horticultural
Society's Council and Committees. He knew too, at first hand, the adventurous
world of the plant collector, having collected in South and East Africa and
accompanied Frank Ludlow and George Sherriff on an expedition in the
Himalayas and south-eastern Tibet. As a taxonomist he had published a book on
that beautiful genus *Meconopsis* and done much work on the aquatic plants
classified in *Podostemaceae* and *Potamogeton*, including extensive field investigations. He took the view that Kew had reached a point where all aspects of its policy
needed re-examination and proposed to the Ministry of Agriculture that a visiting
group of distinguished people should be entrusted with this task. The proposal
was agreed, the group formed under the chairmanship of Sir Eric Ashby and the
examination carried out.

Almost at the same time as the new Director arrived Dr W B Turrill succeeded to the Keepership of the Herbarium and Library. He was one of the first who had begun to look beyond the customary reliance of plant taxonomists on external morphology, which he called 'alpha taxonomy', and insisted on the relevance of criteria from other sources, the newer disciplines of ecology, genetics, cytology and the like. He called this wider approach 'omega taxonomy'. His distinction as a scientist was recognised by his election to Fellowship of the Royal Society in 1958.

One of the first steps of Dr Taylor was the creation of a Heath Garden near the Pagoda, for which about 20,000 *Erica* plants were used, mostly propagated at Kew, but some came from the Edinburgh Botanic Garden. Shortly afterwards the flagstaff was replaced by a new giant presented by the Government of British Columbia. The spar was 225 feet long, having been trimmed from a tree 275 feet high which was about 370 years old. Once again it was from a stand growing on Vancouver Island. It was raised into position on 5 November 1959. While it was being prepared Kew celebrated its Bicentenary at which Her Majesty the Queen and His Royal Highness the Duke of Edinburgh graciously consented to be present. A pergola of brick piers with timbered runners and crossbars was built to extend the length of both of the main paths of the Herbaceous Ground as a permanent commemoration of the Bicentenary, and planted up with roses.

The Visiting Group had recommended a drastic overhaul, sifting and modernisation of the Museums, which had remained largely unaltered from Victorian times. The Orangery was cleared as part of this change and restored and refurbished by the Ministry of Works. The Francavilla statues were moved from King William's Temple to ornament the cleared interior and other statuary loaned by the British Museum was placed in it together with an alabaster sarcophagus or bath of Roman times, all objects of the kind which were prized by eighteenth century collectors and in keeping with the period and classical exterior of the building. To complete the scene orange trees were once more grown by the great windows and ferns in tubs in contrast along the back wall.

When, in the late 1960s, the Orangery showed extensive dry rot, the decay was attributed to the high humidity caused by the watering of the orange trees and it was said that orange trees could not be grown there, ignoring the fact that the Aitons successfully grew oranges in the building for eighty years. The decision was taken to cease growing them and when the dry rot had been removed the other changes were almost wholly obliterated and replaced by what Wilfrid Blunt, in *In For a Penny*, described as 'higgledy-piggledy screens which give the whole a makeshift appearance that suggests a large village hall temporarily partitioned for the reception of blood donors'. The contents of the exhibitions which these

[245]

Three different sections of an exhibition in the Orangery devoted to the work of Kew.

screens display are interesting and impeccable but their presence in the building is out of period. The Francavilla statues have once more disappeared from Kew, a development deplored by those who would like to retain the authentic eighteenth century flavour which they provide, since Prince Frederick bought them to decorate Kew.

The pruning and modernisation of the Museums recommended by the Visiting Group were drastic enough, but the changes recommended for the Jodrell Laboratory were even more extensive, designed to increase the Laboratory's capacity to provide the evidence needed for the pursuit of Turrill's 'omega taxonomy'. The appointment of a cytogeneticist was advocated as a first step. The Group recommended, too, that the vast reservoir of the living collection formed such a fine source for plant material to solve physiological problems that a plant physiologist post should be added. As with the wave of a wand, two new botanical

[246]

disciplines were thus added to the scientific effort of the Gardens. There still remained the problem, however, as to how the extra staff could be housed and this was considered in connection with a similar problem arising in the case of the student-gardeners.

The course had rather fallen away in quality. A total of only six theory subjects was being taught in 1959 on the lecture course and the Kew Certificate which the students were awarded on completion of their course was held in far less esteem than had formerly been the case. The Group recommended that the course be overhauled and redefined in terms of modern requirements. The revised course, plans for which were worked out early in 1960, provided for a stay of three years at Kew instead of two, extended the lecture syllabus to cover 21 subjects, confined lectures to the day time instead of holding them in the evening, to allow more time for private study, and replaced the Kew Certificate with the Kew Diploma, which had an Honours category for those who did exceptionally well. The intake of student-gardeners was raised to twenty per year, so that there would be sixty at Kew at any one time. A new post of Supervisor of Studies was created to take charge of the course. The extra accommodation required for student training was added to the Jodrell Laboratory requirement and a joint building designed, providing laboratories and supporting accommodation for the scientists, class-rooms for the students, and a lecture theatre which could not only be used for student training, but could serve for the use of the whole Gardens, fulfilling a need for a lecture theatre which had been felt for some time. The new building was complete and came into use in May 1965.

Recommendations of the Group on the taxonomic side were mainly concerned with the reorganisation of the work to enable arrears of work in certain areas to be overtaken. The post of Assistant Director was abolished and a new post of Secretary created to bring professional administrative expertise to bear on the problems of the Gardens. The new Secretary took up duty on 3 September 1959. Early in the 1960s Dr Taylor's work was recognised by the award of a knighthood, and he became Sir George Taylor. The years which followed were very much concerned with bringing into being the structure set out by the Visiting Group and the history a chronicle of the changes as they came into being, but there were other pressing matters to pursue. Many of the glasshouses were in a poor state and some beyond repair and a programme had to be formulated to rectify this situation. Between 20 and 30 projects were got under way in the early 1960s, including some quite large schemes, such as the move of the Decorative Department base from the Melon Yard to the Lower Nursery. This Department requires a lot of room because it produces all the bedding plants for the Gardens, and several new

[247]

glasshouses and ancillary buildings had to be built.

The glasshouse heating installations were changed from coke to oil-burning, involving the fitting of a number of new boilers and the reconstruction of some boilerhouses. The Palm House was provided with a new oil-fired boiler house and tanks in the Shaft Yard near the Kew Road and the boiler rooms under the Palm House and the tunnel through which coke used to be laboriously trundled by hand in trucks, which had had so much trouble from flooding over the years, were at last abandoned. Motorised blinds were installed on the glasshouses where required and automatic ventilation began to appear, together with capillary, mist spray, and other watering devices where suitable conditions could be created. The age of automation had begun, soon to be aided by the computer and the silicon chip.

A very considerable number of changes in the horticultural work and layout of the Gardens accompanied these other changes in the 1960s. A number of ecologically-based shrub borders were established, starting at the south end of the rock garden and the Mound but extending to other parts of the Gardens. These, under Sir George Taylor's direction, were created by S A Pearce, an expert in trees and shrubs in the tradition of W J Bean. Rhododendrons and other ericaceous shrubs, magnolias and camellias were planted in great variety in these borders, with scattered groups or single trees, mainly silver birches, here and there, simulating self-sown trees. Groups of hostas were used to provide ground cover, interplanted with candelabra and other types of primulas, lilies, meconopsis and ferns, the whole forming an harmonious community.

The rock garden had been undergoing a gradual transformation for a number of years. Bit by bit the original limestone of the garden, hastily gathered together in 1882 when it was made, was being replaced with more water-retentive Sussex sandstone. This process was speeded up and completed in the 1960s. 'Scree' beds were then constructed next to the T-range in which plants were grown which could be got to tolerate the English climate only if such water as they received drained away very quickly, the desired effect being achieved by raising the beds considerably above the surrounding soil. The surge of new work was accompanied by a great increase in the mechanization of gardening processes, the last horse, Zenobia, being put down in 1961. The pay and welfare of the Gardens staff and of the Constabulary was brought into line with what could reasonably be expected by similar workers elsewhere.

As the decade progressed there were more sophisticated changes. Seed-storage, recording and distribution were brought under scientific centralised control. Plant records of the living collections were also rationalised under scientific direction and a more scientific approach adopted towards plant propagation. The intake and

Some of the Queen's Beasts. Made in wood for Westminster Abbey Annexe at the Coronation of Queen Elizabeth II, a private donor afterwards had them copied in stone and placed in front of the Palm House at Kew.

output of the living collections was also rationalised and controlled, a technical development section created to watch over possible improvements, and an internal training system devised. Steps were taken to integrate the control of the living collections as far as possible into the main scientific structure of the Gardens.

During these traumatic and introspective years there were some additions to the Gardens and some historic events to be chronicled. Sir John Ramsden of Bulstrode Park, who had given to the Gardens the Venetian wellhead in the Queen's Garden, also gave Kew the 'Kylins', the Chinese Guardian Lions which stare majestically across the Palm House Lake. In 1964 the fountain in the centre of that lake, which had hitherto been no more than a pipe-end projecting from the water, was provided with a group of statuary from Windsor depicting Hercules struggling with a snake. The group is a casting by Crozatier of an original by the

[249]

Hercules and the Serpent in the Palm House lake with the jets of the fountain at full bore.

Monegasque sculptor François Joseph Bosio which stands in the Tuileries gardens alongside the Rue de Rivoli in Paris. It had been bought by George IV in 1826.

A more prosaic addition to the Gardens was the erection of a small tea-bar at the northern end of the Gardens on the boundary of the Lower Nursery to fill the need for some source of refreshment at this end of the Gardens, the Refreshment Pavilion proper being at the southern end. Built in a 1960s architectural style, some think it sticks out like a sore thumb in the general eighteenth century scene and that some of the constables' gate boxes, rebuilt in a similar style, appear similarly incongruous against Decimus Burton's superb wrought-iron gates.

For a long time the need had been felt at Kew for more planting space. The

Bedgebury Pinetum had afforded some relief since 1924 but there was still need for more. Kew is too dry for many trees and shrubs to grow well and, if more land were obtained, it would have to be in an area of higher rainfall than Kew and with a more water-retentive soil. Various options came up from time to time, but none was thought to be suitable. Then Sir Henry Price, who died at the end of 1962, left Wakehurst Place near Ardingly in Sussex to the National Trust with an endowment, and the Trust offered it to Kew. Since it had been the home of Gerald Loder, Lord Wakehurst, President of the Royal Horticultural Society, and planted up in the earlier part of the century with many rare plants, had an annual rainfall several inches higher than that of Kew, and was located on the Sussex sandstone ridge, it could not have been bettered. There was difficulty because the endowment was not sufficient to meet the costs of its maintenance but the Treasury was eventually persuaded that the extra cost was a proper charge on national funds and on 1 January 1965 it was taken over as a satellite garden for Kew. The estate has been open to the public since the late 1960s. Its development has, since the beginning, been subject to the advice of a consultative panel.

Shortly after the acquisition of Wakehurst Place, Kew was subject to another watery visitation. Taking everyone by surprise, the Thames overflowed its banks again on Friday 10 December 1965, coming up at Kew to virtually the same points as it reached in 1928, although fortunately this time there was not the loss of life down-river which occurred then. The water was well across the Green and came again into the Queen's Cottage grounds. Presumably the new Thames Barrage will prevent such happenings in the future.

The steady influx of dried specimens into the Herbarium had led Sir Edward Salisbury as early as 1952 to raise the question of additional accommodation. There was also a need to provide better accommodation for the Library. In 1965 a case was accepted for building a fourth wing to the Herbarium, filling in the remaining side of the U-shaped block to turn it into a rectangle, in which space was provided for the Library as well as for the Herbarium specimens and staff. Completed in 1968, the opportunity was taken to combine the opening ceremony with a similar ceremony for the seventeenth century garden behind Kew Palace, which had now also been completed. Her Majesty the Queen kindly consented to the name 'The Queen's Garden' being used for this new creation and to open both the new Herbarium wing and the Garden on 14 May 1969, another day of considerable rejoicing at Kew.

Changes continued into the 1970s, the scientific work of the Herbarium being radically reorganised. The taxonomic work, since Sir William Hooker had directed it on to Colonial floras, had been arranged almost entirely geographically:

it was reshuffled on to a world basis, so that individual scientists, instead of dealing with areas or regions, now dealt with families or genera on a global footing. This was, indeed, a traumatic change, to which it took some time to adjust. It was the last radical change before Sir George Taylor retired on 31 May 1971.

There had been only one period in the history of the Royal Botanic Gardens since they had become a state garden, in which the activity of the institution and the changes effected had been comparable with those brought about during Sir George Taylor's directorship. The fifteen years of his tenure of office between 1956 and 1971 parallel very closely the first fifteen years of Sir William Hooker's reign, from his appointment in 1841 to his first tentative move on Colonial floras in 1856. Sir George Taylor, alone of the Directors who followed the Hookers, stands on a par with them. He took a semi-moribund Kew by the scruff of its neck, just as Sir William had taken W T Aiton's Kew, wrenched it out of its Victorian lethargy, and thrust it into the twentieth century. There was no corner of Kew which did not feel his reforming influence. He combined this with many journeys about the world, serving both botany and horticulture well in a larger sphere than Kew.

I knew Sir George personally as a kind and helpful man, from whom I learnt a great deal. He was great in company, with an enormous sense of humour. He had a tremendous capacity for making friends, from royal personages downwards, and his friends all love him. Kew benefited more than most who worked there knew from this delightful trait. It brought many new funds, for example, into the coffers of the Bentham-Moxon Trust and other gifts in kind, and much kindness and goodwill to Kew from many sources. I am proud to have served under him as his lieutenant, and to have helped him to carry through those reforms and launch those new projects, such as Wakehurst Place, about which he felt so deeply.

The two Directors who followed Sir George Taylor, Professor John Heslop-Harrison and Professor J P M Brenan, both stayed for five years only. Professor Heslop-Harrison, under whom I also served, was also a kind and helpful man with a great sense of humour, but in the end he preferred to return to science, in which he has achieved great distinction. He brought the study of cell physiology to the Gardens and during his time a new subject began to engross the attention of Kew, the need to conserve endangered plant species. The Red Book listing such species was prepared at Kew. There have since been other developments but full assessment of the years since Sir George Taylor's retirement must be left to later historians. I am content to let my own account terminate with the completion of Sir George's heroic and successful effort to wrest for Kew a place in the modern scientific world even greater than it had held in the past.

[252]

INDEX

Numbers in italics, thus *12*, refer to illustrations on pages indicated